Enforcement of Foreign Arbitral Awards and the Public Policy Exception

Bruno Zeller · Gautam Mohanty ·
Sai Ramani Garimella

Enforcement of Foreign Arbitral Awards and the Public Policy Exception

Including an Analysis of South Asian State Practice

Springer

Bruno Zeller
Department of Law
University of Western Australia
Crawley, WA, Australia

Gautam Mohanty
Jindal Global Law School India (JGLS)
O. P. Jindal Global University
Sonipat, Haryana, India

Sai Ramani Garimella
Faculty of Legal Studies
South Asian University
New Delhi, Delhi, India

ISBN 978-981-16-2633-3 ISBN 978-981-16-2634-0 (eBook)
https://doi.org/10.1007/978-981-16-2634-0

This Springer imprint is published by the registered company Springer Nature Singapore Pte Ltd.
The registered company address is: 152 Beach Road, #21-01/04 Gateway East, Singapore 189721, Singapore

Foreword by Justice Deepak Verma

International Commercial Arbitration's importance in the present-day framework of cross-border transactions and International Trade continues to burgeon. The single-handed preference of arbitration as a dispute resolution method between conflicting parties is well documented throughout the world, even more emphatically in South Asian jurisdictions. The rise of South Asian jurisdictions as economic powerhouses and the readiness of legislators to emphasize the use of arbitration is well illustrated by the very fact that the jurisdictions above have long provided for arbitration as part of their legislative fabric. Hence, it comes as no surprise that the number of arbitrations in South Asia is increasing rapidly.

International Commercial Arbitration has been a central interest of mine for about a decade. I have been involved in arbitration and dispute resolution as a member of the Hon'ble judiciary, starting my tenure as a Judge of High Court of Madhya Pradesh (India) and ending my tenure as a Justice of the Supreme Court of India. Even after I retired from the Hon'ble Supreme Court of India, I have continued pursuing my interest in arbitration as an arbitrator. Therefore, I consider myself lucky to have witnessed the development of arbitration in South Asia, and I believe the exponential growth of arbitrations in South Asian jurisdictions has been spectacular.

The present book is not just another book contributing to the endless list of literature already widely used in International Commercial Arbitration on public policy but, in my opinion, is unique in many respects. The distinguishing factor of this book is its regional perspective. The book is much more than a brief overview of the principal aspects of International Commercial Arbitration as in addition to an analysis of the United Nations Convention on the Recognition of Enforcement of Foreign Arbitration Awards ("New York Convention") and the UNCITRAL Model Law on International Commercial Arbitration ("Model Law") and several secondary writings the book also discusses the interpretation of public policy by various national courts. An analysis of the interpretation of public policy by national courts in South Asia is an exercise that is imperative because unless the courts adhere to the international standards set out by the New York Convention and the Model Law, they will not be able to guide the growth of arbitration in the right direction.

The book provides a detailed and comprehensive examination of public policy treatment in South Asian jurisdictions, including India, Bangladesh, Pakistan, Nepal and Sri Lanka. Each of the abovementioned jurisdictions is examined in-depth, and while the book has a South Asian perspective, it is not written in a parochial way. Besides referring to primary and secondary sources from the South Asian region, the book is replete with frequent references to well-known materials outside South Asia. In summation, the book is an excellent compendium and a primer for the reader to comprehend the enforcement of foreign arbitral awards in South Asia jurisdiction vis-à-vis public policy.

Veritably, the chapters of the book provide valuable insights into the panoramic understanding of public policy and is an essential contribution to the literature explaining the advantages, peculiarities and pitfalls of enforcement of foreign arbitral awards in South Asia. I extend my heartiest congratulations to the Learned Authors on coming out with such an excellent book with a unique focus. I am confident that it will be useful to students and practitioners in the region, litigants and advocates in other parts of the world who wish to know more about the impact and role of public policy in each of the diverse jurisdictions.

One of the authors, Mr. Gautam Mohanty, as I know him, is a scholarly and gentle author. He has that bent of mind, to express himself, with absolute and perfect clarity.

This is indeed an extraordinary and brilliant work by the Learned Authors. They have put the best foot forward at a right time, when full view on the subject was indeed needed.

March 2021

Justice Deepak Verma
Former Judge of Supreme Court of India and Arbitrator
New Delhi, India

Foreword by Csongor István Nagy

It would be difficult to question the proposition that arbitration became the standard dispute settlement mechanism of international commercial transactions. This is due not only to its popularity but also to the fact that arbitration, contrary to litigation before state courts, is really capable of being international in every sense. However tolerant they may be to foreign cultural and legal patterns and foreign languages, state courts can hardly be truly international. Judges are local nationals, the procedure is governed by local rules (the *lex fori*) and the court (and also the procedure) will have an "official language." The emergence in Europe of international commercial courts tries to respond to these shortcomings and it will be seen how much these will be able to become an effective competitor for arbitration. For the time being, however, arbitration has two very important advantages. First, it is the only dispute settlement mechanism that ends with a mandatory (legally enforceable) decision and is still international to the core. Arbitrators may come from various regions and have diverse cultural and legal backgrounds. The language and the rules of the procedure can be freely chosen by the parties. Second, the value of an arbitral award in terms of enforceability is second to none.

Culture and legal patterns, even if they are not part of the applicable law, do matter. A good example is the German commercial law notion of "confirmation letter" ("*kaufmännische Beschtätigungsschreiben*"), which is not only a legal institution but a notion deeply rooted in the daily commercial practice. The confirmation letter is sent after the conclusion of the agreement. The fundamental rule is that if the receiver of the letter remains silent, the content of the contract is determined by the confirmation letter, unless the sender does not observe the requirement of good faith or the difference between the initial agreement and the confirmation letter is so great that the sender cannot reasonably expect the receiver to approve it. The confirmation letter works also in cases where the parties "almost" concluded the initial agreement ("*abschlussreif*"): in this case the letter not only confirms or changes but also creates the contract. The receiver is expected to object immediately; otherwise the letter will determine the content of the agreement.

Although confirmation letters may have evidentiary value in different legal systems, the letter's decisive impact on the content of the contractual relationship is peculiar to German law. In most legal systems, silence, in itself, infers no agreement.

The parties' concurrence of wills is based on an offer and an acceptance, and the same rule applies to the amendment of the contract. Hence, the silence of the confirmation letter's recipient, in itself, does not infer agreement. A judge coming from such a jurisdiction may not understand why the German party relied so confidently on its own unilateral declaration (confirmation letter) and why it makes continued references to the other party's failure to object. Was it reasonable for the German party to count on the other party's reply and assume that if the other party did not reply, this was because it was fine with the confirmation letter? May a non-Germany party be expected to be familiar with this commercial norm if it regularly deals with German business customers? An international tribunal may be more prone to recognize the misunderstandings emerging from cultural differences.

The practical value of arbitral awards is second to none. When it gets to state court judgments, the parties face significant uncertainties and hurdles. The enforceability of judgments is normally regulated by national law and this may make enforcement in multi-jurisdiction matters intensely complicated. Furthermore, what is worse, foreign court judgments, at least in commercial matters, are quite often enforced only if backed by an international treaty or reciprocity. Arbitral awards face no such uncertainties and hurdles. The 1958 New York Convention on the Recognition and Enforcement of Foreign Arbitral Awards provides a closed list of grounds of refusal of recognition and enforcement. No foreign arbitral award can be excluded from the domestic legal sphere for reasons not listed in the Convention. Reciprocity is not among these. Of course, states may conclude treaties (mostly on a bilateral basis) and develop reciprocity to ensure the recognition and enforcement of the judgements of particular states. Nonetheless, the purview of the network of these treaties and reciprocal relations may not even compare to the geographical coverage of the 1958 New York Convention, which covers nearly the entire globe. This is why a New York court judgment and an arbitral award rendered in New York may have completely different practical values. To use the example of my country, aside from some exceptions, Hungarian courts do not enforce US judgments, as there is no confirmed reciprocity between the two countries (and no treaty providing for recognition and enforcement). On the contrary, arbitral awards rendered in the US can be smoothly enforced in Hungary, owing to the 1958 New York Convention.

This book addresses this core element of the success story of arbitration: enforcement and refusal to enforce and, hence, its relevance cannot be overstated. As noted above, the 1958 New York Convention created a uniform regime for the recognition and enforcement of foreign arbitral awards. This is a major achievement, nonetheless, it is far from eliminating geographical diversity. Uniform rules create uniform frameworks but may be applied in diverse and diverging ways. It is easier and more advisable to unify law through flexible rules using vague terms, however, these may raise issues when they are interpreted. The requirement of uniform application is embedded in various international instruments but it has raised difficulties in practice and, at times, courts have not been reluctant to read their own laws into the wide categories of uniform law. The notoriously undefinable "public policy" is a perfect example. This ground of refusal is a security valve and the final reservation of all states, which affords courts a very wide playing field. However, if applied improperly, it may put the whole system upside down. This book provides an excellent and comprehensive analysis of the practice of public policy from a very important regional perspective.

Csongor István Nagy
Professor of Law and Head
Department of Private International Law
University of Szeged, Szeged, Hungary

Acknowledgements

A book is a long term project and this has been no exception. The fact that it crystalized into the book the esteemed reader is reading now is the result of support and inspiration of various kinds and from various sources. At the outset, I would like to thank both my co-authors, Prof. Ramani and Prof. Bruno for having me on board for this book and for providing me with unambiguous support and the necessary critique to transform my work into meaningful contribution. Further, I greatly benefited from my personal experiences in arbitration by being associated with Justice Deepak Verma, Former Judge of Supreme Court of India. His guidance and insights in arbitration have truly shaped my understanding of the practical intricacies involved in arbitration which are highlighted throughout the book. On a personal note, I thank my fiancée Aleksandra Cwik, for her unconditional love and support throughout the process of writing the book. Furthermore, I would like to thank my friends who have consistently encouraged me to believe in my abilities to pull though the process of writing this book. At a fundamental level, I would like to thank my sister for instilling in me the love for writing. Above all, this book is dedicated to my parents, my first teachers, for which I am immensely grateful.

—Gautam Mohanty

The authors collectively would like to extend their gratitude to Al-Imran Khan (Bangladesh) and Nirogini Thambaiyya (Sri Lanka) for their timely help with the case law from South Asian jurisdictions. The authors also thank Judge Saleem Marsoof, Judge, Supreme Court of Fiji, and formerly of the Supreme Court of Sri Lanka, for consenting to allow references to his research, as well as making available the recent jurisprudence from Sri Lanka that forms part of this work. The authors also acknowledge the valuable support provided by Sajawal Hussain (Pakistan) and Prakriti Malla (Nepal) in accessing the jurisprudence from those respective jurisdictions. Lastly, the authors would like to thank the publishers for their extensive support, especially for their consideration and the additional time provided during the pandemic.

Contents

About the Authors

Bruno Zeller is Professor of Transnational Law at the University of Western Australia, Perth; Adjunct Professor at Murdoch University, Perth; Fellow of the Australian Institute for Commercial Arbitration, Panel of Arbitrators—MLAANZ; Visiting Professor at Humboldt University, Berlin and a Visiting Professor Stetson Law School, Florida. Prof. Zeller is an international law consultant with Michael Bula Solicitors and specializes in transnational commercial law. He is the author of the seminal work—*Four-Corners—The Methodology for Interpretation and Application of the UN Convention on Contracts for the International Sale of Goods*(2003), amongst a host of research work in the form of books, chapters in edited collections and journals. His research in the area of transnational commercial law and commercial arbitration is much cited.

Gautam Mohanty is an Assistant Professor at Jindal Global Law School (JGLS), O. P. Jindal Global University. He graduated from National Law University Odisha in the year 2015 and has a Master's in International Business Law from Central European University in 2017. He is also an arbitration consultant and has experience advising domestic and international clients in commercial and dispute resolution matters. He has served as an Arbitration Tribunal Secretary to Hon'ble Justice Deepak Verma, Former Judge of Supreme Court of India in several arbitration matters. Further, he has published his work in several reputed journals and his areas of interest include international commercial arbitration, international investment law, private international law, Blockchain and the law. He is currently pursuing his Doctoral Studies at Kozminski University, Warsaw, Poland.

Sai Ramani Garimella teaches international commercial law and arbitration at South Asian University, an inter-governmental organisation of the South Asian Regional group, SAARC. Dr. Garimella also serves as the Visiting Senior Research Associate at the Research Centre on Private International Law in Emerging Countries, University of Johannesburg, Johannesburg, South Africa. Her research on international arbitration has appeared, recently, in the Manchester Journal of International Economic Law. She has co-edited a commemorative volume on the CISG, titled *Contracts for the International Sale of Goods: A Multidisciplinary Perspective.* (A

Commemorative Volume Celebrating 30 Years of The CISG (Sweet & Maxwell, 2019), contributing an essay on Article 42—Third Party IPR Claims in Transnational Commerce—Addressing the Indeterminacy. She has been awarded the Isambard Kingdom Brunel fellowship by the University of Portsmouth in 2019. Her research on international arbitration is appearing in the current volume of Pepperdine Dispute Resolution Journal. She has previously co-edited a collection of essays on Private International Law and the OBOR (Routledge, 2018) and Private International Law—South Asian State Practice for Springer (2017).

Chapter 1
Enforcement of Foreign Arbitral Awards—An Introduction

Overview

This chapter seeks to explain the importance of the enforcement of Arbitral Awards in South Asia with global trade in the South Asia region being at the threshold of a new era. Global trade has been made all the more significant by China's push towards the development of the new Silk Road. International commercial arbitration has been regarded as the norm for resolving international business disputes for many years and the supply chain by road, rail and ship are creating a multinational supply chain through South Asia, South-East and Central Asia into Europe. Hence, it is inevitable that the newly proposed Silk Road would create new challenges to Dispute Resolution practices, especially pertaining to the enforcement process of an Arbitral Award.

This chapter, in particular, will discuss

- The background of the Silk Road
- The importance of the New York Convention ("NYC") on the Recognition and Enforcement of Arbitral Awards
- The UNCITRAL Model Law ("Model Law") on International Commercial Arbitration
- The difficulties encountered in implementing the regime of enforcement of foreign awards.

1.1 Introduction

At the end of April 2017, the first train arrived in China which originated in England through the newly identified Silk Road. It is anticipated that a train can arrive in China every week. The question that then arises is how do the legal systems take into account the new logistics possibilities? A trans-shipment may not be too difficult to understand as it can be accommodated within the current dispute resolution system. However, the issues will be more complex and multifaceted when goods are

B. Zeller et al., *Enforcement of Foreign Arbitral Awards and the Public Policy Exception*,
https://doi.org/10.1007/978-981-16-2634-0_1

off-loaded and new goods are loaded at multiple locations in different countries. In essence, the possibility of damages or breaches of contract may potentially be more frequent. Consequently, how do arbitration and specifically the enforcement process takes into account the multitude of jurisdictions which need to be included in the risk assessment? To answer that, it is argued that diverse legal systems within the supply chain while interacting with each other tend to display a level of diversity. The issue is not as much a question of selecting a governing law, a seat or a procedural framework through an established arbitral institution such as the London Court of International Arbitration ("LCIA"), the International Chambers of Commerce ("ICC"), the Singapore International Arbitration Centre ("SIAC") and the Hong Kong International Arbitration Centre ("HKIAC"). The issue relates to the legal regime impacting the challenge and enforcement of awards in countries with diverse legal systems. The book will argue that the current State practice in this context needs to be appreciated in a holistic manner that factors in the international law on the subject and the local issues that have impacted the development of the law in the States. Such understanding, in view of the authors, is pertinent for commerce to help contracting, risk avoidance and risk management.

The addition of new players from countries along the Silk Road in South Asia and Central Asia is bound to make new challenges inevitable. Given the fact that several countries and nationals are and expected to be involved in the OBOR project, it can be safely presumed that any commercial dispute arising will be a cross border dispute incorporating different legal systems. As with most cross-border infrastructure transactions, the possibility of disputes remains high and in the context of OBOR, the potential is increased further as the scope and scale of the BRI projects finds itself taking place in countries rated as 'high risk' by Transparency International's Corruption Perception Index (CPI).[1]

1.2 The Silk Road—What is Proposed

The Silk Road Initiative, also known as One Belt One Road (OBOR) or Silk Road Economic Belt or Belt Road Initiative (BRI), is a development strategy announced by the President of the People's Republic of China in October 2013[2] involving infrastructure development and investments in countries in Europe, Asia and Africa.[3]

[1] Over 25% of the countries participating in the BRI ranked over 100 on Transparency International's 2017 CPI. https://www.transparency.org/news/feature/corruption_perceptions_index_2017#table, accessed 07/08/2020.

[2] Ministry of Foreign Affairs of the People's Republic of China, 'President Xi Jinping Delivers Important Speech and Proposes to Build a Silk Road Economic Belt with Central Asian Countries', Ministry of Foreign Affairs of the People's Republic of China, 07 September, 2013, https://www.fmprc.gov.cn/mfa_eng/topics_665678/xjpfwzysiesgjtfhshzzfh_665686/t1076,334.shtml, accessed 07/08/2020.

[3] The World Bank, 'Belt and Road Initiative', 29 March, 2018, https://www.worldbank.org/en/topic/regional-integration/brief/belt-and-road-initiative, accessed 28/09/2020.

A perusal of the official paper on the "Vision and Actions on Jointly Building Silk Road Economic Belt and 21st-Century Maritime Silk Road" issued by the National Development and Reform Commission, Ministry of Foreign Affairs, and Ministry of Commerce of the People's Republic of China with State Council authorization in March 2015 encapsulate the principles and framework, the cooperation priorities as well as the cooperation mechanisms. As the title of the official paper reveals, the OBOR is divided into (a) the overland Silk Road Economic Belt and (b) the 21st Century Maritime Silk Road.[4] In other words, 'Belt' refers to the trade routes through land whereas 'Road' refers to sea routes.[5] In essence, the OBOR is an ambitious program setting out the foundations for a trade network and a roadmap for a series of massive infrastructure projects, ranging from high-speed railways to ports and airports. The Silk Road Initiative is aimed at increasing China's global economic dominance and seeks to connect China with East Asia, European and African Countries. From South-East Asia to Eastern Europe and Africa, the initiative includes 71 countries that account for more than half of the global GDP.[6] Notably, the OBOR is perceived as the most international project that China has embarked on in the last decades and as of 2018, China has signed more than 80 cooperation agreements with countries and organizations.[7]

In the context of OBOR, it is noteworthy that Chinese companies, during the period from January 2015 to August 2017, have signed more than 15,300 new construction contracts in BRI countries, with a cumulative value of more than US$300 billion[8] and China has signed cooperation agreements with over 40 countries and international organizations.[9] There is no doubt that the OBOR or the Silk Road is of immense economic value to Asia and requires massive investments to be functioning efficiently. Be that as it may, the redirection of Chinese money overseas will undoubtedly increase the potential for disputes in the construction and trade sectors that can be resolved in Arbitration. Importantly China's BRI has the potential to accelerate economic growth and development in neighboring countries. The ten nations of the Association of Southeast Asian Nations (ASEAN), for example, will see their

[4]Pichler and Meissner [1].

[5]Transparency International, *supra* 1.

[6]Lily Kuo and Niko Kommenda, 'What is China's Belt and Road Initiative?', https://www.theguardian.com/cities/ng-interactive/2018/jul/30/what-china-belt-road-initiative-silk-road-explainer, accessed 30 September, 2020.

[7]Jiang Jiang, 'Belt and Road—An Initiative for Win–win Cooperation', Malta Independent, April 10, 2018, https://www.fmprc.gov.cn/mfa_eng/wjb_663304/zwjg_665342/zwbd_665378/t1549461shtml, accessed 07/08/2020.

[8]Joseph Tam, Karen Lin, Cloris Li, 'A thousand miles begin with a single step: tax challenges under the BRI', *International Tax Review* 28 November 2017, https://www.internationaltaxreview.com/article/b1f7nb45fj2r7y/a-thousand-miles-begin-with-a-single-step-tax-challenges-under-the-bri, accessed 15/10/2020.

[9]Xinhua,'Full text of President Xi's speech at opening of Belt and Road forum', 14 May 2017, http://www.xinhuanet.com/english/2017–05/14/c_136282982.htm., accessed 15/10/2020.

collective urban population expand by 20,000 people every day for the next ten years, creating significant demands for new infrastructure.[10]

Given the enormity of the BRI, China is also in awareness of the expected rise in cross border commercial disputes and has attempted to facilitate such disputes within its legal regime. The establishment of the China International Commercial Court ("CICC") by the Supreme People's Court of China in July 2018 is an attempt by China to adjudicate disputes arising from BRI.[11] Notably, the CICC consists of two courts, one in Xian for adjudicating disputes from overland projects and one in Shenzhen for maritime disputes.[12] The CICC is merely a "permanent adjudication organ" of the Supreme People's Court and not a new court in itself and is assisted by an International Commercial Expert Committee on issues pertaining to foreign law.[13] Nonetheless, a limitation of the CICC that should be taken into due notice is that CICC may only accept a case provided that such a case has a connection to China. Therefore, it follows as a necessary corollary that there is an inherent limitation on the CICC which might leave the disputes unrelated to China in a legal quagmire and hence, disputing commercial parties from different countries may hardly perceive the CICC as a preferred forum to resolve a dispute arising from OBOR projects.

Current discussions in the context of dispute resolution in OBOR disputes essentially have revolved around implementing unified arbitration rules and resolution mechanisms.[14] The International Academy of the Belt and Road(Hong Kong) has been the first to propose unified arbitration and dispute resolution rules for OBOR disputes.[15] A perusal of the aforesaid proposal indicates that the Academy aims to introduce a new set of regulations encapsulating mediation, conciliation, arbitration and appeal procedures titled "Blue Book-Dispute Resolution Mechanism for the Belt and Road".[16] Considering the involvement of several countries, the Blue Book focuses on emphasizing the cultural differences of the disputing parties by permitting the parties to appoint an arbitrator who has the expertise and understanding of local or regional culture and practices.[17]

However, since 2017 a rethink of the BRI has taken place, most specifically in ASEAN countries. In some cases, there have been calls for a renegotiation of contracts. A more prudent approach to the creation of sovereign debt which inevitably

[10]PwC, 'PwC Growth Markets Centre—Realising opportunities along the Belt and Road', June 2017, https://www.pwc.com/gx/en/growth-markets-centre/assets/pdf/pwc-gmc-repaving-the-ancient-silk-routes-web-full.pdf, accessed 15/10/2020.

[11]China International Commercial Court, http://cicc.court.gov.cn/html/1/219/index.html%20 accessed 10/10/2020.

[12]Ministry of Foreign Affairs, PRC, *supra* 2.

[13]Jue Jun Lu, 'Dispute resolution along the Belt and Road: what does the future hold?', Practical Law Arbitration Blog, 2 August, 2018, http://arbitrationblog.practicallaw.com/dispute-resolution-along-the-belt-and-road-what-does-the-future-hold/, accessed 07/08/2020.

[14]See, Wang [2], 11; see generally, Malik [3].

[15]International Academy of Belt and Road, available at: http://interbeltandroad.org/en/major_events/, accessed 07/08/2020.

[16]Ministry of Foreign Affairs, PRC, *supra* 2.

[17]Ibid.

follows infrastructure projects, appears to be taking place which thereby changes the landscape and financing of new projects and increases the potential for dispute resolutions.

In March 2015, China's National Development and Reform Commission, along with its Ministries of Foreign Affairs and Commerce, published the first official document setting out the vision, guiding principles and defining routes with an action plan for the OBOR in the following terms[18]:

> Over 2000 years ago, our ancestors, trekking across vast steppes and deserts, opened the transcontinental passage connecting Asia, Europe and Africa, known today as the Silk Road. Our ancestors, navigating rough seas, created sea routes linking the East with the West, namely, the maritime Silk Road. These ancient silk routes opened windows of friendly engagement among nations, adding a splendid chapter to the history of human progress.
>
> Spanning thousands of miles and years, the ancient silk routes embody the spirit of peace and cooperation, openness and inclusiveness, mutual learning and mutual benefit. The Silk Road spirit has become a great heritage of human civilization . . . Generation after generation, the silk routes travellers have built a bridge for peace and East-West cooperation.
>
> History is our best teacher. The glory of the ancient silk routes shows that geographical distance is not insurmountable. If we take the first courageous step towards each other, we can embark on a path leading to friendship, shared development, peace, harmony and a better future.

In that context, the effects of OBOR can be simply understood as an increase in trade in goods and services affecting rail, road and sea transports. In order to facilitate the smooth functioning, six major cooperation corridors have been proposed, namely:

On land, the plan is to build a new Eurasian land bridge and develop the economic corridors of China-Mongolia-Russia; China-Central Asia-West Asia; the China-Indochina peninsula; China-Pakistan; and Bangladesh-China-India-Myanmar…On the seas, the initiative will focus on jointly building smooth, secure and efficient transport routes connecting major sea ports along the belt and road.[19]

In addition to rail transport, OBOR has attempted to boost maritime trade as below:

China also plans to build a $46 billion economic corridor—pipeline, rail, roads, bridges and more—through Pakistan. The goal is to establish a trade route connecting Gwadar, a port on the Arabian Sea, to northwest China. This enormous project is driven in part by Beijing's desire to build additional routes for its energy imports from the Middle East—to lessen its dependence on sea routes.[20]

The importance of the Silk Road is not so much the building of a connection between China and Europe as both are developed economies, having a predictable

---

[18]The State Council of the Peoples Republic of China, 'Action plan on the Belt and Road Initiative', 30 March, 2015, http://english.www.gov.cn/archive/publications/2015/03/30/content_281475080249035.htm, accessed 07/08/2020.

[19]Geoff Wade, 'China's 'One Belt, One Road' initiative', http://www.aph.gov.au/About_Parliament/Parliamentary_Departments/Parliamentary_Library/pubs/BriefingBook45p/ChinasRoad, accessed 20/10/2017.

[20]Ibid. See also, Jacob Mardell, 'The BRI in Pakistan: China's flagship economic corridor', 20 May, 2020, available at: https://merics.org/en/analysis/bri-pakistan-chinas-flagship-economic-corridor, accessed 20/10/2020.

legal system. The main issue is the fact that countries in Central Asia as well as South Asia which are arguably underdeveloped, will now be playing a pivotal role in the connection between China and Europe. As an example, the five Central Asian states (Kazakhstan, Kyrgyzstan, Tajikistan, Turkmenistan and Uzbekistan) have doubled their trade with China compared to Russia.[21] This suggests that China is redrawing Central Asia's energy economics and more pertinently, Chinese companies now own significant parts of the oil and gas production.[22]

1.2.1 The Response

In response to the BRI, the EU has adopted a politically mixed approach wherein it has openly spoken about the failure of BRI to meet the "*EU agenda for liberalizing trade*" and pushing the balance of power more in favour of China[23] while at the same time recognizing the significance of the BRI in terms of estimated revenue that EU stands to gain from the BRI. Notwithstanding the above signed statement, few countries such as Hungary[24] and Greece[25] have signed bilateral memorandums of understanding (MoU) with China on BRI cooperation. With regard to other EU countries such as France, Germany and the United Kingdom, there is a certain level of scepticism of the BRI; Italy has proceeded to establish an independent bilateral relationship with China to become the "first" G7 partner on the BRI[26] promising to sign a cooperation deal that would include sectors such as railways, airlines, space and culture. Notably, inspite of the aforesaid mixed signals, the EU has, as a collective force, raised concerns regarding BRI projects relating to strict adherence to principles such as openness, interoperability, transparency and sustainability.[27] Summing it up, the EU's position on the BRI can be deciphered as based on engagement rather than attempting to isolate itself from the BRI and rightly so, as the BRI has enormous

---

[21] W. Wilson, China's Huge 'One Belt, One Road' Initiative is Sweeping Central Asia, 27 July, 2016, The National Interest, http://nationalinterest.org/feature/chinas-huge-one-belt-one-road-initiative-sweeping-central-17150 accessed 20/10/2020.

[22] Ibid.

[23] It is to be noted that except for Hungary all EU countries ambassadors to Beijing signed a statement against the approach adopted by China towards the completion of BRI. See, https://www.handelsblatt.com/english/politics/china-first-eu-ambassadors-band-together-against-silk-road/23581860.html?ticket=ST-178239-epxt0YKRtKcMbEYUYr5f-ap3, accessed 01/09/2020.

[24] https://carnegieendowment.org/2018/10/19/europe-s-emerging-approach-to-china-s-belt-and-road-initiative-pub-77536, accessed 01/09/2020.

[25] http://www.chinadaily.com.cn/a/201808/28/WS5b853bdba310add14f3883f1.html, accessed 01/09/2020.

[26] https://www.scmp.com/news/china/diplomacy/article/2165292/italy-aims-be-chinas-first-g7-partner-belt-road, accessed 01/09/2020.

[27] https://eeas.europa.eu/delegations/china/26154/european-commission-vice-president-jyrki-katainen-speech-belt-and-road-forum-leaders-round_en, accessed 01/09/2020.

potential to bring in large scale revenue so long as it adheres to the EU market rules and regulations.

The response of the USA to the BRI, little more than 'unadulterated opposition', has lacked any coherent strategy.[28] However, going by the US National Security Strategy, China is viewed as a competitor seeking to challenge "American power, influence and interests, and attempting to erode American security and prosperity."[29] Pertinently, the document does not directly address the impact of BRI on the US but tacitly recognizes the challenge of the BRI, noting that "China is gaining a strategic foothold in Europe by expanding its unfair trade practices and investing in key industries, sensitive technologies, and infrastructure."

A fact that cannot be overlooked is that Australia is drawn economically—and by necessity—more than ever before into the ASEAN market. Mention must be made here of the recent efforts leading to an interaction of the Australian economy with the ASEAN—The AANZFTA, 2010, ASEAN, Australia and New Zealand Free Trade Agreement[30] and the Indonesia-Australia Comprehensive Economic Partnership Agreement (IA-CEPA) entered into force on 5 July 2020.[31] Australian companies are also extensively involved in cross-border commerce and infrastructure development work, such as the Northern Railways, a subsidiary of Aspire Mining, won "the contract to build and operate a 546 km railway to extend Mongolia's national rail network from the city of Erdenet to Ovoot, the site of the Ovoot Coking Coal Project, a large-scale project in Mongolia."[32] In Australia, a not-for profit organization (ACOBOR) has been established providing information to Australian industry and is supported by the Australian Government and the Australia-China Council.[33]

A significant concern noted within the public discourse with regard to the OBOR has been the slowdown of funding for BRI projects as China is feeling an economic squeeze and the question has been asked whether China is putting scarce resources to the right use.[34] Given that, an expanded view of the project could be an interesting development as new players such as Australia might infuse the project with much needed diversity and larger acceptance. Currently and for the foreseeable future, it can be argued that the economic development in ASEAN is fluid with new players coming in and hence increasing the participation of international companies.

---

[28]https://www.cnas.org/publications/reports/power-play, accessed 11/09/2020.

[29]https://www.whitehouse.gov/wp-content/uploads/2017/12/NSS-Final-12-18-2017-0905.pdf, accessed 11/09/2020.

[30]AANZFTA, General Review 2017–2018, https://aanzfta.asean.org/general-review, accessed 17/11/2020.

[31]Department of Foreign Affairs and Trade, Australia, 'Indonesia-Australia Comprehensive Economic Partnership Agreement (2020).

[32]PWC, *supra* 10.

[33]http://www.australiachinaobor.org.au/, accessed 2008/2017.

[34]See, Zheng S., South China Morning Post 31 January 2019, https://www.scmp.com/news/china/diplomacy/article/2183790/questions-are-raised-about-belt-and-road-projects-slow.

1.3 BRI and the Dispute Resolution Infrastructure—a Role for International Arbitration

In sum, the OBOR is likely to significantly impact the economic landscape by providing access to countries that have so far witnessed limited international interaction or have not excitedly developed their international contacts and connectedness. The economic interaction is also likely to result in legal friction in the form of enforcement of contracts and dispute resolution-related issues, given that the economic activity is being supported on disparate normative regimes of diverse legal traditions.

Signalling that further and significant change may be required, in January 2018, the Leading Group for Deepening Overall Reform of the 19th Central Committee of the Communist Party of China approved a plan to establish a mechanism to legally resolve trade and investment disputes arising from issues related to the BRI, stating[35]:

> The goal is to lawfully settle commercial, trade and investment disputes regarding the Belt and Road Initiative, protect the lawful rights and interests of Chinese and foreign individuals on equal footing and create a stable, fair and transparent business environment with the rule of law, those at the meeting decided.
>
> Efforts to set up the procedure and the organisation to handle disputes should follow the principles of extensive consultation, joint contribution and shared benefits and should be based on China's existing judicial, arbitration and mediation institutions, the leaders agreed.

Pertinently, the advent of BRI has ushered in a change in approach of various arbitral institutions which have invariably responded by allocating resources to facilitate BRI disputes. The International Chamber of Commerce ("ICC") has established a Belt and Road Commission aiming to address dispute resolution opportunities arising from the BRI and aims to promote ICC dispute resolution services.[36] The focus of the ICC in relation to OBOR disputes is concentrated on introducing international mediation standards especially in the context of infrastructure and investment matters to assimilate the aforesaid standards to arbitration disputes in connection with OBOR.[37] In pursuance of its objectives, the ICC has already established a representative office in Shanghai's Free Trade Zone thereby being the first non-Asian dispute resolution institution to establish an office in China.[38]

---

[35]Zhang Yunbi, 'Process eyed to solve Belt, Road disputes', China Daily, 24 January 2018, http://www.chinadaily.com.cn/a/201801/24/WS5a678697a3106e7dcc136198.html, accessed 20/10/2020.

[36]International Chamber of Commerce (ICC), 'Belt and Road Commission', https://iccwbo.org/dispute-resolution-services/belt-road-dispute-resolution/belt-and-road-commission/, accessed 07/08/2020.

[37]Finbarr Bermingham, 'ICC launches Belt and Road arbitration commission', 08 March, 2018, https://www.gtreview.com/news/asia/icc-launches-belt-and-road-arbitration-commission/, accessed 08/08/2020.

[38]International Chamber of Commerce (ICC), 'ICC MoU with Shenzhen Court of International Arbitration extends facilities to arbitration users', 19 October, 2017, https://iccwbo.org/media-wall/news-speeches/icc-mou-with-shenzhen-court-of-international-arbitration-extends-facilities-to-arbitration-users/, accessed 09/08/2020.

Furthermore, ICC has also signed a memorandum of understanding with the Shenzhen Court of International Arbitration in order to cater to the arbitration and mediation disputes arising out of the OBOR.[39] Additionally, the Hong Kong International Arbitration Centre in 2018 announced its "Belt and Road Programme" which consists of (i) an industry-focused "Belt and Road Programme" Committee consisting of independent experts from various fields such as finance, infrastructure, insurance, construction and maritime sectors,[40] (ii) establishing a knowledge database where information relevant to the BRI including reports, articles, expert analysis will be continuously published,[41] and (iii) a model arbitration clause to be incorporated in OBOR contracts.[42] (emphasis supplied).

China has also attempted to revamp its arbitral institutions by merging the Shenzhen Court of International Arbitration and Shenzhen Arbitration Commission into one arbitration centre called the Shenzhen Court of International Arbitration (SCIA) in 2018. Further, the SCIA has also entered into cooperation arrangements with ICC and ICSID for sharing knowledge and facilities in administering international commercial disputes.[43] Moreover, China is also focusing on strengthening its other arbitration institution i.e. CIETAC to adjudicate disputes arising out of the OBOR.[44]

Interestingly, the Astana International Financial Centre("AIFC") established in Kazakhstan in July 2018, has adopted a unique approach to portray itself as an arbitration hub in the backdrop of prospective OBOR disputes.[45] The AIFC has set up two dispute resolution bodies viz.,

(i) The AIFC Court of Justice, and
(ii) An International Arbitration Centre ("IAC").

The AIFC Court of Justice offers a common law court mechanism for the settlement of commercial and civil disputes in the AIFC. The AIFC Court is independent of the courts of Kazakhstan. On the other hand, the IAC has been established for civil and commercial disputes as an alternative to litigation and has included procedures for expedited arbitrations, the appointment of emergency arbitrators, and the resolution of investment treaty disputes.[46]

[39]Ibid.

[40]Stephanie Tang, 'HKIAC's New Belt and Road Programme: Does More Need to be Done?', Kluwer Arbitration Blog, 27 June 2018, http://arbitrationblog.kluwerarbitration.com/2018/06/27/hkiacs-new-belt-roadprogramme-need-done/, accessed 07/08/2020.

[41]http://www.hkiac.org/Belt-and-Road/belt-and-road-knowledge-database accessed 21/07/2020.

[42]http://www.hkiac.org/Belt-and-Road/model-clauses-belt-and-road-contracts accessed 21/07/2020.

[43]Jue Jun Lu, Dispute resolution along the Belt and Road: what does the future hold?, Kluwer Arbitration Blog, August 2, 2018, http://arbitrationblog.practicallaw.com/dispute-resolution-along-the-belt-and-roadwhat-does-the-future accessed 07/08/2020.

[44]Gan and Yang [4], 96.

[45]https://aifc.kz/structure/, accessed 10/08/2020.

[46]https://aifc.kz/files/legals/75/file/iac-arbitration-and-mediation-rules-2018.pdf, accessed 10/08/2020.

As per the current state of things, as of March 2020, it is estimated that 131 to 138 countries have joined the BRI by signing an official Memorandum of Understanding(MoU) with China, although the nature of the MoU remains highly country-specific.[47]

Therefore, it becomes pertinent to consider the stance adopted by the Supreme People's Court, China in relation to the resolution of disputes arising out of OBOR. The Supreme People's Court on 16th June 2015 issued the "*Several Opinions of the Supreme People's Courts concerning Judicial Services and Safeguards provided by the People's Courts for the Belt and Road*".[48] The guidance envisages that the People's Courts would consider their trial function in an enhanced manner and provide effective services for the smooth building and functioning of the Belt and Road initiative.[49] Pending reciprocal arrangements[50] for judicial assistance between China and certain Belt and Road countries, Chinese courts may provide judicial assistance to parties from relevant countries to facilitate the formation of reciprocity.

The *Several Opinions* emphasized the need for the accurate application of international treaties and foreign laws and reiterated upon respect of party autonomy in the context of choice of law as well as the content of such law. People's courts are responsible for ascertaining foreign laws, the focus being on the development of regulations on the identification and application of foreign laws in the relevant countries under the 'Belt and Road Initiative'.[51] Briefly, the aforesaid *Opinions, inter alia*, encapsulate the below mentioned principles:

I. Develop the judicial jurisprudence by delving into the peculiarities of the characteristics of cases and issues arising out of OBOR.
II. Maintaining statistical analyses of cases related to OBOR and providing legal information to concerned authorities to ensure the prevention of any major legal risks.
III. Being aware of applicable rules of international law and the laws and regulations of countries along the OBOR.
IV. Placing rule by law at the highest threshold and ensuring adequate safeguards of the legal process concerning disputes with regard to OBOR.

The effect of OBOR will be an increase in disputes, which necessitates the management of new risks that were not contemplated so far. Additionally, new players

---

[47] https://green-bri.org/countries-of-the-belt-and-road-initiative-bri accessed 01/09/2020.

[48] *Several Opinions on Providing Judicial Services and Guarantee for the Building of One Belt One Road by People's Courts* (No.9 [2015] of the Supreme People's Court) (hereinafter, *Several Opinions*); China Guiding Cases Project (2018).

[49] Supreme People's Court Issues Service to Ensure Belt and Road Initiatives (with Typical Cases) http://szlhqfy.chinacourt.org/article/detail/2015/07/id/1663903.shtml accessed 15/10/2018.

[50] It maybe of interest herein that China has evinced interest in joining the Hague Convention on Choice of Court Agreements, 2005. It has deposited the signature to the Convention on 12th September 2017 https://www.hcch.net/en/news-archive/details/?varevent=569 accessed 10 October 2018.

[51] Supreme People's Court Issues Service to Ensure Belt and Road Initiatives (with Typical Cases) http://szlhqfy.chinacourt.org/article/detail/2015/07/id/1663903.shtml accessed 15 October 2018.

would also become part of the arbitration space. In this scenario, the support of courts towards the arbitral process becomes all the more important, as arbitration cannot stand alone. Such support is most crucial in the enforcement and recognition of arbitral awards. Judicial processes need to be understood in order to rise to the new challenge. This is so as any dispute resolution is only effective once the judgment debt is settled. The influence of the New York Convention and the Model law will prove to be invaluable to overcome new challenges.

The Supreme People's Court has also released eight typical cases, the ratio of which could be a guidance on dispute resolution related to OBOR.[52]

In *Zhejiang Yisheng Petrochemical Co. Ltd v Luxembourg INVISTA Technology Co. Ltd*[53] the Court was called upon to affirm the validity of an arbitration clause that was worded in a seemingly incompatible language with the prevailing arbitration law[54]:

The arbitration shall take place at China International Economic Trade Arbitration Centre (CIETAC), Beijing, P. R. China and shall be settled according to the UNCITRAL Arbitration Rules as at present in force.[55]

The Supreme People's Court, hearing a review from the decision of the Ningbo Intermediate Court, opined:

> The parties used the expression "take place at" in the arbitration clause; the phrase following [this expression] was generally understood to be [a reference to] the place [of arbitration]. However, according to the teleological method of interpretation [that supports the adoption of a meaning] conducive to realizing the parties' wishes to arbitrate, [the phrase] could be understood to also include agreement on the arbitration institution.[56]

The *Zhejiang* ratio is significant as it recognised the validity of arbitration clauses that specified China-seated arbitrations under UNCITRAL Arbitration Rules. Adopting a teleological interpretation of the arbitration clause to ensure its validity, thereby ensuring the realisation of the parties' intention to arbitrate in 'a situation where the arbitration clause did not clearly limit the authority arbitration institution, [the court] determined that the parties' agreement concerning the application by a permanent arbitration institution of another [organisation's set of] arbitration rules should be understood as [an agreement] that the institution would manage the entire arbitration process in accordance with that [set of] arbitration rules'[57] The decision

---

52 Garimella [5].

53 (2012) Zhejiang Ningbo Zhong Zi No. fourth.

54 See, Arbitration Law of the People's Republic of China, Article 16, passed and issued on Aug. 31, 1994, effective as of Sept. 1, 1995, amended on and effective as of Aug. 27, 2009, http://www.npc.gov.cn/wxzl/wxzl/2000-12/05/content_4624.htm and http://www.gov.cn/flfg/2009-08/27/content_1403326.htm (providing for the requirement of designating, in an arbitration agreement, an arbitration commission for handling the case); Stanford Law School, China Cases Guiding Project, case 6 https://cgc.law.stanford.edu/wp-content/uploads/sites/2/2016/11/B-and-R-TC6-English.pdf accessed 14/09/2017.

55 Ibid. case 6, at 3.

56 Ibid.

57 Ibid., at 4.

is significant as it helps promote diversified dispute resolution mechanisms, supports the institutionalisation of arbitration, and enhances the credibility of arbitration.

1.4 Overview of the International Regime on Enforcement of Foreign Arbitral Awards

Increased transnational commercial interaction necessitates the existence of harmonized legal platforms to ensure conformity with the essential feature of human interactions across national boundaries—predictability and certainty of laws. Dispute Resolution has been an area that has received much attention and effort within the harmonization space in the last century and continues to be the focus of international legal harmonization efforts.[58] Success in litigation or arbitration is, for all the stakeholders of international commerce, determined by the successful enforcement of the judgment or award. Today, there is a broad recognition of the proposition that arbitral awards should be enforceable anywhere, regardless of where made.[59] This is the principal advantage of arbitration over litigation and the recognition and enforcement of foreign judgments, which, only recently, saw some efforts at harmonization through the presence of The Hague Convention on Choice of Court Agreements, 2005[60] and the much-discussed Judgments Project of the Hague Conference on Private International Law and regional efforts like the Asian Principles of Recognition and Enforcement of Judgments[61] sponsored by the Asian Business Law Institute, Singapore.

It is thus evident that international arbitration has come to be recognized as an effective mechanism for resolving disputes in international commercial relationships,[62] especially in omnibus economic partnerships between nations. The main

[58] See, the Singapore Mediation Convention (2020); The HCCH Judgments Project, Convention of 2 July 2019 on the Recognition and Enforcement of Foreign Judgments in Civil or Commercial Matters (yet to come into force) https://assets.hcch.net/docs/806e290e-bbd8-413d-b15e-8e3e1bf1496d.pdf, accessed 29/11/2020.

[59] See, generally, Blackaby [6].

[60] HCCH, *Convention of 30 June 2005 on Choice of Court Agreements* https://assets.hcch.net/docs/510bc238-7318-47ed-9ed5-e0972510d98b.pdf accessed 29/11/2020.

[61] Chong [7]; see, also, Chong [8].

[62] 2015 International Arbitration Survey: Improvements and Innovations in International Arbitration, http://www.arbitration.qmul.ac.uk/media/arbitration/docs/2015_International_Arbitration_Survey.pdf. 90% of respondents indicate that international arbitration is their preferred dispute resolution mechanism, either as a stand-alone method (56%) or together with other forms of ADR (34%).

reason for the popularity of arbitration as a means of dispute settlement in international commercial relationships is the flexibility in the procedure, the party-appointment of arbitrators[63] and an almost inherent fidelity to neutrality[64] as well as proven enforceability through an international legal regime.

In light of the above, some of the inherent beneficial features of international arbitration, *inter alia*, such as party autonomy, flexibility, confidentiality also need to be considered when choosing arbitration as a dispute resolution mechanism.[65] Party autonomy can be understood to connote the expressed will of the parties involved in the arbitration process as a source of norms indicating the chosen procedural rules and substantive law governing their arbitral proceedings.[66] The flexibility and neutrality feature of international arbitration is another advantage wherein both Parties have an option to choose a neutral forum for the resolution of their disputes.[67] Additionally, the aspect of confidentiality constitutes one of the most attractive features of arbitration as all proceedings are held in private and are confidential.[68] This is in stark contrast to the hearings held in Court which are generally public. Further, limited court intervention with respect to the appeal of arbitral awards also renders a sense of finality to arbitration as from a commercial standpoint it means that the rendering of an award by the arbitrators will typically mark the end of proceedings.

1.4.1 The Legal Regime Impacting International Arbitration

The two significant instruments within the space of dispute resolution, concerning arbitration, the New York Convention(“***NYC***”)[69] and the UNCITRAL Model Law,[70]

---

[63] Teresa Chang, “Evolution, Not Revolution” The Search for Order within Chaos in the Evolution of ISDS, 45th Alexander Lecture https://www.doj.gov.hk/en/community_engagement/speeches/pdf/sj20200116e1.pdf accessed 02/03/2021. Chang commented that the success of the Alabama Claims Arbitration in resolving the dispute peacefully was very much a result of the party-appointment model under which the five-person arbitral tribunal was formed with one arbitrator nominated by the United States, one nominated by the Great Britain, and three nominated by neutral States.

[64] The 1871 Alabama Claims Arbitration laid the foundations for modern arbitration especially the commissions were composed of members who were not nationals of the claimants’ States. The principle of neutrality in international arbitration had its modern beginnings with this case. See, generally, Bingham [9], Veeder [10].

[65] See, generally, Lowenfeld [11], Watt [12].

[66] Redfern et al. [13] 131. The authors characterised the agreement of the parties as the keystone feature of international arbitration. See, generally, Giuditta Cordero-Moss [14], Cordero Moss [15].

[67] See, generally, Moses [16], Blackaby and Hunter [17]; Born [18], Born [19]; Bernini [20] Pierre [21], Park [22], 103.

[68] See, generally, Paulsson and Rawding [23] 312; Fortier [24]; Brown [25] 974; Jolles et al. [26], Young and Chapman [27], Mistelis [28].

[69] United Nations Convention on the Recognition and Enforcement of Foreign Arbitral Awards (New York, 10 June 1958), https://www.newyorkconvention.org/english, accessed 10/08/2018.

[70] UNCITRAL Model Law on International Commercial Arbitration, 1985, https://www.uncitral.org/pdf/english/texts/arbitration/ml-arb/07-86998_Ebook.pdf, accessed 10/08/2018.

have helped achieve, to a large extent, the much-needed predictability and certainty on the law related to the enforcement of foreign arbitral awards. Such predictability is enhanced by the fact that since 1958 when the Convention came into force, it has now garnered 166 members at the last count.[71] Many countries have taken guidance from the UNCITRAL Model Law (amended and updated in 2006) in drafting and amending their arbitration laws in their quest to ensure harmonized legal platforms.[72]

1.4.1.1 The New York Convention

The vast acceptance of the New York Convention and the fact that arbitral awards are more often recognized in another jurisdiction than earlier is viewed as one of the significant advantages of arbitration over litigation in state courts.[73] The Convention provides what amounts to a universal constitutional charter for the international arbitral process, whose sweeping terms have enabled both national courts and arbitral tribunals to develop durable, effective means for enforcing international arbitration agreements and arbitral awards. Additionally, the Convention also provided the basis for most contemporary national legislation governing the international arbitral process, and in particular, the UNCITRAL Model Law, which has implemented and elaborated upon the Convention's fundamental principles and legal framework. The purpose of the Convention is laid out in Article I.

This Convention shall apply to the recognition and enforcement of arbitral awards made in the territory of a State other than the State where the recognition and enforcement of such awards are sought and arising out of differences between persons, whether physical or legal. It shall also apply to arbitral awards not considered as domestic awards in the State where their recognition and enforcement are sought.[74]

The quintessential characteristic of the Convention is that it concerns itself only with the enforcement and recognition of foreign arbitral awards. Thus, it follows as a necessary corollary that enforcement of an award, as per the terminology of Article I, cannot take place at the seat. This is an obvious point as recognition or enforcement of an award which is sought at the seat will not attract the relevant principles of the Convention as they will still be governed by the same legal system under which the award was made; that is it is left to domestic law principle mainly the Model Law.

Further, since awards can be challenged in other jurisdictions than that of the seat, the NYC created a uniform set of laws under which any challenges can be heard. It promotes the comity principle with very few exceptions, which are embedded within Article V-the subject of this book. Article V, in essence, is the ceiling or

[71] See, https://www.newyorkconvention.org/list+of+contracting+states for the updated list of Contracting States.

[72] Legislation based on the Model Law has been adopted in 85 States in a total of 118 jurisdictions. https://uncitral.un.org/en/texts/arbitration/modellaw/commercial_arbitration/status accessed 28/02/2021.

[73] Gary B. Born, *supra* 67, 3394–3731.

[74] http://www.uncitral.org/pdf/english/texts/arbitration/NY-conv/New-York-Convention-E.pdf.

maximum level of control but States are free to apply more liberal rules than those listed in Article V.[75] Fouchard also suggested that the NYC in Article VII enshrined the pro-enforcement policy which is considered to be one of the cornerstones of the convention.[76] Gaillard and Bermann argued,

> The genius of the New York Convention is to have foreseen, and made provision for, the progressive liberalization of the law of international arbitration. Article VII (1), which governs the relationship between the Convention and other applicable treaties and laws, derogates from the rules that normally govern the application of conflicting provisions of treaties, and provides that in the event that more than one regime might apply, the rule which shall prevail is neither the more recent nor the more specific, but instead that which is more favourable to the recognition and enforcement. Guide on the Convention on the Recognition and Enforcement of Foreign Arbitral Awards.[77]

In addition, Article VII has been drafted in such a form that a revision of the NYC is unnecessary as courts in convention States can innovate and improve on the understanding of the enforcement and recognition aspects of arbitration.[78]

1.4.1.2 The Model Law

The Model Law is a soft law that was drafted by UNCITRAL but has found its way in one form or another into domestic arbitration laws. As an example, Australia has adopted the model law into the International Arbitration Act. UNCITRAL is not a stand-alone inclusion to the International Arbitration Act, 1974 as the Act also contains an enabling legislation that incorporates the New York Convention and the International Centre for the Settlement of Investment Disputes (ICSID). UNCITRAL only deals with international arbitration and domestic arbitral legislation is a matter of policy within the ambit of powers vested with States. Despite the fact that initially, domestic legislations were not in line with the Model Law, nonetheless, in recent years, many states including Australia have amended their domestic legislation in order to bring it in line with international arbitration.

It must be taken to understand the Model Law as it was included into domestic legislation. Unlike a convention, not all states have adopted the Model Law in its entirety. Variations are possible. For example, in Austria, the Model Law does not distinguish between a domestic or international application. It is to be applied for both situations. In Australia, a different issue must be noted. When adopting the Model Law, the Australian parliament prefaced the Model Law which was included as a Schedule in Part V. Hence the Model Law must be read and applied in conjunction with the enabling legislation. Courts and arbitral tribunals, as well as disputant parties, often refer to the enabling legislation and not to the Model Law which

---

[75] Gaillard and Bermann [29].

[76] Fouchard [30].

[77] Gaillard and Bermann, *supra* 75, 7.

[78] See, Gaillard [31].

in essence deals with the same issues. An example is Section 18A in relation to justifiable doubts as to the impartiality of arbitrators' which notes:

(1) For the purposes of Article 12(1) of the Model Law, there are justifiable doubts as to the impartiality or independence of a person approached in connection with a possible appointment as arbitrator only if there is a real danger of bias on the part of that person in conducting the arbitration.
(2) For the purposes of Article 12(2) of the Model Law, there are justifiable doubts as to the impartiality or independence of an arbitrator only if there is a real danger of bias on the part of the arbitrator in conducting the arbitration.

The jurisprudential developments in this regard, as with other aspects impacting enforceability of the awards would be an interesting watch.

While the two aforesaid instruments have enjoyed a large volume of adherence, there is an increasing need to revisit these attempts. The importance lies in the fact that the mechanism for enforceability of foreign arbitral awards conforms to the envisaged purpose within the New York Convention—delocalization and the enforcement of awards, including annulled arbitral awards, interim measures and their enforceability, and the need for a uniform approach on public policy exception to the enforcement of foreign arbitral awards. This book shall address these issues through interfacing the articulation, including the absence of it, of these topics within the NYC and the UNCITRAL Model Law, lacing it with State Practice. The book includes the State practice of a few jurisdictions from South Asia, a region that has, despite adhering to these two instruments, not demonstrated enough consistency in its approach, especially while addressing the areas mentioned above.

Further, the language introducing the enlisted criteria[79] for setting aside of arbitral awards at the seat as well as for refusing enforcement of the same, uses discretionary terms with little guidance within the text on the methodology for the exercise of that discretion.[80] In effect, review systems such as Article V of the NYC, Article 34 of the Model Law and diverse Public Policy considerations[81] designed to protect the accuracy of an arbitration award and ensure legal precision may impede the attainment of "*justice*" through delay by eroding "confidence in the efficiency and fairness of the system."[82]

[79] Albert Jan van den Berg, The New York Convention of 1958: An Overview, https://cdn.arbitration-icca.org/s3fs-public/document/media_document/media012125884227980new_york_convention_of_1958_overview.pdf accessed 28/01/2021.

[80] Amokura Kawharu, 'Articles 34 and 36 of the UNCITRAL Model Law on International Commercial Arbitration: The Court's Discretion' https://www.researchgate.net/publication/228150922_Articles_34_and_36_of_the_Uncitral_Model_Law_on_International_Commercial_Arbitration_The_Court's_Discretion accessed 12/11/2016.

[81] See, Park [32], 656.

[82] Gelander [33].

1.4.1.3 Enforceability of the Annulled Awards

Another pertinent issue for consideration is that the NYC and the UNCITRAL Model Law do not make a definite and an effective statement on the status of the awards set aside by courts at the seat of the arbitration. Setting-aside proceedings are regulated within the local law i.e. the domestic regulation governing arbitration proceedings at the seat of arbitration. Notably, one of the criteria for setting aside arbitral awards namely public policy—which is discussed later in the book—needs to be defined within the relevant forum as it is not an internationally harmonized issue. The UNCITRAL Model Law only provides guidance with regard to such proceedings. The Singapore Court of Appeal in *PT Asuransi Jasa Indonesia (Persero) v Dexia Bank SA*[83] while deliberating upon the feasibility of a cohesive international public policy has opined,

> 59 Although the concept of public policy of the State is not defined in the Act or the Model Law, the general consensus of judicial and expert opinion is that public policy under the Act encompasses a narrow scope. In our view, it should only operate in instances where the upholding of an arbitral award would "shock the conscience" (see Downer Connect ([58] supra) at [136]), or is "clearly injurious to the public good or ... wholly offensive to the ordinary reasonable and fully informed member of the public" (see Deutsche Schachbau v. Shell International Petroleum Co. Ltd. [1987] 2 Lloyds' Rep 246 at 254, per Sir John Donaldson MR), or where it violates the forum's most basic notion of morality and justice: see Parsons & Whittemore Overseas Co. Inc. v. Societe Generale de L'Industrie du Papier (RAKTA) 508 F 2d, 969 (2nd Cir, 1974) at 974. This would be consistent with the concept of public policy that can be ascertained from the preparatory materials to the Model Law. As was highlighted in the Commission Report (A/40/17), at para 297 (referred to in A Guide to the UNCITRAL Model Law on International Commercial Arbitration: Legislative History and Commentary by Howard M Holtzmann and Joseph E Neuhaus (Kluwer, 1989) at 914):
>
> In discussing the term 'public policy', it was understood that it was not equivalent to the political stance or international policies of a State but comprised the fundamental notions and principles of justice... It was understood that the term 'public policy', which was used in the 1958 New York Convention and many other treaties, covered fundamental principles of law and justice in substantive as well as procedural respects. Thus, instances such as corruption, bribery or fraud and similar serious cases would constitute a ground for setting aside. (emphasis supplied).

This judgment has been recently affirmed by the Singapore High Court in *Dongwoo Mann Hummel Co. Ltd. v Mann Hummel GmbH*.[84]

The New York Convention, however, makes a reference to an award set-aside at the seat within Article V (1) (e) stating that such awards "'may' be refused [...] if it has been set aside or suspended by a competent authority of the country in which, or under the law of which, that award was made." Accordingly, it has been a practice in many jurisdictions as well as in scholarly opinion that enforcement of an annulled award is also understood to draw support from Article VII of the New York Convention, which allows for the application of more favourable provisions of local law or other international treaties in order to further strengthen the binding

[83] *PT Asuransi Jasa Indonesia (Persero) v Dexia Bank SA,* [2006] SGCA 41.

[84] *Dongwoo Mann Hummel Co. Ltd. v Mann Hummel GmbH* [2008] SGHC 67.

nature of arbitral awards.[85] Therefore, if the local law does not view the annulment of the foreign arbitral award at the seat of arbitration as a sufficient reason to refuse recognition and enforcement, setting aside such an award will not in itself have adverse consequences.[86]

However, it is necessary that the international regime posits this approach into binding instruments to ensure there is adherence to the vision of the NYC that foreign arbitral awards are binding and enforceable, and courts at the seat would not perceive their '*supervisory*'[87] role to extend to review of awards in pleas of serious irregularity, as was evident in the case of *Pacific China Holdings Ltd.(In Liquidation) v Grand Pacific Holdings*[88] where there were two-stage proceedings challenging an award on due process irregularities in Hong Kong, resulting in a rejection of the appeal by the Court of Final Appeal and setting a high threshold for such pleadings in future.[89]

Notably, in the aforesaid case, Pacific China Holdings Ltd. ("PCH") filed a motion to set aside the arbitral award based on the violation of Article 34 (2) (a) (ii) and 34 (2) (a) (iv) of the UNCITRAL Model Law. The Court of First Instance granted the claim of PCH and concluded that PCH had convincingly established violations of Article 34 (2) of the Model Law. On the other hand, the Court of Appeal and Final Appeal dismissed PCH motion to set aside the award while observing that such provisions advanced by PCH were not reasonably premised on essential grounds and while dismissing the motion made a pertinent observation within the ratio:

> The rulings complained of were made by the tribunal in the proper exercise of its procedural and case management discretions, reflecting its assessment of the requirements of procedural fairness as appropriate to the circumstances. There is no basis for interference by the Court. No reasonably arguable basis has been disclosed for granting leave to appeal.[90]

In this case, the precedent set by the Hong Kong courts pertaining to the dismissal of the case on the grounds of violation of Article 34(2)(a) of the UNCITRAL Model Law serves as a valuable signpost guiding the judiciary on preserving the effectiveness of arbitration practice in relation to requiring significant reasons that must be egregious for the application for setting aside the arbitral award to succeed.

---

[85] See, Davis [34] 55; See, generally, Brekoulakis [35]; Reisman and Iravani [36], 36—Reisman and Iravani observed, "A critical strut of the architecture of international commercial arbitration is the guarantee of the finality of arbitral awards once they are issued...."; See, also, Silberman [37], Gharavi [38].

[86] Paulsson [39], Paulsson [40], Li [41], 387.

[87] Bělohlávek [42].

[88] CACV 136/2011; Date of judgment: 9 May 2012.

[89] *Pacific China Holdings Ltd.(In Liquidation) v Grand Pacific Holdings* FAMV No. 18 of 2012 https://legalref.judiciary.hk/lrs/common/ju/ju_frame.jsp?DIS=85755&currpage=T accessed 02/03/202.

[90] Ibid., [5].

1.4.2 International Arbitration and the Role of the National Courts: Interesting Insights

International arbitration as a method of dispute resolution is not beyond scrutiny though. The themes of the scrutiny includes, amongst others, the reconciliation of freedom of contract with the inherent feature of the legal personality of the State—the administration of justice. The discussion on the relationship between national courts and international arbitration is almost legendary and a part of the folklore of arbitration. Yet, it continues to play a dominant part of the debate around the regulation of international arbitration. Despite its inherent benefits like party autonomy, neutrality, expediency, expertise, confidentiality and finality associated with arbitration, privatization of justice has the intrinsic weakness of being distinct from the legal system—jurisdictional as well as with regard to substantive law. It is therefore pertinent to understand how national courts have found a role for themselves in the context of international arbitration, especially because it effects the enforcement of the resultant arbitral award.

One of the prominent theories surrounding the role of the national courts in the context of international arbitration is the jurisdictional theory. The jurisdictional theory, in simple parlance, contemplates that "although the jurisdictional theory does not dispute the idea that an arbitration has its origin in the parties' arbitration agreement, it maintains that the validity of arbitration agreements and arbitration procedures needs to be regulated by national laws and the validity of an arbitral award is decided by the laws of the seat and the country where the recognition or enforcement is sought."[91] The proponents of the jurisdictional theory often argue that all arbitration procedures, per se, have to be regulated by two different legal regimes, i.e., the law chosen by the parties and the law governing the place of arbitration. The proponents also further put forth the argument that arbitrators resemble judges of national courts, since both derive their powers from a common source- the laws governing the place of arbitration and both are expected to judiciously apply the laws of their state to settle the disputes submitted to them. Another notable feature that is propagated by the proponents of the jurisdictional theory is that the seat of the arbitration assumes specific significance and that the will of the parties will only be put on the highest threshold in an arbitration proceeding to the extent that the lex fori permits.[92]

The arbitrators' role encapsulates a bounden duty to achieve a delicate yet significant balance between the will of the parties and the mandatory rules of the *lex fori*. To quote Yu,

> Any acts of arbitrators that contradict the mandatory rules and public policy of the place of arbitration are regarded as judicially unjustified.[93]

---

[91] Yu [43].

[92] Mann [44].

[93] Hong-Lin Yu, *supra* 91, 259.

Furthermore, the territorial principle provides a strong basis for the national courts exercising supervisory powers over the arbitration. Such supervisory powers are also confirmed in the New York Convention 1958. A perusal of a few of the provisions of the convention demonstrates that in the absence of party agreement on the following issues, it ought to be decided in accordance with the law of the seat of arbitration. Such issues include the validity of arbitration agreements,[94] arbitral awards,[95] the composition of the arbitral authority and the arbitral procedures.[96] While the courts in the seat of arbitration and in the enforcing jurisdiction step in to perform this important role, their increased presence, citing public policy reasons, can also be an interference with the arbitral process and could also lead to vitiation of the award. The jurisprudence from the Indian courts, discussed in this chapter as well as extensively throughout the course of this book, is but emblematic of the problem of judicial interference that the territoriality principle unwittingly ushers in. This could also impact upon the enforceability of the award, given the ground of the award being set aside being a possible consideration for refusing to enforce an award, courtesy Article V (1) (e).

1.4.2.1 UNCITRAL Model Law and the Territoriality Principle

Article 1(3) states the territoriality nature of the law. It reads as follows,

(3) An arbitration is international if:
(a) The parties to an arbitration agreement, have, at the time of the conclusion of that agreement, their places of business in different States; or
(b) One of the following places is situated outside the State in which the parties have their places of business:
(i) The place of arbitration if determined in, or pursuant to, the arbitration agreement;
(ii) Any place where a substantial part of the obligations of the commercial relationship is to be performed or the place with which the subject-matter of the dispute is most closely connected; or
(iii) The parties have expressly agreed that the subject-matter of the arbitration agreement relates to more than one country.

Many arbitration laws have attempted to limit court involvement in international commercial arbitration.[97] The explanatory note of the Model Law opined that it seemed justified in view of the fact that the parties to an arbitration agreement make

---

[94] New York Convention, *supra* 69, Article V (1) (a).

[95] Ibid., Article V(1)(e).

[96] Ibid., Article V(1)(d).

[97] See, for example, Section 103 of The English Arbitration Act, 1996. **103—Refusal of recognition or enforcement.**

[…].

a conscious decision to exclude court jurisdiction and, in particular in commercial cases, thereby preferring expediency and finality to protracted battles in court.[98]

The Model Law foresaw court involvement only in the limited areas of appointment, challenge and termination of arbitrators (articles 11,13 and 14), jurisdiction of the arbitral tribunal (article 16) and setting aside of the arbitral award (article 34). Beyond these instances in these articles, no court shall intervene in matters governed as according to the provisions of the Model Law.

As Kaufmann-Kohler commented, one of the Model Law's 'main purposes was to free the proceedings from the constraints of local law, so as to avoid the parties' expectations from being frustrated by conflicting provisions of such law'.[99] This is also reflected in UNCITRAL reports leading up to the establishment of the Model Law:

> Probably the most important principle on which the Model Law should be based is the freedom of the parties in order to facilitate the proper functioning of international commercial arbitration according to their expectations. This would allow them to freely submit their disputes to arbitration and to tailor the 'rules of the game' to their specific needs. It would also enable them to take full advantage of rules and policies geared to modern international arbitration practice as, for example, embodied in the UNCITRAL Arbitration Rules.[100]

As a precursor to the detailed discussion in the following paragraphs regarding state practice pertaining to public policy in the enforcement mechanism of foreign arbitral awards in South Asia it is noteworthy, as an example, to take into consideration the enforcement mechanism prevalent in India concerning foreign NYC arbitral awards, as most states in South Asia, follow a similar procedure. In India, foreign awards are governed by Part II of the Indian and Arbitration Act, 1996 (Act, 1996) wherein a foreign award is not a decree by itself, which is executable as such under Section 49 of the Act, 1996. The enforcement of a foreign award in India occurs

---

(3) Recognition or enforcement of the award may also be refused if the award is in respect of a matter which is not capable of settlement by arbitration, or if it would be contrary to public policy to recognise or enforce the award.

(4) An award which contains decisions on matters not submitted to arbitration may be recognised or enforced to the extent that it contains decisions on matters submitted to arbitration which can be separated from those on matters not so submitted.

(5) Where an application for the setting aside or suspension of the award has been made to such a competent authority as is mentioned in subsection (2)(f), the court before which the award is sought to be relied upon may, if it considers it proper, adjourn the decision on the recognition or enforcement of the award.

[…].

https://www.legislation.gov.uk/ukpga/1996/23/section/103 accessed 02/03/2021.

[98] UNCITRAL, UNCITRAL Model Law on International Commercial Arbitration (as revised in 2006), 26–27. https://uncitral.un.org/sites/uncitral.un.org/files/media-documents/uncitral/en/19-09955_e_ebook.pdf accessed 02/03/2021.

[99] Kaufmann-Kohler [45], 355.

[100] Yearbook of the United Nations Commission on International Trade Law, 1981, Volume XII, 'Report of the Secretary-General: possible features of a model law on international commercial arbitration, A/CN.9/207', [107] https://undocs.org/pdf?symbol=en/A/CN.9/207, accessed 20/10/2020. ("Yearbook of the UNCITRAL").

only after the court indulges itself in the exercise of determining whether the foreign award before it satisfies the enforceability requirements as meted out under Chap. 1 in Part II of the Act,1996. It is only pursuant to the completion of stages enunciated in Section 47 and 48 of the Act, 1996, the foreign award becomes enforceable as a deemed decree, as provided by Section 49 of the Act, 1996. Pertinently, the scheme of the Act, 1996 for enforcement of New York Convention awards is as follows.[101]

> (a) Part II Chapter 1 of the Arbitration and Conciliation Act, 1996 pertains to the enforcement of New York Convention awards. Under the 1996 Act, there is no requirement for the foreign award to be filed before the seat court, and obtain a decree thereon, after which it becomes enforceable as a foreign decree. This was referred to as the "double exequatur," which was a requirement under the Geneva Convention, 1927 and was done away with by the New York Convention, which superseded it.[102] There is a paradigm shift under the 1996 Act. Under the 1996 Act, a party may apply for recognition and enforcement of a foreign award, after it is passed by the arbitral tribunal. The Applicant is not required to obtain leave from the court of the seat in which, or under the laws of which, the award was made.
>
> (b) Section 44 of the 1996 Act provides that a New York Convention award would be enforceable, if the award is with respect to a commercial dispute, covered by a written agreement in a State with which the Government of India has a reciprocal relationship, as notified in the Official Gazette.

Further, in *Fuerst Day Lawson Ltd. v Jindal Exports Ltd.*,[103] the Supreme Court of India has held that a proceeding seeking recognition and enforcement of a foreign award in India has two different stages viz., (1) In the first stage, the Court is required to decide about the enforceability of the award in the backdrop of Section 47 and Section 48 of the Act, 1996 and (2) Only when the Court finds the foreign award enforceable it would proceed to take further steps for the execution of the award. Notably, the Supreme Court of India has observed that both the abovementioned stages are to be conducted in the same proceeding and no two separate proceedings are required.

Section 48 of the Act, 1996 replicates Article V of the NYC, and postulates the conditions on which the enforcement of a foreign award may be refused. The courts, via subsections (1) and (2) of Section 48 of the Act, 1996 consider any one of the enlisted seven grounds for refusal to enforce a foreign award. Sub-Section (1) contains five grounds which may be raised by the losing party for refusal of enforcement of the foreign award, while Sub-Section (2) contains two grounds which the court may ex officio invoke to refuse enforcement of the award[104] i.e. non-arbitrability of the subject-matter of the dispute under the laws of India; and second, the award is in conflict with the public policy of India.

It is noteworthy that the enforcement court, if situated in India, cannot set aside a foreign award, even if the conditions under Section 48 of the Act, 1996 are made

[101] *Government of India v Vedanta Limited and Ors.*, Civil Appeal No. 3185 of 2020 (Arising out of SLP (Civil) No. 7172 of 2020.

[102] *Renusagar Power Co. Ltd. v General Electric Co.*, (1994) Suppl. (1) SCC 644, Para 41. See also, *Escorts Limited v Universal Tractor Holding LLC*, (2013) 10 SCC 717.

[103] *Fuerst Day Lawson Ltd. v Jindal Exports Ltd.*, (2001) 6 SCC 356.

[104] Malhotra [46].

out. The power to set aside a foreign award vests only with the court at the seat of arbitration, since the supervisory o primary jurisdiction is exercised by the curial courts at the seat of arbitration. The enforcement court may "refuse" enforcement of a foreign award, if the conditions contained in Section 48 of the Act, 1996 are made out. This would be evident from the semantics employed in Section 48 of the Act, 1996, which provides that enforcement of a foreign award may be "refused" only if the Applicant furnishes proof of any of the conditions contained in Section 48 of the Act,1996.

1.4.2.2 The Public Policy Exception to Enforcement of Arbitral Awards

While the public policy does not find any categorical international definitional articulation in the *travaux preparatoires* of the New York Convention, it has, nevertheless, enjoyed universal acceptance tempered upon each country's national needs. Some common features found within the conceptual understanding in many national jurisdictions are public good and public interest.

Definitional guidance on public policy could be derived from the decision in *Parsons & Whitemore Overseas Co. v Societe Generale de L'Industrie du Papier*,[105] wherein it was held that enforcement of a foreign award may be denied on public policy grounds only where enforcement would violate the State's most basic notions of morality and justice.

A perusal of the *travaux preparatoires* of the UNCITRAL Model Law indicates that during the course of discussion in the Commission it was observed that the term "public policy" in the common law systems could be interpreted as having a narrower meaning that its ostensible equivalent—"*ordre public*"- as prevalent in civil law systems. It was further observed that term "*ordre public*", used in the French text of the Model Law, was said to include principles of procedural justice, while the former term, used in the English text, was thought by some to be susceptible to an interpretation that would exclude notions of procedural justice.[106] Nevertheless, the common understanding between the members of the Commission was that the term "*Public Policy*" was not to be equated with the political stance or international policies of a State but in essence comprised the fundamental notions and principles of justice.[107] However, in the end, the Commission decided to incorporate the broader interpretation of the term "public policy" into the Commission Report which states as below:

---

[105] *Parsons & Whitemore Overseas Co. v Societe Generale de L'Industrie du Papier* 508 F. 2d 969 (2nd Cir. 1974).

[106] UNCITRAL Report on the work of its 18th session, UN Doc: A/40/17, [296], June 3–21, 1985, https://undocs.org/en/a/40/17(supp), accessed 21/01/2021; See also, 'UNCITRAL Model Law, Chapter VII, Article 34 [Application for setting aside as exclusive recourse against arbitral award]', in Holtzmann and Neuhaus [47].

[107] Ibid.

> It was understood that the term "public policy," which was used in the 1958 New York Convention and many other treaties, covered fundamental principles of law and justice in substantive as well as procedural respects. Thus, instances such as corruption, bribery or fraud and similar serious cases would constitute a ground for setting aside. It was noted, in that connection, that the wording "the award is in conflict with the public policy of this State" was not to be interpreted as excluding instances or events relating to the manner in which an award was arrived at.[108]

The starting point for any discussion involving the interpretation of "public policy" is that an award can be enforced in any jurisdiction subject to the restrictions as noted in Article 36 of the Model Law and Article V of the NYC. However, Article 34 allows the setting aside of an award and hence enforcement and recognition of foreign awards is closely tied to Article 34 of the Model Law. This is so as Article V of the New York Convention mirrors Article 34 of the Model Law. Thus, the threshold question at this juncture is whether an award which has been set aside can be enforced in another jurisdiction under either Article 36 of the Model Law or Article V of the New York Convention. While the necessity of public policy exception has been much discussed,[109] the discourse[110] on international arbitration has called for delimitation of the content of this exception, to ensure conformity to the purpose of the NYC, recognition and enforcement of foreign arbitral awards. However, as this book will demonstrate the problem is how court charged with the enforcement of an award will view the strength of the seat. This is specifically a problem–as discussed in a later chapter—when the award has been set aside at the seat.

Article V (1) (e) of the NYC contemplates that an arbitral award may be refused recognition if it "has been set aside or suspended by a competent authority of the country in which, or under the law of which, that award has been made."[111] Notably, the UNCITRAL Model Law and other national arbitration legislations modelled as per the NYC contain similar provisions.[112] The applicability of Article V (1) (e) hinges on the analysis conducted on the touchstone of whether the national court judgement purports to deny the legal effect of an arbitral award. Even though, in practice, it is relatively rare for international award to be annulled in the courts of the arbitral seat,[113] however, in a situation where an award is annulled pertinent questions

[108] UNCITRAL Report, *supra* 105, [297].

[109] see, generally, Garcia de Enterra [48]; Buchanan [49], Miller [50].

[110] see, generally, International Law Association, 'Resolution 2/2002, Recommendation on the Application of Public Policy as a Ground for Refusing Recognition or Enforcement of Foreign Arbitral Awards' (2004) 29 *Yearbook of Commercial Arbitration* 345; Yang [51], Hanson [52].

[111] New York Convention, *supra* 69, Article V (1) (e).

[112] UNCITRAL Model Law, *supra* 70, Article 36(1)(a)(v); English Arbitration Act, 1996, §103(2)(f); Swiss Law on Private International Law, Art. 194 (referring to New York Convention); German ZPO, §1061(1); Netherlands Code of Civil Procedure, Arts. 1075, 1076(1)(e); Scottish Arbitration Act, 2010, §20(3)(d); Norwegian Arbitration Act, §46(f); Singapore International Arbitration Act, 2012, §31(2)(f); Hong Kong Arbitration Ordinance, 2013, §89(2)(f); Japanese Arbitration Law, Art. 45(2)(vii); Australian International Arbitration Act, 2011, §8(5)(f); Indian Arbitration and Conciliation Act, §48(1)(e); New Zealand Arbitration Act, §7, Schedule 1, Art. 36(1)(a)(v).

[113] Gary B. Born, *supra* 67, 3394–3731.

arise. In this regard it is important to note that there is no controversy that setting aside must be undertaken at the seat. Article 34 of the UNCITRAL Model Law uses the term "*this State*" which confirms that the process must take place at the seat of the arbitration. Article 36 of the Model Law-duplicating the language of Article 34–also uses the term "*this State*". Hence the inevitable conclusion is that if the enforcement is also contemplated to take place at the seat and it is doubtful if not impossible to enforce an award at the seat where the award was set aside.

The issue becomes complicated when the enforcement of an award which has been set aside at the seat of arbitration is being enforced in another jurisdiction than the seat. It is well accepted that an award can be enforced in any jurisdiction other than the seat which is highlighted by Article V of the New York Convention which uses the word "*that country*" meaning the country where the enforcement is to take place. The NYC provides limited express guidance on the issue of an annulled award. The National Court decisions in France, Belgium, Austria and the United States of America have all held that an arbitral award may, and in some circumstances, must be recognized by foreign courts even if the award has been annulled in the arbitral seat.[114] Alternatively, it is also the position of some states that the annulment of an award at the seat renders the award a nullity, which other states should not recognize or enforce.[115]

It is clear that the seat is a mere convenience in order for courts to oversee the proper function of the procedural aspects which in the end either confirms the award or sets it aside. However, Gaillard has argued,

> Arbitral tribunals need not operate like the national courts of a particular State simply because they have their seat there. Arbitrators do not derive their powers from the State in which they have their seat but rather from the sum of all the legal orders that recognize, under certain

---

[114]See, e.g., *Chromalloy Aeroservs. v Arab Republic of Egypt*, 939 F.Supp. 907 (D.D.C. 1996); Judgment of 29 June 2007, *PT Putrabali Adyamulia v Rena Holding et Société Mnogutia Est Epices*, 2007 Rev. arb. 507 (French Cour de cassation le); Judgment of 10 June 1997, *Omnium de Traitement et de Valorisation v Hilmarton*, XXII Y.B. Comm. Arb. 696 (French Cour de cassation) (1997); Judgment of 23 March 1994, *Société Hilmarton v Société OTV*, 1994 Rev. arb. 327 (French Cour de cassation civ. le); Judgment of 14 January 1997, *Arab Repub. of Egypt v Chromalloy Aeroservs., Inc.*, XXII Y.B. Comm. Arb. 691 (Paris Cour d'appel) (1997); Judgment of 6 December 1988, *Société Nationale pour la Recherche, le Transport et la Commercialisation des Hydrocarbures (Sonatrach) v Ford, Bacon & Davis, Inc.*, XV Y.B. Comm. Arb. 370 (Brussels Tribunal de Première Instance) (1990); Judgment of 20 October 1993, *Radenska v Kajo*, XXVIa Y.B. Comm. Arb. 919 (Austrian Oberster Gerichtshof) (1999). See also Judgment of 24 February 1994, *Ministry of Public Works v Société Bec Frères*, XXII Y.B. Comm. Arb. 682 (Paris Cour d'appel) (1997) (recognizing award notwithstanding fact that it was made while challenges to impartiality of arbitrators were pending in courts of arbitral seat; fact that arbitrators were subsequently removed held irrelevant); Judgment of 24 January 2003, XXX Y.B. Comm. Arb. 509 (Hanseatisches Oberlandesgericht Hamburg) (2005) (decision in arbitral seat (Poland) denying enforcement of award not res judicata in German recognition proceedings).

[115]See, *TermoRio SA v Electranta SP*, 487 F.3d 928, 935 (D.C. Cir. 2007); *Baker Marine Ltd v Chevron Ltd*, 191 F.3d 194, 196–97 (2d Cir. 1999); *Spier v Calzaturificio Tecnica, SpA*, 71 F.Supp.2d 279, 287–89 (S.D.N.Y. 1999), reargued, 77 F.Supp.2d 405 (S.D.N.Y. 1999).

conditions, the validity of the arbitration agreement and award. Therefore, it is often said that arbitrators have no forum.[116]

An award issued in the seat creates a link between the arbitration and the domestic legal order. It follows that if the award is set side in the seat the same argument applies. However, if an award is enforced the link between the legal order of the seat and the place of enforcement is broken. This is made clear by Article V of the New York Convention which uses the term "*that country*" (emphasis supplied) instead of "*this state*" (emphasis supplied) as noted in Articles 34 and 36 of the Model Law. This issue is further supported by Article I of the New York Convention which notes that it only applies to "awards made in the territory of a state other than the state in which enforcement and recognition of such awards are sought." The book in the following chapters would attempt an extensive discussion of the interplay between these two instruments.

The public policy defense has in recent times resorted to extensively to refuse recognition and enforcement of foreign and non-domestic awards under the Convention.[117] For example, in *Dongfeng Garments Factory of Kai Feng City & Tai Chu Int'l Trade (H.K.) Co. v Henan Garments Imp. & Exp. (Group) Co.*[118] which was later overruled, a Chinese court denied enforcement of a foreign award against a Chinese party on the grounds that enforcement of the same would be against the economic interests of China.

The book remains sensitive to the discussion surrounding the public policy and would attempt to map the various theoretical constructs that have been identified in the literature in the context of the diversity in State practice.

1.5 The Difficulties in Implementing the Regime on Enforcement of Foreign Awards

As a preliminary comment, the legal regime for setting aside an award is contained only within Article 34 of the Model Law. The pertinent question for inquiry is, almost always, whether the governing law of the arbitration agreement has been applied properly. Nonetheless, if a tribunal deliberately ignores the applicable law and reaches a conclusion based entirely on its own view of the prevailing equities, then there may be very narrow circumstances in which an award may properly be annulled.[119] In these cases, however, the award is not annulled because the tribunal makes a substantive mistake, which necessarily implies that the arbitrators were seeking to

---

[116] Gaillard [53].

[117] Gary B. Born, *supra* 67, 3394–3731.

[118] Judgment of 28 September 1992, *Dongfeng Garments Factory of Kai Feng City & Tai Chu Int'l Trade (H.K.) Co. v Henan Garments Imp. & Exp. (Group) Co. (Zhengzhou Zhongji Fayuan)*, discussed in Peerenboom [54], 289. This case was later overruled by the Supreme People's Court. See also, Gary B. Born, *supra* 67, 3394–3731.

[119] Gary B. Born, *supra* 67, 3394—3731.

apply the relevant legal rules and erred, but because the tribunal deliberately chose to ignore its mandate to apply the law and instead effectively acted *ex aequo et bono.*[120] However, any such analysis must be conducted with great circumspection, to avoid encroaching on the arbitrators' mandate and violating the rule against the substantive review of the arbitrators' decision; nonetheless, where an arbitrator does ignore his or her mandate, an annulment is generally both appropriate and necessary. Simply put, a limited measure of substantive judicial review arguably serves to safeguard the integrity of the arbitral process by permitting annulment of truly perverse decisions and by providing arbitrators with an enhanced incentive to do their job properly. Ramos J explained this issue well when he noted,

> Merely an error or misunderstanding of the applicable law does not constitute manifest disregard (Id.). Judicial review of arbitration awards is extremely limited. An arbitration award must be upheld when the arbitrator "offer[s] even a barely colourable justification for the outcome reached.[121]

There is no issue with the application of Article 34 in setting aside an award. However, the problem arises when an award is to be enforced or recognized by a jurisdiction other than the one of the seat as already noted above. It is argued that Article 34 of the Model Law creates more problems than it solves. Jurisprudence specifically in the United States and France indicates that having an award set aside does not automatically guarantee that enforcement via the NYC in a forum other than the seat is not possible. In effect, this rule is firmly established in France. The conclusion is that Article 34 is problematic and only enforcement is the defining moment when an award is either enforced or not enforced. Simply put Article 34 of the Model Law and Article V of the NYC are in most parts identical and hence arguments to set aside an award can also be used to deny enforcement. The only difference is that Article V is applying the arguments within a different legal system than the one used at the seat under Article 34 and hence will or can trump Article 34. For example, the Australian International Arbitration Act also in the enabling legislation does not note Article 34 but exclusively addresses Article 36 of the Model Law.

1.6 Conclusion

This chapter has demonstrated that the commercial landscape is changing in the coming years as China is investing vast amounts of money into the creation of a network of roads, rail and shipping lines in order to connect Europe with Asia. Many countries along the Silk Road (OBOR) will be increasing their participation in world trade and hence new challenges will be created. This does not only affect contract law and transport law but will also create new challenges in dispute resolution

---

[120]Ibid.

[121]*Daesang Corp. v Nutrasweet Co.,* Slip Copy (2017) 55 Misc.3d 1218(A), 2017 N.Y. Slip Op. 50,646(U) [4].

mechanisms. Specifically, the enforcement of arbitral awards—the subject matter of this book—will become a crucial element in the successful execution of trade and commerce.

However, challenges such as the enforcement of awards are still not resolved and arguably never will be. The Model Law on Arbitration and the New York Convention have created a harmonized approach to arbitration. In addition, institutional rules such as the Singapore Arbitration Rules have created a predictable approach to the resolution of disputes. The importance of the rules is that the seat of arbitration that is the system with which the arbitration has its procedural connection has arguably been resolved if parties have not done so.

In addition, the Model law makes a distinction between "court intervention" and "court assistance and supervision." Despite the distinctions made in the Model Law the greatest challenge, however, is the interrelationship between setting aside an award and the enforcement process. The fact that an award has been set aside at the seat does not necessarily block its enforcement in another jurisdiction. The issue is that the interpretation of Article V(1)(e) and Article VII of NYC has produced inconsistency. The question is whether the seat has primacy over the arbitration or whether the court of the seat is interfering with international arbitration. The issue is one of primacy and it has been argued that "[t]he relationship between national courts and arbitral tribunals swings between forced cohabitation and true partnership."[122] A secondary question also can be posed namely "when does 'involvement' by a court become 'intervention' in the arbitral process; and when does 'intervention' become 'interference' with a process which is supposed to stand on its own feet?".[123]

The problem is that in relation to the interpretation of Articles V and VII of the NYC, an agreement in an international sense has not been achieved. Whether an award which has been set aside can still be enforced depends on the enforcing country and hence which of the two approaches namely the Traditional or the Denationalised view is applied, is still unknown. France certainly does enforce awards that have been set aside at the seat and other countries such as the U.S and Belgium to mention a few have on occasions also followed the French lead.

After having reviewed the available literature pertaining to the origin and current status of setting aside in international arbitration, the practical approach for any losing party in an arbitration would be to simply bypass the setting side process under Article 34 of the Model Law. Notably, one of the main issues as identified by Van den Berg, with which the authors agree upon, is the issue of potential double control of the judiciary by having a judicial review of the award on similar grounds in enforcement proceedings and setting aside proceedings.[124] Of course, it is recognised that there are potential legal differences in the seat and the enforcement country which could lead to a different result. However, while the uncertainty concerning enforcement of awards

[122]Blackaby [55].

[123]Ibid., 443.

[124]Albert Jan van den Berg, 'Should the Setting Aside of the Arbitral Award be Abolished' (2014) ICSID Review, 1–26 https://cdn.arbitration-icca.org/s3fs-public/document/media_document/media213982548067270van_den_berg_setting_aside_icsid_review_2014.pdf accessed 02/01/2021.

which were set aside persist, arbitral parties must take this issue into consideration when selecting a seat and be aware of the potential enforcement country and its view on the enforcement process.

About the Book

This book attempts to be relevant and of utility to academicians and practitioners alike. Further, the book would attempt to extensively resort to State practice in jurisdictions discussed in contemporary literature on the subject and also to jurisdictions that have not been extensively discussed, especially in a comparative analysis method. The geography that the book attempts to traverse is spread across continents in an attempt to showcase within the book the State practice in major regions. Inputs related to statutory provisions and judicial opinion would be resourced from England, Australia, the US, South Africa, Singapore, Hong Kong and India and few other South Asian jurisdictions, detailed in the chapter structure.

The methodology for this research would be analytical, based largely on primary sources—Conventions, Legislations, and judicial decisions. Understanding the immense contribution of secondary sources to the strengthening of literature on public policy exception in international commercial arbitration, this research would attempt at paraphrasing this contribution to supplement the critique on the topic.

The roadmap of the book is that it commences with a brief introduction of dispute resolution in the context of OBOR, highlighting the potential impact of OBOR on cross-border transactions and its trickling effect on dispute resolution while specifically focusing on the role of the public policy exemption in the same.

The second chapter of the book conducts an incisive analysis of UNCITRAL Model Law provisions concentrating upon the various facets surrounding the enforcement of awards in several jurisdictions. The chapter sets out by analyzing the relevant portions of the *travaux* of the Model Law pertaining to Article 34 and Article 36 of the Model Law and attempts to bring forth the origin of the public policy exemption in Article 34 and Article 36. Further, the second chapter on Model Law illustrates with examples from state practice the domestic manifestation of the enforcement provisions of the Model Law, the exceptions to enforcement provisions of Model Law and the interpretations attributed to them by the municipal courts. The varied interpretations of the Model Law provisions are courtesy of the fact that Model law is a soft law regime aimed at supporting countries in developing their legal regimes on international commercial arbitration and harmonizing it with their domestic laws.

In the above backdrop, the book transits to the third chapter of the book which deals with the exceptions to the enforcement of foreign arbitral awards within the New York Convention i.e. Article V of the New York Convention. The New York Convention is arguably the most significant cornerstone of International arbitration as it attempts to standardize the enforcement of foreign awards on a global scale by creating a single framework for foreign awards. Inspite of the fact that New York Convention is a precursor to the formation of UNCITRAL Model Law, the chronology of the chapters in the book, dealing with UNCITRAL Model Law and the New York Convention is such, solely because the applicability of the New York Convention is confined to foreign arbitrations. Hence, as per the authors, it was pertinent for the reader to garner a holistic understanding of the interplay between enforcement provisions in the Model Law and the interpretations attributed to them by municipal courts setting out the perfect roadmap of understanding public policy in domestic arbitrations in Chap. 2 leading to understanding public policy in foreign arbitrations in Chap. 3.

Moving ahead, the fourth chapter of the book deals with the public policy exception to enforcement and maps its origins in Private International Law whilst discussing the international standard of public policy and the need for ensuring uniformity within the application of the Public Policy exception.

The fifth chapter of the book draws the attention of the reader to the uniqueness of this book i.e., state practice in south Asian jurisdictions in the context of Public policy. The chapter focuses on compiling relevant literature from India, Bangladesh, Pakistan, Nepal and Sri Lanka effectively sewing them together as a compendium for easy reference on public policy in the aforesaid jurisdictions. The chapter at the outset traces the treatment of public policy exception and related enforcement concerns in south Asian jurisdictions as a whole before detailing the public policy exception in each of the abovementioned jurisdictions. The chapter concludes with few pointers for improving the regime on recognition and enforcement of foreign arbitral awards in South Asia. The last chapter of the book is the conclusion of the book and summarizes the findings of the authors and contains a few observations with regard to public policy which might pave the way for future research.

Some of the notable topics covered within this book include.

- The interface between the NYC and the UNCITRAL Model Law with regard to the exceptions of enforcement of foreign arbitral awards
- The State practice with regard to the exceptions listed with Article V(1) (a–e) and V(2)
- The need for uniformity with regard to the public policy exception to the enforcement of foreign arbitral awards.
- The interpretation of public policy exception with regard to enforcement of foreign awards in South Asian nations of India, Pakistan, Sri Lanka and Bangladesh.

References

1. Pichler, N., & Meissner, A. (2019) The arbitration agreement and arbitrability: The impact of the one belt, one road initiative on international arbitration. In C. Klausegger, & P. Klein (Ed.),*Austrian Yearbook on International Arbitration* (Vol. 1, pp. 79), Stämpfli.
2. Wang, G. (2017). The belt and road initiative in quest for a dispute resolution mechanism. *Asia Pacific Law Review, 25*(1), 1.
3. Dahlan, M. (2018). Dimensions of the new belt and road international order: An analysis of the emerging legal norms and a conceptionalisation of the regulation of disputes. *Beijing Law Review, 9* 87.
4. Gan, L., & Yang, S. (2017). Issues in the recognition and enforcement of foreign arbitral awards in China. *Asian International Arbitration Journal, 13*(1), 95.

5. Garimella, S. R. (2018). OBOR and the syncretic private international law rules in India: Time for accession to harmonised legal regimes. In P. Sooksripaisarnkit & S. R. Garimella (Eds.), *China's one belt one road initiative and private international law*, Routledge.
6. Blackaby, N., Constantine Partasides, Q. C. , Redfern, A., & Hunter, M. (2015) In *Redfern and hunter on international arbitration* (6th edn.), OUP.
7. Chong, A. (ed.) (2020) In *Asian principles on the recognition and enforcement of foreign judgments,* Asian Business Law Institute.
8. Chong, A. (2020). Moving towards harmonisation in the recognition and enforcement of foreign judgment rules in Asia. *Journal of Private International Law, 16*(1), 31.
9. Bingham, T. (2005). The alabama claims arbitration. *International and Comparative Law Quarterly, 54*(1), 1–25.
10. Veeder, V. V. (2015). The historical keystone to international arbitration: The party-appointed arbitrator—From Miami to Geneva. In D. D. Caron, S. W. Schill, A. C. Smutny & E. E. Triantafilou (Eds.), *Practising virtue: Inside international arbitration* (Vol. 1, pp. 127), OUP.
11. Lowenfeld, A. F. (2005). In *Lowenfeld on international arbitration: Collected essays over three decades,* Jurisnet.
12. Watt, H. M. (2010). Party autonomy in international contracts: From the makings of a myth to the requirements of global governance. *European Review of Contract Law, 6*(3), 250.
13. Redfern, A., Hunter, M., Blackaby, N., & Partasides, C. (2004). *Law and practice of international arbitration* (4th ed., p. 131). London: Sweet and Maxwell.
14. Cordero-Moss, G. (ed.) (2013). In *International commercial arbitration: Different forms and their features,* CUP.
15. Moss, G. C. (2008). International arbitration and the quest for the applicable law. *Global Jurist, 8*(3), 1.
16. Moses, M. L. (2017). In *The principles and practices of international commercial arbitration* (3rd edn., Vol. 1, pp. 140–41), CUP.
17. Blackaby, N., Partasides, C., Redfern, A. & Hunter, M. (2015). In *Redfern and hunter on international arbitration* (6th ed., Vol. 1, pp. 255), OUP.
18. Born, G. B. (2016). *International Commercial Arbitration* (2nd ed. Kluwer, 2014) 1, 99–105
19. Bernini, G. (1989). Cultural neutrality: A prerequisite to arbitral justice. *Michigan Journal of International Law, 10*, 39.
20. Born, G. (2016). In *International arbitration: Law and practice* (2nd ed. pp. 1–2).
21. Lalive, P. (1984). On the neutrality of the arbitrator and of the place of arbitration. *Recueil De Travaux Suisses Sur L'arbitrage International,* 24.
22. Park, W. W. (1995). Neutrality predictability and economic co-operation. *Journal of International Arbitration, 12*, 99.
23. Paulsson, J. & Rawding, N. (1995). The trouble with confidentiality. *Arbitration International, 11,* 303.
24. Yves Fortier, L. (1999). The occasionally unwarranted assumption of confidentiality. *Arbitration International, 15*(2), 131.
25. Brown, A. C. (2001). Presumption meets reality: An exploration of the confidentiality obligation in international commercial arbitration. *American University International Law Review, 16*(4), 969.
26. Jolles, A., Stark-Traber, S., & de Cedie, M. C. (2013). Confidentiality. In E. Geisinger, N. Voser, & A. M. Pett (Eds.), *International arbitration in Switzerland—A handbook for practitioners,* Kluwer.
27. Young, M., & Chapman, S. (2009). Confidentiality in international arbitration, does the exception prove the rule?; Where now for implied duty of confidentiality under English law?". *ASA Bulletin, 27*(1), 26.
28. Mistelis, L. A. (2005). Confidentiality and third party participation UPS v. Canada and Methanex Corporation v. United States. *Arbitration International, 21*(2), 211.
29. Gaillard, E., & Bermann, G. A. (1958). In *Guide on the convention on the recognition and enforcement of foreign arbitral awards: New York 1958.* (Vol. 1, pp. 7), Brill.

30. Fouchard, P. (1998). Suggestions pour accroître l'efficacité internationale des sentences arbitrales. *REV. ARB ., 653*, 663.
31. Gaillard, E. (2009). The urgency of not revising the New York convention. In A. J. Van den Berg (Ed.), *50 Years of the New York Convention: ICCA International Arbitration Conference*, ICCA Congress Series, Dublin (Vol. 14, pp. 689–696), Kluwer Law International.
32. Park, W. W. (1989). National law and commercial justice: Safeguarding procedural integrity in international arbitration. *Tulane Law Review, 63*, 647.
33. Gelander, J. L. (1997). Judicial review of international arbitral awards: Preserving independence in international commercial arbitrations. *Marquette Law Review, 80*, 625.
34. Davis, K. R. (2002). Unconventional wisdom: A new look at Articles V and VII of the convention on the recognition and enforcement of foreign arbitral awards. *Texas International Law Journal, 37*, 43.
35. Brekoulakis, S. (2008). Enforcement of foreign arbitral awards: Observations on the efficiency of the current system and the gradual development of alternative means of enforcement. *American Review of International Arbitration, 19*, 415.
36. Michael Reisman, W. & Iravani, H. (2010). Conflict and cooperation: The changing relation of national courts and international commercial arbitration. *American Review of International Arbitration, 21*, 5.
37. Silberman, L. (2009). The New York convention after fifty years: Some reflections on the role of national law. *Georgia Journal of International and Comparative Law, 38*, 25.
38. Gharavi, H. G. (2002). In *The international effectiveness of the annulment of an arbitral award* (Vol. 1, pp. 50), Kluwer Law International.
39. Paulsson, J. (1983). Delocalisation of international commercial arbitration: When and why it matters. *International and Comparative Law Quarterly, 32*, 53.
40. Paulsson, J. (1981). Arbitration unbound: Award detached from the law of Its Country of origin. *International and Comparative Law Quarterly, 30*, 358.
41. Li, J. (2011). The application of the delocalization theory in current international commercial arbitration. *ICCLR, 22*(12), 383.
42. Bělohlávek, A. J. (2015). Seat of arbitration and supporting and supervising function of Courts. *Czech Yearbook Of Arbitration, 5*, 21.
43. Yu, H.-L. (2008). A theoretical overview of the foundations of international commercial arbitration. *Contemporary Asian Arbitration Journal, 1*(2), 255.
44. Mann, F. A. (1983). Lex facit arbitrum. *Arbitration International, 2*(3), 245.
45. Kaufmann-Kohler, G. (1998). Identifying and applying the law governing the arbitration procedure—The role of the law of the place of arbitration. *ICCA Congress Series, 9*, 336.
46. Malhotra, I. (2020). In *Malhotra's commentary on the law of arbitration Vol. 2* (Vol. 1, 4th edn, pp. 1163–64). Wolters Kluwer.
47. Holtzmann, H. M., & Neuhaus, J. (1989). In *A guide to the UNCITRAL model law on international commercial arbitration: Legislative history and commentary*, (Vol. 1, pp. 910–1003), Kluwer Law International.
48. De Enterra, J. G. (1989). The role of public policy in international commercial arbitration. *Law and Policy in International Business, 21*, 389.
49. Buchanan, M. A. (1988). Public policy and international commercial arbitration. *American Business Law Journal, 26*(3), 511.
50. Miller, D. (1993). Public policy in international commercial arbitrations in Australia. *Arbitration International, 9*(2), 167.
51. Yang, I. (2015). A comparative review on substantive public policy in international commercial arbitration. *Dispute Resolution Journal, 70*(2), 49.
52. Hanson, J. (2014). Setting aside public policy: The PEP decision and the case for enforcing international arbitral awards set aside as contrary to public policy. *Georgetown Journal of International Law, 25*, 825.
53. Gaillard, E. (1999). Enforcement of awards set aside in the Country of origin: The French experience. In Van den Berg, A. J. (Ed.), *Improving the efficiency of arbitration agreements and awards: 40 Years of application of the New York convention, ICCA Congress Series No. 9* (Vol. 505, pp. 506), ICCA & Kluwer Law International.

54. Peerenboom, R. (2001). Seek truth from facts: An empirical study of enforcement of arbitral awards in the PRC'. *American Journal of Comparative Law*, *49*(2), 249.
55. Blackaby, N., Partasides, C., Redfern, A. & Hunter, M. (2009) In: *Redfern and hunter on international arbitration* (Vol. 1, pp. 438), OUP.

Chapter 2
UNCITRAL Model Law

Overview
This chapter discusses the exceptions to the enforcement of arbitral awards as noted in the UNCITRAL Model Law.

In particular, the chapter will discuss the following points.

- mapping the work of Working Group II on Articles 34 and 36;
- UNCITRAL Model Law on recognition and enforcement of arbitral awards;
- Article 34—set aside of arbitral awards;
- the importance of the "exclusive" in Article 34;
- the role of the seat in arbitration proceedings;
- Article 36—refusal of recognition or enforcement of foreign arbitral awards.

2.1 Introduction

The framework for the successful resolution of cross border and domestic commercial disputes through arbitration was revolutionized upon the arrival of the New York Convention; however, it is the work of the United Nations Commission on International Trade Law (UNCITRAL) that streamlined the enthusiastic, yet extremely diverse national attempts at operationalizing the Convention. One instrument that helped achieve that is the UNCITRAL Model Law on international commercial arbitration, 1985. International commercial arbitration as we know it today premises itself on a triad of achievements of the international community of which the NYC is the first and foremost important achievement as it enabled the States to give effect to arbitration agreements and eased the process of enforcement of foreign arbitral awards. The second important achievement in the triad is the UNCITRAL Model Law, 1985 (revised in 2006) which constituted a model act for national legislations which is the subject of this chapter. The last of the three is the UNCITRAL Arbitration Rules, 1976 (last revised in 2013 to incorporate provisions related to transparency for Treaty-based Investor-State arbitration) which provide for the settlement of a broad

B. Zeller et al., *Enforcement of Foreign Arbitral Awards and the Public Policy Exception*,
https://doi.org/10.1007/978-981-16-2634-0_2

range of disputes, including disputes between private commercial parties where no arbitration institution is involved, Investor-State disputes, State-to-State disputes and commercial dispute administered by arbitral institutions.[1]

The UNCITRAL Model Law was conceived as an instrument to assist States in reforming and modernizing their laws on arbitral procedure so as to take into account the particular features and needs of international commercial arbitration.[2] Notably, "legislation based on the Model Law has been adopted in 85 States in a total of 118 jurisdictions."[3] The reason that the number of jurisdictions exceeds the number of States is the fact that in federations such as Australia, Canada and in some federal units of the United States, some territories and States have also adopted the Model Law to govern domestic arbitrations. Some States, such as Austria, do not make any distinction between the rules governing international and domestic arbitration. In sum, the UNCITRAL Model Law has been found to be very useful in legislating arbitration, whether domestic or international.

To start with, the processes involved within an arbitration proceeding could be split into two parts—first, the arbitration process as such, and secondly, the judicial process as and when so required. This arrangement leads to an important question—is there an autonomous, arbitral legal order? Arguably this is not the case. "In arbitration, the ad hoc nature of arbitration and its finality and privacy militate against overall consistency."[4] In addition, an award, despite being set aside, can still be enforced in some jurisdictions, and such enforcement would be discussed extensively elsewhere in this book. Suffice it to say here that notwithstanding the possibility of enforcement of annulled arbitral awards, Article 34 is still of some utility, especially in cases where the entire arbitral process takes place in one jurisdiction, that is the seat. In other words, the award, the possibly setting aside motion, and the enforcement are all tied to the seat. In this situation, an award once set aside cannot be enforced. However,

> a deep distinction should be drawn between cases where the intrusion comes from the court at the place of the arbitration and cases where a "foreign" or "third" court interferes with an arbitration that is seated in a different country.[5]

Hence, the role of the seat and the interplay between the Model Law—Articles 34 and 36—and the New York Convention—Article V—is essential to understand the aforesaid distinction. Furthermore—as already noted—arbitrators do not have judicial functions and hence must rely on the court system in situations where according

---

[1]United Nations Commission on International Trade Law, UNCITRAL Arbitration Rules 1976, https://uncitral.un.org/en/texts/arbitration/contractualtexts/arbitration, accessed 08/06/2020.

[2]See, generally, Ilias Bantekas, Pietro Ortolani, Shahla Ali, Manuel Gomez, Michael Polkinghorne, *UNCITRAL Model Law on International Commercial Arbitration: A Commentary* (CUP:2020).

[3]United Nations Commission on International Trade Law, https://uncitral.un.org/en/texts/arbitration/modellaw/commercial_arbitration/status accessed 04/03/2021.

[4]Lord Mance, "Arbitration—a Law unto itself?", 30th Annual Lecture organised by The School of International Arbitration and Freshfields Bruckhaus Deringer', https://www.supremecourt.uk/docs/speech-151104.pdf, accessed 05/05/2020.

[5]G. Carbone, "The Interference of the Court of the Seat with International Arbitration", (2012) *Journal of Dispute Resolution* 217, 219.

to Article 5 of the Model Law, "no court shall intervene except where so provided in this Law."

The Model Law, as contemplated by its drafters, attempted to achieve a balance between ensuring that arbitration remains loyal to its essentially private nature of dispute resolution and the issues/concerns that are addressed within enforcement procedures before the courts.[6]This balance is evident throughout its content and is especially reinforced within the provisions related to judicial procedures, if any, after the tribunal's work has been completed, in provisions related to challenges to the arbitral awards—Articles 34 and 36 of the Model Law. This is not surprising as the functions described in these two Articles are judicial in nature and hence must be decided by a court. To put it, succinctly,

> The two articles contain an almost identical list of grounds which justify the setting aside or refusal of enforcement of arbitral awards. In both articles, the grounds are divided into two main groups: the first group lists grounds that have to be proven by the party invoking them, whereas the second group names grounds which the court can take into consideration itself.[7]

The conditions for setting aside an arbitral award are specified within Article 34 of the Model Law. In other words, Article 34 postulates the minimum threshold for the courts in the Model Law States to decide upon the challenges to an arbitral award. The regime has, as is evident within its text, seemed to have preferred a high threshold in Article 34 as the exceptions to enforcement of an award are not easily overcome in practice. Article 34 restricts the involvement of courts and is a tool of last resort for the opposing parties only if what appear as procedural issues were not adhered to in the tribunal's proceedings. Article 34(4) permits the court "where appropriate and if so requested by the parties suspend the setting aside proceedings [and]… give the arbitral tribunal the opportunity to resume the arbitral process." Thus, the Article's content seems to allow a possibility for the tribunals to correct their mistakes regarding such concerns as were made aware to the court. This Article thus allows the court an opportunity to ask the tribunal whether its proceedings comply with all the requirements of procedural justice in a manner that would eliminate a challenge to the award, pleading for its annulment.[8]

In a related vein, Article 18 of the Model Law—equal treatment of parties—is of much relevance and significance:

---

[6]See, generally, Aron Broches, *Commentary on the UNCITRAL Model Law on International Commercial Arbitration* (Kluwer Law and Taxation Publishers, 1990).

[7]UNCITRAL Report on the work of its 18th session, UN Doc: A/40/17, [296], June 3–21, 1985, ("UNCITRAL Report") https://undocs.org/en/a/40/17(supp), accessed 21/01/2021; See also, "UNCITRAL Model Law, Chapter VII, Article 34 [Application for setting aside as exclusive recourse against arbitral award]", in Howard M. Holtzmann and Joseph Neuhaus, *A Guide to the UNCITRAL Model Law on International Commercial Arbitration: Legislative History and Commentary*, (Kluwer Law International 1989) 1, 910—1003.

[8]UNCITRAL Model Law on International Commercial Arbitration, 1985, ("UNCITRAL Model Law").

https://www.uncitral.org/pdf/english/texts/arbitration/ml-arb/07-86998_Ebook.pdf, accessed 10/08/2018.

See, Article 34(4) Model Law.

…The purpose of Article 18 is to protect a party from egregious and injudicious conduct by an arbitral tribunal, and it is not intended to protect a party from its own failures or strategic choices…[9]

On the other hand, as soon as there is court interference, privacy and confidentiality are lost, and the issue becomes one of public interests; hence, public policy becomes an important factor when reviewing arbitral awards. Any decisions—in this case, in relation to Articles 34 and 36—dealt with in one and the same jurisdiction—that is the seat—should be consistent. However, as with all international legal issues, there is no guaranteed consistency between different municipal legal orders.[10] Therefore, one can confidently argue that there is no "arbitral legal order."[11] A question of this chapter is what can Article 34 do which cannot be achieved using Article 36 or Article V of the New York Convention for that matter?

2.2 The Significance of "May"

An important issue regarding Articles 34 and Article 36 of the Model Law, which is noteworthy at this juncture is that both use a permissive word: an arbitral award "may" be refused or may be set aside by a court. In relation to interpreting the term "may", the Working Group had suggested that the term "may" in the opening sentence of Article 34(2) did in fact vest the relevant court with discretion not to set aside an award even if grounds for doing the same were present.[12] However, the Commission Report eventually concluded that "it was understood that an award might be set aside on any of the grounds listed in paragraph (2) irrespective of whether such ground had materially affected the award."[13]

In spite of the apparent friction between the interpretations of the Working Group and the Commission pertaining to the term "may", it is crucial to note that the interpretation of the Commission when viewed as a single unit, instead of, in isolation

---

[9]UNITED NATIONS COMMISSION ON INTERNATIONAL TRADE LAW (UNCITRAL), 2012 Digest of Case Law on the Model Law on International Commercial Arbitration, 7, 98. ("UNCITRAL Digest"). https://uncitral.un.org/sites/uncitral.un.org/files/media-documents/uncitral/en/mal-digest-2012-e.pdf, accessed 10/01/2021.

[10]Lord Mance, *supra* 4.

[11]For a different view see, Emmanuel Gaillard, *Legal Theory of International Arbitration*, (BRILL & Nijhoff, 2010).

[12]United Nations Commission on International Trade Law (UNCITRAL), "Summary records for meetings on the UNCITRAL Model Law on International Commercial Arbitration, 318th Meeting", ("Summary Records"). http://www.uncitral.org/pdf/english/travaux/arbitration/ml-arb/318meeting-e.pdf, accessed 18/09/2020.

[13]United Nations Commission on International Trade Law (UNCITRAL), "Report of the Secretary–General: study on the application and interpretation of the Convention on the Recognition and Enforcement of Foreign Arbitral Awards (New York, 1958), A/CN.9/168", [46]–[47] ("Report of the Secretary-general") https://undocs.org/en/A/CN.9/168, accessed 10/08/2020.

clearly highlights that there is a certain level of consistency between both interpretations. As noted in the Commission Report itself, a non-material error can give rise to grounds for setting aside the award, but as agreed during the debates, the court adjudicating a setting aside application does have the discretion not to set aside the award when such grounds are present.[14] Arguably, therefore, the permissive word "may" must be approached with a pro-arbitration view, which will give force to Article 34 and Article 36 of the Model Law. It allows a court to consider particular domestic principles when enforcing or setting aside an arbitral award. This is demonstrated by the word "this state" instead of "that state" as found envisaged in Article V of the New York Convention. As the discretion exists, the critical question relates to the scope of the discretion. One issue is clear: courts in various jurisdictions have not always used the discretion permitted under the Model Law. Notably, a Hong Kong court in *Brunswick Bowling & Billiards Corp v Shanghai Zhonglu Industrial Co Ltd*[15] observed

> Even though the Respondent established a valid ground under Article 34(2)(a)(ii), the court still has to consider whether the award under this head should be set aside as a matter of discretion. I find it somewhat surprising that despite the diligence of counsel no decided case on how the discretion under article 34 should be exercised has been found.[16]

The above-mentioned observation appears to be an indication that the import of the word "may" has not gone unnoticed by the Hong Kong court. However, the court also averred on the pertinent issue, namely how the discretion should be exercised. It observed that the court "may refuse to set aside an award if what is established is a minimal or trivial infraction of the procedural rules",[17] thus allowing an inference that this articulation could serve as a guidance on the exercise of discretion. The arguments of the Counsel for the Appellant also open a window to understanding the above-mentioned observation of the court. The Counsel averred that "even where there was a violation, the court may exercise its discretion to uphold the award if the party attacking it could not show the result would have been different if there was no violation."[18]

The important takeaway from the above-mentioned observation is that courts hearing the setting aside application are under no obligation to set aside the arbitral award even in a scenario where it appears that one or more grounds for setting aside might be present.[19] Hence, the threshold question pertaining to the role of courts in Model Law jurisdictions is how do courts utilize this discretion vested with them? The complexity of the issue is well highlighted in the fact that there is no concrete guidance within the text of the Model Law nor directly in the *travaux preparatoires* of the Model Law. It is therefore left to the local courts of the relevant jurisdiction to interpret

---

[14] Holtzmann and Neuhaus, *supra* 7, 910–1003.

[15] *Brunswick Bowling & Billiards Corp v Shanghai Zhonglu Industrial Co Ltd*, [2009] HKCFI 94.

[16] Ibid, 29.

[17] Ibid, 30.

[18] Ibid, 32.

[19] See, Ilias Bantekas et al., *supra* 2, 864. It is without a doubt that Article 34 of the Model Law like other provisions of the Model Law are derived from the New York Convention.

the word "may" which will invariably have an effect in the application of both articles within the local regime. Pertinently, some national arbitration legislations specifically provide that the power to annul an award is discretionary.[20]

Further, a glance over the State practice confirms that there have been instances wherein the discretion vested with the courts has been resorted to in order to avoid annulling an award for procedural errors. In *Grand Pacific Holdings v Pacific China Holdings*,[21] the Hong Kong Court of Appeal was presented an appeal from the High Court of Hong Kong which had set aside an arbitral award for the reason that Respondent had been able to establish proof of violation of the grounds enumerated in Article 34(2)(a)(ii), i.e. lack of opportunity to present its case. The facts of the case which are relevant for the present discussion were that an award had been passed in Hong Kong in an ICC arbitration in 2009 ordering Claimant, Grand Pacific Holdings (GPH) to pay Respondent, Pacific China Holdings Ltd (PCH) a sum in excess of US$55 million together with interest.

Thereafter, PCH filed a setting aside application in Hong Kong, relying on Article 34(2)(a)(ii) and (iv) of the Model Law claiming that it was unable to present its case and that the arbitral procedure was not in accordance with the agreement of the Parties. The Hong Kong Court of Appeal, after reviewing the relevant commentaries on Articles 18 and 34 of the Model Law, opined that in order to set aside an award, "the conduct complained of must be sufficiently serious or egregious so that one could say a party has been denied due process."[22] Additionally, the court also agreed with the observation of the High Court of Hong Kong that "if the violation had no effect on the outcome of the arbitration that is a good basis for exercising one's discretion against setting aside."[23] Thus, in the above backdrop, the Court of Appeal concluded that the conduct as alleged did not constitute a valid ground for setting aside the award as was done by the High Court of Hong Kong. Hence, the Award as passed was reinstated. The relevant paragraphs from the above-mentioned judgement germane for the present discussion are quoted herein below:

> 55. As the learned authors in Craig, Park and Paulsson in International Chamber of Commerce Arbitration (3rd ed., 2000) put it at para 16.04 when dealing with art.15(2) of ICC Rules:
>
> Except in the most egregious cases, the wide discretion of arbitrators and the flexibility of the arbitral process have been confined by national courts which quite regularly reject the procedural arguments of disappointed parties.
>
> 68. The learned Judge concluded at para.129 that the refusal to receive and consider the additional authorities prevented PCH from presenting its case and therefore a violation of art.34(2)(a)(ii) has been established. With respect, I cannot agree with Saunders J. I do not believe he was entitled to interfere with a case management decision, which was fully within the discretion of the Tribunal to make.

---

[20] See, e.g., British Columbia Commercial Arbitration Act, 1986. Section 30(2) states that: "where…court finds that arbitrator has "committed an arbitral error," but that "the error consists of a defect in form or a technical irregularity," court may refuse to set aside award where "refusal would not constitute a substantial wrong or miscarriage of justice".

[21] *Grand Pacific Holdings v Pacific China Holdings*, [2012] 4 H.K.L.R.D.1.

[22] Ibid, [92].

[23] *Grand Pacific Holdings, supra* 21, [104].

...

81. I agree with the observation by Johnson Lam J in Brunswick Bowling & Billiards Corp v Shanghai Zhonglu Industrial Co Ltd that:

[40] ... if the Tribunal gave several reasons for the award, with any single one of those being sufficient for its decision, the court may decline to set aside the award even if the Tribunal had not heard the parties on one of the reasons provided that the court is satisfied the result would be the same in the light of the other reasons given.

86. In A Guide to the UNCITRAL Model Law on International Commercial Arbitration: Legislative History and Commentary, Holtzmann and Neuhaus (Holtzmann & Neuhaus), the learned authors said: ... Article 18 has been rightly described as a key element of the "Magna Carta of Arbitral Procedure." Likewise, it might well be called the "due process" clause of arbitration, akin to similar provisions in national constitutions that establish the requirement of procedural fairness as the indispensable foundation of a system of justice. (at p.550)

...

88. There was a suggestion at the drafting stage that the language of art.18 should be incorporated into art.34(2)(a)(ii). Holtzmann & Neuhaus explained at p.915: ... This change in fact initially was adopted, but the decision was later reversed on the understanding that a violation of art.18 was already covered by the text of art.34...

89. Then at p.1003, they stated: 302... it was the Commission's understanding that, in spite of the resulting difference between the test of art.18 bis and art.34(2)(a)(ii), any violation of art.18 bis [sic] would constitute a ground for setting aside the award under art.34(2) sub-paragraph (a)(ii), sub-paragraph (a)(iv) or sub-paragraph (b) and that the concerns which led to the proposal to amend sub-paragraph (a)(ii) were, therefore, already met.

...

93. In International Chamber of Commerce Arbitration (3rd ed., 2000), Craig, Park and Paulsson in discussing art.15(2)32 of the ICC Rules said at p.302:

16.04 ... The application of these requirements has given rise from time to time to controversy, and challenge of arbitration awards before national courts in a number of cases involving such issues as fair notice, the setting of time limits and the handling of hearing and evidence. Except in the most egregious cases, the wide discretion of arbitrators and the flexibility of the arbitral process have been confirmed by national courts which quite regularly reject the procedural arguments of disappointed parties."

105. I am of the view that only a sufficiently serious error could be regarded as a violation of art.18 or art.34(2)(a)(ii). And that an error would only be sufficiently serious if it has undermined due process. A party who has had a reasonable opportunity to present its case would rarely be able to establish that he has been denied due process. Even so, the Court may refuse to set aside the award if the Court is satisfied that the arbitral tribunal could not have reached a different conclusion. How a court may exercise its discretion in any particular case will depend on the view it takes of the seriousness of the breach. Some breaches may be so egregious that an award would be set aside although the result could not be different.

The aforesaid discussion holds forth that the discretion vested with the Municipal Courts is significant so far as it ensures that the enforcement of an award set aside at the seat on national policy grounds,[24] which are not in alignment with internationally acceptable standards, will not be hampered in any other country. However, it has been argued that the term "may" in the context of Article 34 allows for minimal

[24] *Chromalloy Aeroservices. v Arab Republic of Egypt*, 939 F.Supp. 907 (D.D.C. 1996); Judgment of 29 June 2007.

manoeuvering.[25] In practice, the court's refusal to set aside an award in spite of the presence of one of the grounds for annulment postulated in Article 34 may be interpreted as a denial of justice. Hence, taking the argument further, it has been argued that from a practical standpoint, courts may not be inclined to utilize this discretion vested with it by the term "may" for setting aside an award but will resort to relying on the argument that there is insufficient evidence warranting setting aside of the award.[26]

2.3 Mapping the Work of Working Group II on Articles 34 and 36

An examination of the *travaux preparatoires* of Articles 34 and 36 at this juncture of the chapter is a pivotal step as it allows the reader of the Model Law to understand and comprehend the issues that remained unclear within the drafting process or are otherwise ambiguous. The utility of *the travaux prepartoires* lies in the fact that they offer much insight to the drafting process, thus enabling the correct interpretation of the Model Law, and provide a tangible repository to gauge the intention of the drafters of the Model Law.

2.3.1 Article 34

A perusal of the *travaux préparatories* related to Article 34 of the Model Law indicates that drafting the grounds for setting aside of arbitral awards presented much difficulty and many roadblocks.[27] Apprehensive of concerns related to having a viable text that articulated the structure for judicial intervention on arbitral awards, the Secretariat, at the outset, had predicted that finalizing the issues pertaining to Article 34 would be "amongst the most difficult ones to be settled in the model law."[28] Further, the Secretariat also cautioned for careful consideration of the role of the courts in the context of arbitral awards, stating that the success of the Model Law as a whole hinged upon the successful resolution of all concerns of participating States concerning Article 34 of the Model Law.[29]

---

[25] Ilias Bantekas et al.,*supra* 2, 864.

[26] Ilias Bantekas et al.,*supra* 2, 864.

[27] Emmanuel Gaillard & George A. Bermann, *Guide on the Convention on the Recognition and Enforcement of Foreign Arbitral Awards: New York 1958.* (BRILL, 2017)1, 7.

[28] Yearbook of the United Nations Commission on International Trade Law, 1981, Volume XII, "Report of the Secretary-General: possible features of a model law on international commercial arbitration, A/CN.9/207", [107] https://undocs.org/pdf?symbol=en/A/CN.9/207, accessed 20/10/2020. ("Yearbook of the UNCITRAL").

[29] Ibid.

The complexity of the entire task of the Secretariat is well illustrated by the fact that the *travaux préparatories* of Article 34 are longer than any other single article of the Model Law except the *travaux* for Article 1.[30] The preliminary questions that were addressed by the Secretariat were

(i) what grounds would justify setting aside an arbitral award, and.

(ii) whether the grounds for setting aside an award should be the same as those envisioned under the New York Convention.

In response to the second question posited above, the Secretariat during discussions urged that the grounds for setting aside an arbitral award under New York Convention are incorporated into Article 34 as according to the Secretariat, the grounds under the treaty "are internationally accepted bases for attacking an award"[31] and incorporating them would "help prevent…an international award [from] fall[ing] victim to local particularities of law."[32] Subsequently, several discussions regarding grounds to be incorporated in Article 34 amongst the Working Group and the Commission were convened; however, there was no objection to the adoption of the grounds in the New York Convention in addition to other possible grounds.

Moving ahead, the *travaux preparatoires* on Article 34 suggest that it was discussed for the first time in the 317th meeting. Given the importance of Article 34 as a novel feature for an international instrument, it is of pertinent value to examine the *travaux préparatories* of the Working Groups in order to shed light on issues that were not settled in the draft and more importantly the concerns expressed by the members of the Working Group. This expedition into the endeavour of the Working Groups enables the reader to develop a holistic understanding of the nuances involved in Article 34.

In addition to the adoption of the grounds for setting aside almost like a parallelism to grounds for refusing recognition and enforcement of an award as enumerated under the New York Convention into the Model Law,[33] the Secretariat proposed to incorporate a single exclusive method of judicial recourse against the award other than recognition or enforcement, thereby laying down the foundations of Article 34 in the Model Law.[34] Interestingly, the Working Group was presented with several additional grounds for inclusion in Article 34;[35] however, it decided against adopting

---

[30]Gaillard and Bermann, *supra* 27.

[31]*Daesang Corp. v Nutrasweet Co.,* Slip Copy (2017) 55 Misc.3d 1218(A), 2017 N.Y. Slip Op. 50,646(U) [4].

[32]Ibid, 110, 925.

[33]See, Ilias Bantekas et al.,*supra* 2, 863.

[34]Yearbook of the UNCITRAL, *supra* 28, [108]; See also, UNCITRAL, INTERNATIONAL COMMERCIAL ARBITRATION ANALYTICAL COMMENTARY ON DRAFT TEXT OF A MODEL LAW ON INTERNATIONAL COMMERCIAL ARBITRATION, Report of the Secretary-General, A/CN.9/264, Article 34, 1, 71 ("Analytical Commentary") https://undocs.org/en/A/CN.9/264, accessed 10/01/2021, (noting that national laws "set varied and sometimes extremely long periods of time and set forth varied and sometimes long lists of grounds on which the award may be attacked").

[35]UNCITRAL Sixteenth Session Report of the Working Group on International Contract Practices, A/CN.9/233, [186] – [187] ("Working Group Report") https://undocs.org/en/A/CN.9/233, accessed

any of them and chose to align itself with the grounds in Article V in the New York Convention. It made the following observation

> That solution would facilitate international commercial arbitration by enhancing predictability and expeditiousness and would go a long way towards establishing a harmonized system of limited recourse against awards and their enforcement. It was [further] stated in support that the reasons set forth in article V of the New York Convention provided sufficient safeguards, and that some of the grounds suggested as additions to the list were likely to fall under the public policy reason.[36]

Subsequently, the delegation from the United Kingdom raised the issue of adding additional grounds for setting aside an award citing reasons that it doubted that the grounds postulated in the New York Convention fully addressed the additional grounds that it proposed for inclusion in Article 34.[37] The grounds proposed by the United Kingdom were (a) when evidence is found to have been perjured; (b) the award was obtained by corruption of the arbitrator or of a witness of the losing side; (c) the award is subject to an admitted mistake that does not fall into the "clerical errors" provision of Article 33; and (d) new evidence is discovered.[38] The proposal was rejected. Notably, while declining the inclusion of the above proposed grounds by the United Kingdom, the Working Group stated that there was disagreement amongst States as to whether an award should be set aside in all of the cases cited by the United Kingdom.[39]

The United Kingdom noted that the exclusive list of grounds for setting aside an award was not covering all cases of procedural fairness. Sir Mustill commented that the concept of public policy as mentioned in paragraph (2) (*b*) (ii) did not exist in English laws.[40] In this context, the views of Sir Mustill on public policy are quoted hereinbelow.

> The structure of English arbitration law is such that there has been no need to create any doctrine of public policy in relation to instances such as those stated above: the express

---

10/01/2021. It also decided against an alternative suggestion to replace some or all of the grounds listed in Article 34 with a single, broad standard of whether the award was infected with "procedural injustice."

[36] Working Group Report, *supra* 35, [187].

[37] United Nations Commission on International Trade Law (UNCITRAL), "Analytical compilation of comments by Governments and international organizations on the draft text of a model law on international commercial arbitration, Report of the Secretary-General Addendum", (1985) (UK Comments), A/CN.9/263/Add.2, [29] – [35] https://undocs.org/en/A/CN.9/263/Add.2, accessed 07/08/2020.

[38] Gaillard & Bermann, *supra* 27.

[39] UNCITRAL Report, *supra* 7, [279]. The Commission Report comments, "One view was… that only some and not all of the grounds presented in the…illustrative cases justified setting aside an award."

[40] United Nations Commission on International Trade Law (UNCITRAL), "Yearbook of the United Nations Commission on International Trade Law, 1981, Volume XII, Travaux préparatoires: UNCITRAL Model Law on International Commercial Arbitration (1985)-317th Meeting" 446–448, [4]. ("UNCITRAL Yearbook").

https://uncitral.un.org/sites/uncitral.un.org/files/media-documents/uncitral/en/317meeting-e.pdf

> statutory power to intervene is sufficient. The United Kingdom is not in a position to say how "public policy" would be understood in the courts of other States, but the decisions referred to in *Van den Berg* "The New York Arbitration Convention of 1958" at pp. 359 et seq. would appear to suggest that these words are not in general widely construed. If this continues to be the approach, there will be a risk that an injured party will be powerless to protect himself, even in the case of serious procedural injustice.[41]

The Indian as well as the Mexican representatives agreed with the comments made by Sir Mustill. However, the consensus appeared that the current list is an exhaustive one and no changes were needed. It is interesting to see that an attempt was made to give courts more oversight in arbitral decision making. However, a clear distinction can be drawn from the comments that only procedural issues should be included in Article 34 and not issues of a substantive nature and hence the door to rehearing the case has been closed or has never been opened. The Chairman did observe that "most countries would find it difficult to accept an open list since their legislation provided for an exhaustive list."[42]

Further, the Working Group also felt that the grounds raised by the United Kingdom could be adequately covered, tacitly through a broader interpretation of the language of Article 34 and precisely that of "public policy". The discussions of the Working Group also reveal that public policy as understood in common law regimes and civil law regimes was acknowledged as according to the Working Group public policy in common law systems was of narrower scope excluding notions of procedural justice in comparison with "*ordre public*" which included all principles of procedural justice.[43] In the end, the broader interpretation of the term public policy was incorporated in the following terms:

> The Commission, after deliberation, was agreed that the provision should be retained, subject to deletion of! the words "or any decision contained therein", which were superfluous. It was understood that the term "public policy," which was used in the 1958 New York Convention and many other treaties, covered fundamental principles of law and justice in substantive as well as procedural respects. Thus, instances such as corruption, bribery or fraud and similar serious cases would constitute a ground for setting aside. It was noted, in that connection, that the wording "the award is in conflict with the public policy of this State" was not to be interpreted as excluding instances or events relating to the manner in which an award was arrived at.[44]

Interestingly, an incisive analysis of the *travaux préparatories* reveals the emphasis of the Working Group on aligning the provisions pertaining to setting aside with those addressing recognition and enforcement. The Working Group deemed the above alignment as central to the furtherance of the basic policy of the Model Law of reducing the importance of the place of arbitration.[45] Further, it was felt that were there to be different grounds for setting aside and for recognition or enforcement,

---

[41] Gaillard & Bermann, *supra* 27.

[42] UNCITRAL Yearbook, *supra* 40, [17].

[43] UNCITRAL Report, *supra* 7, [296].

[44] UNCITRAL Report, *supra* 7, [297].

[45] Analytical Commentary, *supra* 34, 70–74.

then the setting aside concepts embedded in national laws of the place of arbitration would assume prominence,[46] because once an award has been set aside in the place of arbitration, it may not be enforced under the New York Convention.[47]

In relation to Article 34(1) of the Model Law, it is to be noted that it merely attracted one comment: the wording "competent court" should be included to ensure linkages with Article 6. This proposal was accepted and the discussion then moved to Article 34(2).

A further issue occupied the delegates, namely whether the incapacity of only one person to the arbitration agreement would be adequate. The corresponding clause of the New York Convention-Article V(1)(a) provides for the refusal of recognition and enforcement where "the parties to the agreement referred to in Article II were, under the law applicable to them, under some incapacity." The Working Group deemed the aforesaid clause as being "too simplistic and not accepted in all legal systems."[48] Succinctly stated, it is obvious that it only really requires the incapacity of the applicant in order to activate Article 34.[49] This position was eventually accepted. In effect, the majority of the conversation and suggestions centred around the issues of procedural fairness and injustice.

In the 318th meeting, the conversation moved to Article 34(2)(b).[50] Mr. Peliched, the observer representing the Hague Conference on Private International Law (HCCH), suggested that Article 34(2)(b)(i) seemed unacceptable as there could be the danger of expanding the scope of its application to have the award set aside in any State as, in the absence of an express (implied choice as well) choice of law, the law governing the substance of the dispute would be deemed as the applicable law for the question of arbitrability.[51] The meeting appeared to be split in relation to the question of whether the sub-paragraph should be deleted or not. In the end, the Chairman suggested that most delegates favoured the retention of the sub-paragraph and it should therefore be left unaltered.[52]

The ambit of public policy in sub-paragraph 2(b)(ii) of Article 34 was the focus of extensive debates during its drafting. Two initial proposals concerning public policy were discussed, i.e. (1) deletion of arbitrability as a ground of setting aside and (2) formulation of international public policy. However, neither of the above proposals were accepted. In relation to the proposal to delete the provision that allows an award to be set aside where the subject-matter is not arbitrable under the law of the Model Law State, it was premised on the view that the law of Model State should not govern

[46] Gaillard & Bermann, *supra*, 27.

[47] Article V (1) (e), United Nations Convention on the Recognition and Enforcement of Foreign Arbitral Awards (New York, 10 June 1958), https://www.newyorkconvention.org/english, accessed 10/08/2018.

[48] Working Group Report, *supra* 35, [141].

[49] Ibid.

[50] Summary Records, *supra* 12.

[51] Ibid, [1].

[52] Summary Records, *supra* 12, [11] - [12], [32].

the question of arbitrability.[53] The proposal to incorporate international public policy into Model Law was made by the Secretariat,[54] which had noted that judgments under the New York Convention distinguished between international public order and the domestic public order where recognition and enforcement of a foreign award was sought.[55] However, as already stated above, despite support of the above observation of the Secretariat, the Working Group rejected the proposal[56] because the "underlying idea was not generally accepted and, above all, the term "international public policy" lacked precision.[57]

The meeting then turned its attention to the term of "public policy." In general, it was felt that it was not warranted to include a definition of public policy into subsection (b)(ii). Several speakers—specifically the United States delegate—noted that whatever definition is included it should not be as broad as, to include mistakes by arbitrators, mistakes of fact of any kind or newly discovered evidence, but should be restricted to situations where the award was procured by fraud, corruption or undue means.[58]

Specifically, the delegate from France noted that he "would prefer to have some objective elements which implicitly involve the principles of a party's motive to act"[59] The Hungarian delegate noted with approval the French comments and stated that the word "may" in the opening sentence of paragraph (2) covered all the necessary elements.

In relation to Article 34(2)(b)(ii), the argument again turned to its exclusion as the Indian delegate stated that the term "public policy" was too vague.[60] Mr. Sekhon, the representative of the Indian delegation, expressed that public policy should be deleted from Article 34(2)(b) because it had little to do with the law of arbitration. Mr. Olukolu, representative of Nigeria, was also of the view that public policy should be deleted owing to its vagueness. His view was mirrored by Mr. Jarvin, observer from the International Chamber of Commerce, who in addition to admitting that public

---

[53]United Nations Commission on International Trade Law (UNCITRAL), "Report of The Working Group on International Contract Practices on The Work of its Seventh Session", ("Report on International Contract Practices"), [136] https://undocs.org/en/A/CN.9/246, accessed 20/10/2020.

[54]United Nations Commission on International Trade Law (UNCITRAL), "Yearbook of the United Nations Commission on International Trade Law, 1982, Volume XIII, Working paper submitted to the Working Group on International Contract Practices at its third session (New York, 16–26 February 1982): Note by the Secretariat: possible features of a model law on international commercial arbitration: questions for discussion by the Working Group", A/CN.9/WG.II/WP.35, [30].

https://uncitral.un.org/sites/uncitral.un.org/files/media-documents/uncitral/en/acn9-wg2-wp35-e.pdf, accessed 10/08/2020.

[55]Report of the Secretary–General, *supra* 13, [46].

[56]United Nations Commission on International Trade Law (UNCITRAL), "Report of The Working Group on International Contract Practices on The Work of its Fourth Session", [16] – [17] https://undocs.org/en/A/CN.9/232, accessed 20/10/2020.

[57]Ibid, [20–25].

[58]Summary Records, *supra* 12, [61].

[59]Ibid, [64].

[60]Gaillard & Bermann, *supra* 27.

policy was a vague concept suggested that it should be developed in the Model Law and a distinction should be made between international and national public policy. Alternatively, Mr. Hoellering, representative of the United States of America, was in favour of retaining public policy as deleting the same, as per him, was a radical departure from the New York Convention and would have an adverse impact on the acceptability of the Model Law. Mr. Graham, observer for Canada, while favouring the aforesaid view of the United States of America, stated as below:

> …In Canada, the common law and the civil law systems were both present and problems such as that under discussion had had to be faced…The concept of public policy *(ordre public)* was included in many international conventions and deleting it from the model law would be tantamount to refusing to tolerate the civil law concept…[61]

In addition, there was also the suggestion that the phrase "a decision contained therein" should be deleted if the public policy expression is to be retained as it is superfluous.[62] The arguments are best summed up by the comments of Sir Mustill, who noted:

> …The question was linked with the general problem of whether there should be a general provision encompassing all cases of serious procedural injustice. It was important to know therefore, whether a case of serious procedural injustice would be regarded as contrary to public policy. If the term would allow a court to intervene in such cases, this delegation would regret the deletion of the subparagraph.[63]

Sir Mustill was also of the view that public policy could not be equated to "ordre public" unlike the suggestion of the Secretariat as the former did not encompass procedural injustice. Mr. Lebedev, the representative of the Union of Soviet Socialist Republics (USSR, the former Soviet Union), while tendering his attention to the concerns of the United Kingdom, argued that in some countries the notion of natural justice was not used and in some countries public policy or ordre public was not used. Nonetheless, Mr. Lebedev pointed out that in international Conventions the terms public policy and *ordre public* had proved quite satisfactory to the international community even though it was extremely difficult to define them.[64]

In the end, the Chairman agreed that the public policy expression is to be retained, whereas the phrase "a decision contained therein" should be deleted.[65] It was decided to leave subsection (b)(ii) as it stood.

---

[61] Ibid.

[62] Summary Records, *supra* 12, [34].

[63] Summary Records, *supra* 12, [41].

[64] Gaillard & Bermann, *supra* 27.

[65] Summary Records, *supra* 12, [56]. In the opinion of the representative from Yugoslavia, the distinction made in paragraph (2)(b)(ii) between "the award" and "any decision contained therein" appears to be unclear, and the question is whether it is useful. Such formulation may lead to the interpretation, incompatible with contemporary trends towards restrictive interpretation of public policy that an award could be set aside on a ground which did not influence the decision on the merits of the case.

2.3.2 *Article 36*

Article 35 of the Model Law envisages the procedure for obtaining recognition and enforcement. Following up on that intent, Article 36 of the Model Law sets forth the grounds for refusal of recognition or enforcement of an arbitral award. A reading of both the articles indicates that they are closely related to each other as both are oriented towards laying down a general framework for recognition or enforcement to be declined by the courts. Hence, it came as no surprise when the first question which was posed during discussions pertaining to Article 36 was whether Articles 35 and 36 should be retained.[66] The general argument in favour of deletion was that the New York Convention already addressed this issue and hence Articles 35 and 36 added nothing to the Model Law. The general consensus in favour of retaining the two articles was that not all States had ratified the New York Convention and hence a substantial gap would be left in the Model Law. The majority seemed to favour the retention, and hence, detailed discussion of the articles was proposed.

The first issue which was discussed in the above context was a discussion on the applicability of the Model Law. It was noted that the Model Law dealt with domestic as well as foreign awards and that the same provisions did not always apply to both. Given that, therefore Article 36(1)(b) should not apply for domestic awards, and to ensure that the observers from Switzerland and Sweden suggested that the article is reworded.[67] Towards that end, Mr Volken, the observer from Switzerland, suggested that the words "irrespective of the country in which it was made" should be deleted and the word "foreign" should be inserted before the word "arbitral award."[68] However, Mr Szasz, the member from the Hungarian delegation, observed

> One of the main points during the discussion … had been that the Model Law was not a simple repetition of the 1958 New York Convention but an innovation in that it established a unified common regime for international commercial arbitration. … If the scope of article 36 was to be limited to foreign awards as understood under the 1958 New York Convention, article 35 and 364 would be entirely superfluous and could be deleted.[69]

The proposal as to the insertion of "foreign" was withdrawn.

---

[66]See, generally, United Nations Commission on International Trade Law (UNCITRAL), "Summary records for meetings on the UNCITRAL Model Law on International Commercial Arbitration, 329th Meeting". ("Summary Records-329th Meeting"). https://uncitral.un.org/sites/uncitral.un.org/files/media-documents/uncitral/en/329meeting-e.pdf, accessed 08/08/2020. It needs to be recalled here that at the 320th Meeting, Sir Micheal Mustill, the representative of the United Kingdom, proposed that before discussing Article 35, it was imperative for the Commission to consider the general question of utility surrounding Article 35 and Article 36 and whether they should be retained at all. See also, United Nations Commission on International Trade Law (UNCITRAL), "Summary records for meetings on the UNCITRAL Model Law on International Commercial Arbitration, 320th Meeting", [38] ("Summary Records-320th Meeting") https://uncitral.un.org/sites/uncitral.un.org/files/media-documents/uncitral/en/320meeting-e.pdf, accessed 08/08/2019.

[67]Summary records -329th Meeting, *supra* 66, [65] – [67].

[68]Ibid, [66].

[69]Ibid, [69].

It is worth noting here that the Indian delegate persisted for the withdrawal of the term "public policy" from Article 36; however, the observer from Canada noted that his delegation understood the term "public policy" in the sense of the French "*ordre public*" rather than in the restricted common law sense.[70] The commission agreed to retain the reference to "public policy" in Article 36(1)(b)(ii).[71]

The arguments advanced against the inclusion of Article 35 and Article 36 could be summed up as being two pronged, i.e. dealing with foreign awards and domestic awards, respectively. In relation to recognition and enforcement of foreign awards, it was thought that the New York Convention was sufficient to handle the matter while in the context of domestic awards it was argued that the aforesaid articles would not serve the cause of easing enforcement of arbitral awards because of the national laws. The national laws, as per the opponents, provide less onerous requirements for easing the enforcement of arbitral awards as compared to the proposed provisions of the Model Law.[72] Per contra, the primary reason rallied by the proponents in favour of retaining Articles 35 and 36 was that a single set of provisions for both foreign and domestic awards would serve to de-emphasize the importance of the place of arbitration in international commercial arbitration[73], thereby furthering the cause of uniformity and "enhance the vitality of international commercial arbitration."[74] Overall, the Commission felt that the argument against the inclusion of Articles 35 and 36 was unpersuasive as it was said that the Model Law would be lacking without provisions pertaining to recognition and enforcement.

Some of the observations made in this regard by the representatives of States are worth noting. Mrs. Ratib, the representative of the Republic of Egypt, pointed that the issues covered by Articles 35 and 36 were already covered by the New York Convention which was a successful Convention. Hence, incorporating Articles 35 and 36 would merely result in useless duplication within the domestic legislation of States which had already acceded to the New York Convention. The main thrust of the arguments against the inclusion of Articles 35 and 36 in the Model Law is best summed up by the observation of Mr. Schuetz, the representative of the Austrian delegation, in his averments,

> There was an internationally recognized and satisfactory convention on the subject already and the incorporation of similar provisions in the model law would cause difficulties in respect of awards made outside a State adopting it. It was moreover unnecessary to provide for recognition and enforcement of awards made inside the territory of a State because under the law of many countries, including his own, an award had the same legal effect as a court ruling.[75]

---

[70] United Nations Commission on International Trade Law (UNCITRAL), "Yearbook of the United Nations Commission on International Trade Law, 1982, Volume XVI, 330th Meeting", [9]. https://uncitral.un.org/sites/uncitral.un.org/files/media-documents/uncitral/en/330meeting-e.pdf, accessed 04/09/2020.

[71] Ibid, [10].

[72] Holtzmann and Neuhaus, *supra* 7, 1006–1052.

[73] Analytical Commentary, *supra* 34, 25, 72. See, also, Holtzmann and Neuhaus, *supra* 7, 1040.

[74] Ibid.

[75] Summary Records-320th Meeting, *supra* 66, [36]. See also, Holtzmann and Neuhaus, *supra* 7.

Mr. Loefmarck, the representative of Sweden, observed that even though his delegation had advocated for deletion of Articles 35 and 36 from the Model Law, it was later realized that the absence of the aforesaid articles from the Model Law would result in a substantial gap. Further, it was also suggested that the articles would prove useful to those States which had not acceded to the New York Convention. The arguments in favour of retaining the provisions are best explained by the suggestions of the delegations of France and Russia. Mr. Roehrich, representative of France, averred

> …although his country had ratified the 1958 New York Convention, he would prefer articles 35 and 36 to be retained. If they were deleted, the model law would contain no reference to ways of facilitating the recognition and enforcement of arbitral awards.[76]

Mr. Lebedev, representative of Soviet Socialist Republics, had argued that

> …the model law was intended to promote both consolidation and comprehensiveness of national legislation. Some countries might have legislation that was superior to the provisions of the model law, but others did not. The only substantial argument advanced against articles 35 and 36 had been that they were superfluous, but that was not the case for all countries. The Commission was expected to produce a finished product, and without provisions on recognition and enforcement, the model law would be incomplete. Even if the articles did not embody a better régime than that provided for in the 1958 New York Convention, some provisions on recognition and enforcement would still be useful in the model law. Moreover, since article 1(1) provided that the model law did not affect multilateral or bilateral agreements, there would be no problem of conflict with such agreements.
>
> Even though it had been highly praised, the 1958 New York Convention had been adopted by only 60 or 70 countries. At least some of those which had not so far adopted the Convention could, by using the model law, make essential changes in their domestic legislation. […][77]

The 331st meeting continued its conversational engagements on the content of Article 34 and 36. It was suggested that the wording of Articles 34 and 36 should be identical—that is—Article 34 should be in line with Article 36 specifically as the New York Convention was not concerned with setting side an award. The meeting endorsed this point of view.[78]

---

[76] Summary Records-320th Meeting, *supra* 66, [44].

[77] Ibid, [47] – [48].

[78] United Nations Commission on International Trade Law (UNCITRAL), "Yearbook of the United Nations Commission on International Trade Law, 1982, Volume XVI, 331st Meeting", [8], https://uncitral.un.org/sites/uncitral.un.org/files/media-documents/uncitral/en/331meeting-e.pdf, accessed 06/05/2020.

2.4 Article 34—Setting Aside of Arbitral Awards

2.4.1 Merits of Recognizing Awards Which Have Been Set Aside

The arguments are mostly based on three criteria, namely first the New York Convention, secondly the arbitration policy and the third argument looks on the entitlement of States to focus entirely on their own domestic requirements.

2.4.1.1 Arguments Based on International Documents

It is difficult to draw a convincing argument from the text alone perhaps with the exception of the word "may" which allows an understanding that the obligation to refuse recognition is not mandatory. Scholarship on the English law suggests that this is indeed the case. The flexibility arguably must have been intended by the drafters of the Convention. The word "shall" in the 1927 version (the Geneva Convention) was replaced by the word "may" in the 1958 New York Convention.[79] Mance noted a second pointer, namely that "in the other situations covered by Article V minor failures to comply with the law or procedure of the seat might, for example, well appear immaterial at an international level."[80]

Interestingly, a Singapore court, hearing an enforcement-related application, attempted to articulate the nature of these two obligations in *Aloe Vera of America Inc. v Asianic Food (S) Pte Ltd and Another*[81] Judith Prakash J's opinion is quoted hereinbelow,

> [...] It is axiomatic that an application to a supervisory court to set aside an award has to be based on one of the grounds which the jurisdiction of that court provides for such an order. In a jurisdiction applying the Model Law, an award by the arbitral tribunal on jurisdiction may be challenged in court and, at common law too, an award may be overturned by the supervisory court on the basis that the tribunal did not have jurisdiction. It is also axiomatic that an application to an enforcement court to resist a grant of leave to enforce must be based on one of the grounds as the jurisdiction of that court provides for such setting aside. It is not necessary nor is it logical that the grounds for both types of application would be identical. It is a question of what the law of the respective jurisdictions provides for. As was pointed out by Sir Anthony Mason NPJ in the *Hebei* case (Hebei Import & Export Corporation V. Polytek Engineering Co. Ltd. [1999] HKCFA 40; [1999] 1 HKLRD 665; (1999) 2 HKCFAR 111; FACV10/1998 (9 FEBRUARY 1999) at 229: Under the Ordinance [the Hong Kong equivalent of the Act] and the Convention, the primary supervisory function in respect of arbitrations rests with the court of supervisory jurisdiction as distinct from the enforcement court ... But this does not mean that the enforcement court will necessarily defer to the court

[79] Lord Mance, *supra* 4, 18.

[80] Ibid.

[81] *Aloe Vera of America Inc. v Asianic Food (S) Pte Ltd and Another*, [2006] SGHC 78, https://www.supremecourt.gov.sg/docs/default-source/module-document/judgement/2006-SGHC-78.pdf accessed 05/03/2021.

> of supervisory jurisdiction. The Convention distinguishes between proceedings to set aside an award in the court of supervisory jurisdiction (arts V 1(e) and VI) and proceedings in the court of enforcement (art V(1)). Proceedings to set aside are governed by the law under which the award was made or the law of the place where it was made, while proceedings in the court of enforcement are governed by the law of that forum. The Convention, in providing that enforcement of an award may be resisted on certain specified grounds, recognises that, although any award may be valid by the law of the place where it is made, its making may be attended by such a grave departure from basic concepts of justice as applied by the court of enforcement that the award should not be enforced.[82] (details supplied by the authors)

It seems, therefore, possible to derive that national courts, necessarily do not seem to be under an obligation to annul the arbitral ruling, even when it appears that one or more of the grounds set forth in the provision are present. The content of Article 34 of the Model Law having been inspired by the vision of the New York Convention, however, the justification for a ruling refusing to set aside the arbitral award, is more likely to be founded upon insufficient evidence for ordering the nullity of the award.[83]

The other word namely "only" is merely a limiting term which is confirmed by Article VII which suggest that the drafters only intended to set a minimum standard and hence left each State the freedom to act less restrictively.[84]

However, by looking at the language of Article V(I), it can be argued that the drafters clearly intended to impose on the State where enforcement is sought to recognize the decision of the courts in the seat, hence creating an internationally harmonized approach to the enforcement and recognition mandate of courts. Importantly, Article V allows courts in the enforcing State to review awards and limiting the right not to recognize them, and hence, the intention is clear that the control over the awards is not centralized to the seat. Gaillard correctly argued that "the New York Convention is perfectly neutral on the fate of awards set aside in the State of Origin."[85] Article V(1)(e) does not require recognition due to the word "may" nor does it bar recognition under Article VII as already explained above. Simply put the textual approach is not mandating that an award which is set aside in the seat cannot be enforced in another State.

2.4.1.2 Arguments Based on Policy Considerations

If the New York Convention endeavoured to grant Contracting States of the seat the right to regulate arbitral law in respect of the whole world Article V would have been obsolete and contrary to its vision. Indeed, a distinction is drawn between the authorities of the seat and States other than the seat where enforcement is sought.

[82] Ibid, [55].

[83] Ilias Bantekas et al.,*supra* 2, 863–864.

[84] Emmanuel Gaillard, "Enforcement of Awards Set Aside in the Country of Origin: The French Experience", in Albert Jan Van den Berg (ed), *Improving the Efficiency of Arbitration Agreements and Awards: 40 Years of Application of the New York Convention, ICCA Congress Series No. 9* (ICCA & Kluwer Law International 1999), 517.

[85] Ibid, 519.

The wording and distinction in words between Articles 34 and 36 and Article V is important and clear that a State has sovereignty over its territory. After all, an award which is valid in the seat might still not be recognized in the State of enforcement because one of the criteria listed in Article V has not been satisfied. Simply put the State of enforcement and/or recognition of an award exercises its sovereignty over legal matters within its territory. The situation therefore remains as such—as there is no supranational court in arbitral matters—the conflict between the seat and the place of enforcement will persist as in any case one of the parties will win to the detriment of the other one.

2.4.1.3 Arguments Based on the Legitimacy of the Review

The starting point is the fact that arbitration is a private act and only becomes "judicial" once courts are involved. The point in many of the arguments is whether a review conducted at the seat is so thorough that the courts at the enforcement stage must defer to the result obtained at the seat? The presumed intent of the parties in choosing a seat is not persuasive as in many cases the procedural rules are empowered to nominate a seat if the parties have not done so. Hence, the intent of the parties is not persuasive to elevate the seat to more what it is namely a fictional place. The simplest and at the same time compelling reason to enforce an award which has been set aside at the seat is to imply the fact that both courts are equally competent to recognize and enforce an award.[86] Gaillard commented

> The State of the enforcement of the award, by contrast, has very real interest in ensuring that the award meets the standard of what it considers to be a decision worthy of public support. On a very basic level, between the State of the seat which provides hotel rooms and conference centers for an arbitration, and the State of enforcement which permits the seizure and sale of assets in its territory, there can be little doubt that the latter has a stronger interest in reviewing the award.[87]

This view is supported by the New York Convention which via Article V (2) allows the State where enforcement is sought to apply its own concept of public policy and its own laws in judging whether an award is capable of settlement by arbitration.

Article 34 enlisted the conditions that need to be fulfilled in order that an award may be set aside by courts at the seat of arbitration. It is obvious that reasons of fact and law cannot be part of Article 34 as institutional rules state clearly that an award is final and binding. This is reinforced by the word "only" in Article 34(2) which in essence gives the court power to set aside an award but only based on circumstances as prescribed in Article 34. However, this article also states that setting aside of an award "may" be made which is discretionary. Born noted:

> It is … clear that the grounds specified in Article 34(2) of the Model Law are permissive and discretionary, not mandatory. That is, a court may annul an award if one or more of the

[86] Emmanuel Gaillard, *supra* 84.

[87] Ibid, 526.

> Article 34(2) grounds are satisfied, but the court is not mandatorily required to annul the award, even where one of these grounds applies.[88]

Lor Mance extensively observed on the nature of discretion and was of the view that it is not unfettered. He observed

> [...] it would be a remarkable state of affairs if the word "may" enabled a court to enforce or recognise an award which it found to have been made without jurisdiction, under whatever law it held ought to be recognised and applied to determine that issue.[89]

Wigney J's observation, quoted hereinbelow, seems to be an apt reflection of the judicial thinking on the discretionary application of Article 34.

> Judicial restraint in this context would suggest both that arbitral awards should not be scrutinised upon by overzealous judicial review, and that the discretion to set aside awards should be exercised sparingly and only in clear cases.[90]

Also, the US 2nd Circuit court—already in 1974—stated that the policy of both the New York Convention and the Model Law is pro-enforcement.[91] A further observation needs to be highlighted, namely that the governing rules are not always the ones of the seat of arbitration but the ones of the legal system where the recourse against the arbitral award has been lodged. It is only usual but not mandatory that the challenge takes place in the court of the seat.[92] Lord Mance observed

> The French law view is that an international arbitral award is 'not anchored in any national legal order', but 'is a decision of international justice, whose validity must be ascertained with regard to the rules applicable in the country where its recognition and enforcement are sought.'[93]

This point rises the issue how the word "this state" in the Model Law needs to be interpreted. The word "this state" arguably must be read as suggesting the court where jurisdiction has been seized and is synonymous with "that state" as noted in Article V of the New York Convention. Several issues point to this interpretation such as the validity issue noted in Article 34(2)(a)(i). This point was already discussed in the 317th meeting at UNCITRAL where Mr Pelichet, the observer for the Hague Conference on Private International Law, commented

---

[88]Gary B. Born, *International Commercial Arbitration* (2nd ed. Kluwer, 2014) 3, 3177. The court has held similar views, and the same has also been considered favourably in *CRW Joint Operation v PT Perusahaan Gas Negara (Persero) TBK* [2011] 4 SLR 305, *Downer-Hill Joint Venture v Government of Fiji* [2005] 1 NZLR 554 at [103*]; Cargill International SA v Peabody Australia Mining Ltd* [2010] NSWSC 887 at [242] and *Grand Pacific Holdings, supra* 21, just to mention a few.

[89]*Dallah Real Estate and Tourism Holding Co v Ministry of Religious Affairs of the Government of Pakistan* [2010] UKSC 46, [2011] 1 AC 763, [68]. https://www.supremecourt.uk/cases/docs/uksc-2009-0165-judgment.pdf.

[90]*Hebei Jikai Industrial Group Co Ltd v Martin* [2015] FCA 228 [97]. https://www6.austlii.edu.au/cgi-bin/viewdoc/au/cases/cth/FCA/2015/228.html.

[91]Gary B. Born, *supra* 88.

[92]Nigel Blackaby, Constantine Partasides, Alan Redfern & Martin Hunter, *Redfern and Hunter on International Arbitration* (OUP, 6th ed. 2015), 10, [10.04] – [10.05].

[93]Lord Mance, *supra* 4, 5.

> It did not seem right that the question of validity of the arbitration agreement should be submitted to the law of the country of arbitration, since many arbitration proceedings were held in a country which had no connection with the main contract or the parties to it. Under most systems of private international law, validity of an arbitration agreement was decided by the law governing the main contract.[94]

Further, Mr Herrmann noted that the Working Group "had decided to use the wording of the 1958 New York Convention … because that had enabled Article 34 to be aligned with Article 36."[95] Emphasizing upon the correctness of this view taken at the UNCITRAL meeting, Holtzmann and Neuhaus commented that Article 34 was drafted to "align the grounds for setting aside with the grounds for recognition and enforcement that were listed in Article V of the New York Convention."[96]

It suggests that all the three articles in effect point to the same jurisdictional issue. In other words, "that state" is synonymous with "this state" reinforcing that a challenge can be heard anywhere unless the terms of the arbitration agreement indicate otherwise.

In any case not all jurisdictions will refuse to entertain the motion of enforcing an award even if it has been set aside elsewhere.[97] However, the crucial issue is that awards may be set side and are subject to the law of the seat but enforcement of an award is another issue. It normally takes place where the assets are as it gives the winning party a chance to use the jurisdiction to obtain security over the assets. Article 34(2)(a)(ii) also reinforces the view that any challenge to an award must be on the grounds as listed in Article 34 and cannot be on grounds that the losing party either raised or should have raised during the arbitration. Arguably if a court would allow such a claim, it would sanction an attempted to re-argue an issue.

2.5 The Importance of the "exclusive" in Article 34

Article 34 is the only article in relation to recognition and enforcement of arbitral awards which uses the word "exclusive" in the head note. An explanation as to its meaning can be derived from Article 35 which in essence states that an award shall be "recognized as binding … and shall be enforced." The word "shall" is used contrary to the permissive word "may" in Articles 34 and 36 of the Model Law. Hence as an award is binding. The exclusive exceptions as to setting aside an award are contained in Article 34. The UNCITRAL Secretariat in the Explanatory Note stated that the Model Law,

> (a)llow[s] only one type of recourse, to the exclusion of any other recourse regulated in any procedural law of the State in question. Article 34 (1) provides that the sole recourse against

---

[94]UNCITRAL Yearbook, *supra* 40, [9].

[95]Ibid, [19].

[96]Holtzmann and Neuhaus, *supra* 7, 912.

[97]*PT Putrabali Adyamulia v Rena Holding et Société Mnogutia Est Epices*, 2007 Rev. arb. 507 (French Cour de cassation le); Judgment of 10 June 1997, *Chromalloy Aeroservices*, *supra* 24.

an arbitral award is by application for setting aside, which must be made within three months of receipt of the award (article 34 (3)).[98]

2.5.1 The Role of the Seat

As noted above, courts can only intervene when the procedural law allows the court to do so. Setting aside an award pursuant to Article 34 is said to be usually taking place in the court of the seat.[99] There is no dispute that the choice of a seat is crucial. Greenberg et al. explained that the choice of a seat would be determined by the content of the law applicable to arbitrations in that jurisdiction. They described

> .... legitimizes and provides a general legal framework for international arbitration. The relevant law might itself be found in an independent statute on international arbitration or it might be a chapter in another law, such as a civil procedure or a law also governing domestic arbitration. [It] can also include other statutes and codes (even those not specifically dealing with arbitration) and case law which relates to the basic legal framework of international arbitrations seated there.[100]

The role of the seat has been shaped by two theories, namely territorialism and delocalization.[101] The point of the debate is to answer the question where and how arbitrators derive their powers to perform what might be termed a quasi-judicial function. In brief, under the territorialism theory, arbitrators derive their power from the place where they perform their duties. The procedural laws and the choice of law rules of the seat therefore govern the process.

The delocalization theory on the other hand proposed that international arbitration tribunals are detached from the control of the seat of arbitration. Parties under this

---

[98]United Nations Commission on International Trade Law (UNCITRAL), "UNCITRAL Model Law on International Commercial Arbitration 1985-with amendments as adopted in 2006", ("Model Law 2006 version"). https://uncitral.un.org/sites/uncitral.un.org/files/media-documents/uncitral/en/19-09955_e_ebook.pdf, accessed 29/05/2020.

[99]Nigel Blackaby et al., *supra* 84.

[100]Simon Greenberg, Christopher Kee & J.Romesh Weeramantry, *International Arbitration: An Asia–Pacific Perspective* (CUP, 2011) [2.11]; See, also Alastair Henderson, "Lex Arbitri, Procedural Law and the Seat of Arbitration: Unravelling the Laws of the Arbitration Process" (2014) 26 *Singapore Academy Law Journal* 886.

[101]For a detailed discussion see Jean Francois Poudret, Sebastien Besson, & Stephen Birti, *Comparative Law of International Arbitration*, (Sweet & Maxwell, 2007), 2; see, generally, Jan Paulsson, "Delocalisation of International Commercial Arbitration: When and Why It Matters" (1983) 32(1) *International and Comparative Law Quarterly* 53; Eric Schwartz, "Do International Arbitrators Have a Duty to obey the orders of Courts at the Place of the Arbitration? Reflections on the Role of the Lex Loci Arbitri in the Light of a Recent ICC Award" in Gerald Aksen, Karl-Heinz Bockstiegel, Michael Mustill, Paolo Michele Patocchi, Anne Marie Whitesell (eds), *Global Reflections on International Law, Commerce and Dispute Resolution – Liber Amicorum in honour of Robert Briner* (ICC Publishing, 2005) 796; Jan Paulsson, "The extent of independence of international arbitration from the law of the *situs*" in JDM Lew (ed) *Contemporary Problems in International Arbitration* (Springer, Dordrecht, 1987) 141; William W. Park, "Duty and Discretion in International Arbitration" (2017) 93(4) *American Journal of International Law* 803.

theory will hold their arbitrations at a common convenient place[102] and hence derive their power from the international legal community.[103] The end effect is that an award set aside in one country can be enforced in another one as demonstrated by the French practise.

Article 34 is not expressly stating that setting aside an award must be made at the seat of the arbitration. In subsection (1), it merely states that recourse "to a court" can be made. However, by implication Article V (1) (e) of the New York Convention can be interpreted to suggest that an award can or should be set aside at the seat of the arbitration. The specific provision of the article reads

> [...] The award has not yet become binding on the parties, or has been set aside or suspended by a competent authority of in which, or under the law of which, that award was made.

The conclusion is that "in which, or under the law of which, that award was made" arguably can be interpreted as being the jurisdiction of the seat of the arbitration. The question whether an award which has been upheld can be challenged at the enforcement stage by the losing party is also of suitable interest. The answer is dependent on the reasons to challenge the enforcement process. However, whatever theory is in command the "interference" of local courts cannot be avoided as arbitrators do not have a judicial function and hence must rely on courts. The very reason of this restriction can be demonstrated by the fact that none of the institutional rules have included an article like Article 34 or 36 of the Model Law into their regime. These articles can only be invoked by courts as the very applicability rests within the jurisdictional function of courts. Hence, the seat is of diminished importance depending whether the legal system adheres to the delocalization or territorialism theory.

The English High Court decision of *Nikolay Viktorovich Maximov v Open Joint Stock Company "Novolipetsky Metallurgichesky Kombinat"*[104] explains the importance of the seat. In that case, the claimant asked the court to enforce an annulled agreement. Despite the fact that the annulment of the award by the Moscow Arbitration Court was based on the wrong application of Russian law, the English High Court—though critical—was not persuaded that the errors were so severe as to deprive the claimant of natural justice. However, it is noteworthy that the claimant sought to enforce the award also in France and the Netherlands. The French courts did enforce the award, whereas the Dutch decision—after an initial refusal to enforce—is still pending. This case again indicates that a selection of a seat must be a careful decision and not merely one of convenience.

---

[102] M. Moses, *Principles and Practice of International Commercial Arbitration*, (CUP, 2008), 56.

[103] Emmanuel Gaillard and John Savage (eds), *Fouchard Gaillard Goldman on International Commercial Arbitration*, (Kluwer Law International 1999).

[104] *Nikolay Viktorovich Maximov v Open Joint Stock Company "Novolipetsky Metallurgichesky Kombinat"*, [2017] EWHC 1911 (Comm).

2.5.2 Jurisprudence of Article 34

The first point to note is that only a final award can be set aside. In addition, a further issue was discussed in *Blanalko Pty Ltd v Lysaght Building Solutions Pty Ltd*,[105] (*Blanalko Pty Ltd*) which is whether an arbitrator not making a decision is a ground to set aside the award. The arbitrator in this case did not decide the issue of costs because he decided that he lacked the necessary information.[106] Hence, the issue turns on the application and interpretation of Article 33 of the Model Law in conjunction with the requirements of setting aside of the award in Article 34 of the Model Law. The reason advanced by the parties was that as the arbitrator did not make a decision the award must be set aside.

To begin with the court, correctly, noted that if the arbitrator did not make a decision at all, recourse to Article 34(2)(a)(iii) will fail.[107] This article states

> (2) An arbitral award may be set aside by the court specified in article 6 only if:
>
> (a) the party making the application furnishes proof that:
>
> (iii) the award deals with a dispute not contemplated by or not falling within the terms of the submission to arbitration, or contains decisions on matters beyond the scope of the submission to arbitration, provided that, if the decisions on matters submitted to arbitration can be separated from those not so submitted, only that part of the award which contains decisions on matters not submitted to arbitration may be set aside; […].

It must be remembered that the parties did ask the arbitrator to rule on the cost issues and hence the decision when made will fall within the submission to arbitrate. The court came to the conclusion—examining the critical part in the decision—that the arbitrator considered the answer to the question whether to make an award on the Supreme Courts costs. Croft J noted

> […] All the arbitrator has done is not discharge his whole mandate; he has not gone beyond it. As to the latter, particularly, there is no delegation to, or direction to, the parties to take the Supreme Court Costs claim to a "third party" decision maker; namely the Court in this instance.[108]

Croft J extensively referred to the primary sources—he consulted the predecessor to the New York Convention, the Geneva Convention on the Execution of Foreign Arbitral Awards[109] that contained the words "[…] that the award does not deal with the differences contemplated by or falling within the terms of the submission to arbitration […]"[110] and which were not considered for inclusion within Article 34

---

[105] *Blanalko Pty Ltd v Lysaght Building Solutions Pty Ltd,* [2017] VSC 97. https://www8.austlii.edu.au/cgi-bin/viewdoc/au/cases/vic/VSC/2017/97.html.

[106] Ibid, [4].

[107] Ibid, [48].

[108] Ibid.

[109] *Geneva Convention on the Execution of Foreign Arbitral Awards* (1927) L.N.T.S. 301. Art 2(c) ("the Geneva Convention").

[110] Ibid, Article 2 (c).

of the Model Law and Article V of the New York Convention hence "a decision not to make a decision" is not a decision that may be set aside under s 34(2)(a)(iii).[111]

It is obvious that an arbitrator is not allowed or should not make a decision without sufficient evidence and hence he should never merely guess or act on assumptions. However, the question is whether it is within the power of an arbitrator not to make a decision. If it is not, then the arbitrator exceeded his power, and hence, the award can be set aside.

On this issue, the Singapore Court of Appeal in *CRW Joint Operation v PT Perusahaan Gas Negara (Persero) TBK*[112] observed

> It is useful, at this juncture, to set out some of the legal principles underlying the application of Art 34(2)(a)(iii) of the Model Law... [I]t applies where the arbitral tribunal improperly decided matters that had not been submitted to it or failed to decide matters that had been submitted to it. In other words, Art 34(2)(a)(iii) addresses the situation where the arbitral tribunal exceeded (or failed to exercise) the authority that the parties granted to it [...].[113]

However, an important proviso does apply, namely

> [I]t must be noted that a failure by an arbitral tribunal to deal with every issue referred to it will not ordinarily render its arbitral award liable to be set aside. The crucial question in every case is whether there has been *real or actual prejudice* to either (or both) of the parties to the dispute.[114]

Croft J and the Singapore Supreme Court demonstrated clearly that the fact that an arbitrator did not deal with the issue of costs is decisive but the crucial question is: has there been "real or actual prejudice" to each party in the arbitral process? Importantly, Article 34 only applies to a final award. Hence, the court addressed the issue whether the award is final or not.

Article 34 can only be invoked if the award is final. The court...quoting Mustill and Boyd[115]—made the points that an award isn't final if the arbitrator leaves certain issues to another party to decide. The exception is that if an arbitrator reserves certain matters for future decisions then he only issued an interim award. After carefully considering the jurisprudence underpinning Mustill and Boyd, Croft J concluded that

> I find that, in spite of its labelling, it was clearly not a final award. The Award did not decide all issues put to the arbitrator within the arbitrator's mandate and did not involve an order or direction that might be characterised as an invalid delegation of power to a third party.[116]

The result was that the arbitrator only delivered an interim award and until the entire matter is resolved access to setting aside provisions postulated in Article 34 is barred.

---

[111] *Blanalko Pty Ltd*, supra 105, [49].

[112] *CRW Joint Operation v PT Perusahaan Gas Negara (Persero) TBK*, [2011] 4 SLR 305, 31.

[113] Ibid, [31].

[114] Ibid, [32].

[115] Sir M J Mustill and S.C. Boyd, *The Law and Practice of Commercial Arbitration in England* (Butterworths, 1989) 2, 387.

[116] *Blanalko Pty Ltd, supra* 105, 66.

Several high-profile cases were considering attempts by one of the arbitral parties to set aside an arbitral award. It goes without saying that the principle of confidentiality is lost once a dispute moves from arbitration to litigation. As a case cannot be reheard, there is a fine line to extract facts from the arbitral award which support the claim that Article 34 has been breached. The temptation is ever present for counsel to move beyond the confines of Article 34 and attempt to have the matter reheard that is appeal either in fact or law. This issue was explained clearly in *Emerald Grain Australia Pty Ltd v Agrocorp International Pte Ltd*[117] wherein Pagone J stated

> [Article 34] preserves the court's ability to give effect to public policy in its jurisdiction, and is in part directed to protecting the integrity of the judicial system of the court, but does not authorise new grounds to be relied upon by a party in adversarial proceedings where the application does not otherwise sufficiently do so on a fair reading. The words "if [...] the court finds" in Article 34(2)(b) do not impose upon the court an obligation to embark upon its own inquiry into matters which were not properly, or sufficiently, raised by an applicant in adversarial proceedings; nor do the words enlarge a claim made by an applicant to include matters that were not properly, or sufficiently, relied upon as grounds to set aside an award.[118]

In *Cargill International SA v Peabody Australia Mining Ltd*[119], Ward J dismissed the plaintiffs appeal. The parties were subject to the ICC rules; however, it was not clear where the seat of arbitration was. Notably, the plaintiff claimed that the award was in conflict with public policy. Ward J noted that "by reference to s 19 of the [International Arbitration] Act, there is a conflict with the public policy of Australia if there has been a breach of the rules of natural justice."[120] The court observed that "a breach of the hearing rule is one of the twin pillars of natural justice, the other being the bias rule."[121] However, to put it differently, the public policy rule notes that "the Award was in conflict with both the 'hearing rule' and the 'no evidence' rule of the rules of natural justice."[122] In the end, the plaintiff's application was dismissed as they could not satisfy a breach of the public policy rule.

Brereton J in *Carbotech-Australia Pty Ltd & anor v Yates & 14 ors.*[123] explained that at the most basic level, the hearing rule requires a decision-maker to hear a person before making a decision affecting that person's interests.

In *Dranichnikov v Minister for Immigration and Multicultural Affairs*, the High Court of Australia was asked to decide upon a constructive failure by the tribunal to exercise jurisdiction amounted to violation of natural justice. The court held "[t]o fail to respond to a substantial, clearly articulated argument relying upon established facts was at least to fail to accord Mr Dranichnikov natural justice."[124]

---

[117] *Emerald Grain Australia Pty Ltd v Agrocorp International Pte Ltd (Emerald Grain),* [2014] FCA 414.

[118] Ibid, [9].

[119] *Cargill International SA v Peabody Australia Mining Ltd*, [2010] NSWSC 887.

[120] Ibid, [225].

[121] Ibid, [226].

[122] *Emerald Grain Australia Pty Ltd, supra* 117.

[123] *Carbotech-Australia Pty Ltd & anor v Yates & 14 ors*, [2008] NSWSC 540. See, specifically, [39], [46] – [47].

[124] *Dranichnikov v Minister for Immigration and Multicultural Affairs* [2003] HCA 26, [24].

A New Zealand High Court decision in Sinke v Remarkable Residential Homes Ltd.[125] is instructive of the approach of the courts in deciding Article 34-related applications when pleas of natural justice are involved. The applicant before the court pleaded the breach arising from a delayed conveyance of material information leading to a violation of an opportunity to be heard. Durie J observed that proper consideration was given to Mr. Sinke's final submissions. He noted

> There may have been some lacuna in the approach taken to Mr Sinke's submissions but it was small insofar as the arbitrator was concerned to weed out new material or information. Without wishing to diminish the primacy of adhering to the rules of natural justice I take into account that relief under article 34 is discretionary. There is no error of sufficient magnitude to invoke the exercise of discretion in the plaintiff's favour.
>
> The High Court in New Zealand has approached the discretion under Article 34 in a relatively open way, taking into account causation and materiality considerations when deciding whether to set aside an award once a ground for setting aside has been established. Thus, even if such a ground is present, the Court may consider the magnitude of the defect and the extent to which it had or might have had an impact on the outcome of the dispute, and particularly whether the tribunal might have reached a different conclusion had it adopted the correct approach.[126]

Importantly, it must not be forgotten that a breach of natural justice will be closely tied to facts and the circumstances of the matter. It is therefore not a fixed body of rules.[127] In essence, the court—considering the basic proposition of the hearing rule—still needs to rely on factual appraisal which could have been aired during the arbitral process.

In *Emerald Grain*[128], the issue involved was a breach of public policy, i.e. a breach of natural justice. Pagone J noted that to challenge on the basis of a lack of probative evidence is difficult as

> [...] The distinction between a permissible error of fact and a decision based upon no probative evidence may be difficult, but is essential, to maintain. The difficulty in maintaining the distinction, and the need for the challenge to be firmly based upon the "no evidence" rule or the hearing rule as a breach of the rules of natural justice, points to the need for the most precise identification of what is challenged, of the basis for that challenge, and of how that fits firmly within the basis of a legitimate claim of a breach of the "no evidence" rule (as distinct from a complaint that facts were found incorrectly or not as the losing party had wished) or of the hearing rule (as distinct from a complaint that submissions were rejected or not accepted as the losing party had wished).[129]

Arguably, the difficulty as pointed out by Pagone J is to find the boundary between the lack of probative evidence and the issue of a rehearing of the case which is not within the confines of Article 34 or any other articles in the Model Law or the New York Convention for that matter. In addition, a further difficulty lies with the fact

---

[125] *Peter Sinke v Remarkable Residential Homes Ltd.*, (2000) NZHC CP No, 274/98.

[126] Ibid, [21].

[127] *Mobil Oil Australia Pty. Ltd. v Federal Commissioner of Taxation* [1963] HCA 41, [13].

[128] *Emerald Grain Australia Pty Ltd, supra* 117.

[129] *Emerald Grain Australia Pty Ltd, supra* 117, [11].

that the content of the rules of natural justice is connected to facts and hence varies depending on the context.[130]

It is therefore obvious, as held in *Skiwing Pty Ltd v Trust Company of Australia*,[131] that a claimant must first explain and set out the context in which a breach of natural justice occurred. In its simplest form, the no evidence rule has been proven if the tribunal acts without probative evidence. This must be distinguished with making the wrong finding of facts or come to an illogical conclusion which is not an error of law, and hence, there is no breach of natural justice.

In Singapore, the approach adopted for setting aside of arbitral awards is no different than the one in Australia. In *Triulzi Cesare SRL v Xinyi Group (Glass) Company Limited*[132] *(Triulzi Cesare SRL)*, the original arbitration was governed by the ICC Rules of Arbitration 2012. The plaintiff argued that the award should be set aside pursuant to Article 34(2)(a) specifically the breach of the hearing rule and the public policy exemption pursuant to Article 34(2)(a)(iv). The court first described the general purpose of Article 34 that "there can be no basis whatsoever to set aside the Award under Art 34(2)(a) of the Model Law… if Triulzi's complaints are not premised upon circumstances attributable to the Tribunal."[133] The court further observed

> […] It cannot be the case that any breach of an agreed arbitral procedure, even that of a technical provision or minor formality, will invariably result in an award being set aside. Most supervising courts inquire into the *materiality* of the procedural requirements that was not complied with and the nature of the departures from the parties' agreed arbitral procedures. […][134]

In essence, the court pointed out that setting aside an award must be based on a material and not a minor issue which again is based on facts and reflects the minimal interference rule. It cited with high commendation the decision of the United States District Court in US District Court decision of *Karaha Bodas Company, LLC v Perusahaan Pertambangan Minyak Dan Gas Bumi Negara*[135] wherein it was held that a party "must show that there is a violation of an arbitration agreement between the parties and that the violation actually caused [that party] substantial prejudice in the arbitration."[136]

The court in *Triulzi Cesare SRL* came to the conclusion that the claimant engaged in the "second bite at the cherry"[137] approach that was previously frowned upon by

---

[130] *Emerald Grain Australia Pty Ltd, supra* 117, [12].

[131] *Skiwing Pty Ltd v Trust Company of Australia* [2006] NSWCA 276, 52.

[132] *Triulzi Cesare SRL v Xinyi Group (Glass) Company Limited.*, [2014] SGHC 220.

[133] Ibid, 20.

[134] Ibid, 54.

[135] *Karaha Bodas Company, LLC v Perusahaan Pertambangan Minyak Dan Gas Bumi Negara* 190 F Supp 2d 936 (SD Tex, 2001.

[136] *Ibid*, 945.

[137] *Triulzi Cesare SRL, supra* 134, [67, 76, 80, 148].

the Court of Appeal in *BLC and others v BLB and another*.[138] The court observed that the application was without merit in the following terms:

> Triulzi's characterisation of its case as an award that was not in accordance with Art 18 in order to engage Art 34(2) of the Model Law … simply ignores the evidential foundation of Triulzi's complaints. … Triulzi must bear the consequences of its own failures and choices (tactical or otherwise) that it made at the Arbitration.[139]

The conclusion is that very few, if any, recourses to Article 34 are successful and hence support the view that Article 34 is of no practical benefit to an aggrieved party.

2.6 Article 36—Refusing Recognition or Enforcement of Foreign Arbitral Awards

This article sets out the grounds on which a court can refuse recognition or enforce an award irrespective of the country where the award has been made. Like Article 34, this article is also permissive in character as it contains the word "may." However, two issues need to be observed, first all the sup-paragraphs in Article 36 are the same as in Article 34, and no additional comments are required. Secondly and more importantly—the only difference is Article 36(1)(a)(v) which is not included in Article 34.

The argument—as far as the similar sub-paragraphs are concerned—is that if a party is not successful under Article 34 there is very little chance of succeeding under Article 36 that is block enforcement. The reason is that the same arguments or facts will fit both articles. To put it differently, the real test is not Article 34 but Article 36 or better still Article V of the New York Convention.

As far as Article 36(1)(a)(v) is concerned, two practical differences must be noted

> First the grounds relating to public policy, including non-arbitrability, may be different in substance, depending on the State in question (i.e. State of setting aside or State of enforcement). Secondly, and more importantly, the grounds for refusal of recognition or enforcement are valid and effective only in the State (or States) where the winning party seeks recognition and enforcement, while the grounds for setting aside have a different impact: The setting aside of an award at the place of origin prevents enforcement of that award in all other countries by virtue of article V(l)(e) of the 1958 New York Convention and article 36(1)(a)(v) of the Model Law.[140]

However, this is not always true. As noted above, an award even if annulled can still be enforced depending which theory courts will adopt such as in France. The conclusion is that it is best to wait for enforcement than try to set aside an award.

---

138 *BLC and others v BLB and another* [2014] 4 SLR 79.

139 Ibid, [166].

140 Benjamin Horn and Roger Hopkins, *Arbitration Law Handbook*, (Routledge, 2007), 44,19.

2.6.1 Jurisprudence of Article 36

Enforcement of an arbitral award—once rendered—pursuant to Article 35 must be recognized as binding and "shall" be enforced subject to provisions of Article 36.

It must be noted that this article uses the word "shall" instead of "may" and hence recognition and enforcement is mandatory. However, as Article 35 is subject to Article 36, arguably enforcement of an award has become discretionary only if one of the exceptions in Article 36 are met. In *Europcar Italia S.p.A. v Alba Tours International Inc.*[141], the court found that it is "therefore clear that even should one of the circumstances [set out in article 36(1)] exist, enforcement could still be ordered in the exercise of judicial discretion".[142] The court in this case also made it clear that once a process of setting aside an award under Article 35—which is Italy—is still in progress an enforcement application must be stayed pursuant to Article 36(2). The court stated

> As a matter of international comity this court should refrain from appearing to interfere in any way with the Italian judicial process. It should rather defer to the review being conducted in Italy.[143]

A further point must be noted, namely that the jurisprudence applying Article 36 will show variations depending whether the territorial or delocalization theory is in command. As noted above already—in brief—even though an award has been set aside in one jurisdiction, it can still be enforced in another State.

2.7 Conclusion

This chapter has shown that to invoke Article 34 creates more problems than it solves. It is not suggested that Article 34 should never be invoked however if an application to set aside an award is made the applicant should understand the risks and no doubt good reasons might persuade a party to do so. In general, the arguments which need to be put forward are very similar if not identical in Articles 34 and 36 of the Model Law and V of the New York Convention. There is no doubt that the setting aside at the seat must also consider public policy. However, if the enforcement is also at the seat, then Article 36 or Article V can be enlivened, and hence, public policy must be part of it again. Article 36 is more appropriate if the enforcement is also at the seat. It does not matter really if "that state" or "this state" in this instance is the same State.

To illustrate the point *TCL Air Conditioner (Zhongshan) Co Ltd v Castel Electronics Pty Ltd*[144] is instructive. The court commented that

---

[141] *Europcar Italia S.p.A. v Alba Tours International Inc* [1997] O.J. No. 133, 23 O.T.C. 376 (Gen. Div.).

[142] Ibid, [12].

[143] Ibid, [22].

[144] *TCL Air Conditioner (Zhongshan) Co Ltd v Castel Electronics Pty Ltd*, [2014] FCAFC 83.

> The grounds for TCL's two claims (the setting aside of the award under Art 34 and the resistance of enforcement under Art 36) were identical: the asserted failure by the arbitrators to accord TCL procedural fairness such that there had been a breach of the rules of natural justice in connection with the making of the award, and so, it was asserted, the award was in conflict with, or contrary to, the public policy of Australia.[145]

As already the primary judge noted—and referred to in the appeal, "public policy in Article 34 and 36 is the same", and "the asserted breach of the rules of natural justice must be of a sufficiently serious character to offend fundamental notions of fairness and justice before the relevant discretion under either Article 34 or Article 36 would be exercised."[146] Similar view was expressed by the Supreme Court of Victoria when it noted,

> [that] …However – as the authorities set out below in relation to public policy suggest – the content of this ground for setting aside an award under art 34 is the same as the ground for refusing enforcement under art 36, as is the public policy ground under s 8(7)(b) of the Act, and art V(2)(b) of the New York Convention.[147]

In effect even if a party is successful in setting aside an award, it does not automatically suggest that enforcement at a later stage is not possible as demonstrated in *Corporación Mexicana De Mantenimiento Integral, S. De R.L. De C.V., v PEP–Exploración Y Producción.*[148]

Pursuant to Article V of the New York Convention, an award which is valid in the seat might not be enforced as it is contrary to public policy of the enforcing jurisdiction. The obvious exception is if the seat of the arbitration is not only the place of setting aside an award but is also the jurisdiction where enforcement is likely to be lodged.

In sum, it is argued that the defining point in an arbitration is not the awarding of the award but the enforcement of it. Enforcement is the only binding event in the arbitration process which can only be challenged if an appeal is allowed. In contrast if an award has been set aside pursuant to Article 34 an enforcement is still possible as the setting aside might not be recognized in all jurisdictions. From a practical point of view, a party contemplating a challenge ought to think whether tactically they would be better served to wait for the enforcement and then mount the arguments they would have used in challenging the award anyway. In any event, a party must be mindful not to re-package or re-characterize their original case as otherwise challenges or enforcements of arbitral awards will fail.

---

[145] Ibid, 6.

[146] Ibid, 13.

[147] *Indian Farmers Fertiliser Cooperative Ltd v Gutnick* [2015] VSC 724, 28.

[148] *Corporación Mexicana de Mantenimiento Integral S. De R.L de CV v Pemex-Exploración y Producción*, No.10 Civ. 206 (AKH), 2013 WL 4517225, (S.D.N.Y. 27 August 2013).

Chapter 3
The Exceptions to the Enforcement of Foreign Arbitral Awards Within the New York Convention—Jurisprudence from State Practice

Overview

This chapter is premised upon the observation that arbitral awards are binding and enforceable. However, certain exceptions are noted in the Model Law and the New York Convention. In particular, the following will be discussed in order to gain a general understanding of Article V.

- Article V(1)
    - Article V(1)(a)
        - Party(s) to the agreement being under an incapacity to the arbitration agreement
        - the arbitration agreement being invalid under its applicable law
    - Article V(1)(b)
        - absence of proper notice to the party(s) about the arbitration proceedings
        - State Practice on 'notice'—the phraseology of notice and its interpretation in State practice
    - Article V(1)(c)
    - Article V(1)(d)
    - Article V(1)(e)
        - when an arbitral award has been set aside
        - binding nature of an award
        - distinction between 'set aside' and 'suspended'
        - space for enforcement of annulled arbitral awards
    - Article V(2)
        - Article V(2)(a)—subject-matter arbitrability
        - Article V(2) (b)—public policy exception

B. Zeller et al., *Enforcement of Foreign Arbitral Awards and the Public Policy Exception*,
https://doi.org/10.1007/978-981-16-2634-0_3

3.1 Introduction

Arbitration being a binding contractual obligation founded upon the freedom of contract, arbitral awards are perceived as binding and enforceable by parties, courtesy of the law on binding contractual obligations. However, the problem is that not all awards are honoured and must be enforced or recognized by a court. This is so as specifically enforcement is a judicial function and is beyond the arbitrators ability. The New York Convention[1] has been specifically drawn up to regulate this aspect. Article 1 states

> This Convention shall apply to the recognition and enforcement of arbitral awards made in the territory of a State other than the State where the recognition and enforcement of such awards are sought, and arising out of differences between persons, whether physical or legal.

However, at the same time, enforcement and recognition is not automatic as in the end domestic legal systems need to evaluate the requests taking recourse to domestic legal principles. Hence, Article V notes that recognition and enforcement *may* be refused.

The New York Convention in Article V notes the exclusive grounds for refusing the enforcement of an award which has been rendered in the seat. Enforcement can either be affected at the seat or in a foreign jurisdiction. Either way the New York Convention is applicable. However, Article V distinguishes between the applicable laws as all exceptions noted in V(1) utilize the law of the seat, whereas in V(2), it is the law where the recognition or enforcement is sought. Also, the reasons for setting aside noted in Article V(1) are mainly procedural in nature and hence obviously only applicable in the seat and not in the enforcement country where different procedural rules may apply. To put in another way, Article V(1) lists the grounds that must be raised "at the request of the party against whom [the ward] is invoked", and Article V(2) lists the grounds on which a court may refuse enforcement based on the municipal law of the country where the enforcement is sought. Hence, Article V is clear on the issue that the burden of proof rests on the party opposing the enforcement or recognition of an award.

At this time, it is noteworthy to consider the illuminating observations of the UN Secretary-General commenting on the interplay between the arbitrators and the judges of the domestic courts enforcing a foreign arbitral award:

> It seems generally agreed that, on the one hand, courts should remain free to refuse the enforcement of a foreign arbitral award if such action should be necessary to safeguard the basic rights of the losing party or if the award would impose obligations clearly incompatible with the public policy of the country of enforcement. On the other hand, if the enforcing authorities were to proceed in each case with a full re-examination of such awards … the purpose of the Convention might be defeated. … The extent of judicial control over the recognition and enforcement of arbitral awards must be defined with precision, so as to avoid

[1] United Nations Commission on International Trade Law (UNCITRAL), Convention on the Recognition and Enforcement of Foreign Arbitral Awards (New York, 1958), https://uncitral.un.org/sites/uncitral.un.org/files/media-documents/uncitral/en/new-york-convention-e.pdf, accessed 27/09/2020.

> the possibility that a losing party could invoke without adequate justification a multiplicity of possible grounds for objections in order to frustrate the enforcement of awards rendered against it.[2]

Interestingly, a perusal of the drafting history of Article V of the New York Convention highlights that even though Article V enlists all the grounds on which a competent authority will be able to refuse recognition or enforcement their applicability will not be uniform across the entire spectrum.[3] Courts are vested with discretion to either refuse the enforcement of the award or enforce the award in the absence of sufficient proof adduced by Respondent to not enforce the award. Hence, it can be reasonably deciphered from a holistic reading of the drafting history of Article V that the drafters included "all the safeguards that can reasonably be expected in a multilateral Convention."[4]

However, an important point cannot be overlooked, namely that Article V does not allow a court to refuse to recognize an award on grounds of mistakes in the application of law or fact by the tribunal. Hence, a court is not allowed to review the merits of the tribunals decision. Ramos J *in Daesang Corp. v Nutrasweet Co.*[5] set aside an award on the grounds that the ICC Tribunal manifestly disregarded clearly established laws in order to come to their decision.[6] He clearly stated the pro-enforcement attitude of courts and the limited reasons pursuant to Article V of the New York Convention. In the aforesaid judgement, it was observed that:

> Merely an error or misunderstanding of the applicable law does not constitute manifest disregard (*Id.*). Judicial review of arbitration awards is extremely limited [and] An arbitration award must be upheld when the arbitrator offer[s] even a barely colorable justification for the outcome reached.[7]

The point is that even if a court would rule otherwise this would not be a sufficient ground under the New York Convention to refuse recognition of an award. These are

---

[2]United Nations Commission on International Trade Law (UNCITRAL), "Travaux Préparatoires: Convention on the Recognition and Enforcement of Foreign Arbitral Awards (New York, 1958), Comments on the Draft Convention on the Recognition and Enforcement of Foreign Arbitral Awards: Note by the Secretary-General: 6 March 1958", https://undocs.org/E/CONF.26/2, accessed 10/10/2020,9,5.

[3]International Chamber of Commerce, "Enforcement of International Arbitral Awards", ICC International Court of Arbitration Bulletin Vol. 9 No. 1, https://library.iccwbo.org/content/dr/COMMISSION_REPORTS/CR_0011.htm?l1=Bulletins&l2=ICC+International+Court+of+Arbitration+Bulletin+Vol.+9%2FNo.1+-+Eng, accessed 10/07/2020.

[4]United Nations Commission on International Trade Law (UNCITRAL), "Travaux Préparatoires: Convention on the Recognition and Enforcement of Foreign Arbitral Awards (New York, 1958), Recognition and Enforcement of Foreign Arbitral Awards Comments by Governments on the draft Convention on the Recognition and Enforcement of Foreign Arbitral Awards", U.N. Doc. E/2822/Add.4 (Apr. 3, 1956), 9 https://undocs.org/E/2822/Add.4, accessed 17/06/2019.

[5]*Daesang Corp. v Nutrasweet Co.,* Slip Copy (2017) 55 Misc.3d 1218(A), 2017 N.Y. Slip Op. 50,646(U) [4].

[6]Ibid, 4.

[7]*Daesang Corp, supra* 5.

important distinctions and must be kept in mind when resort to Article V is sought. The pro-enforcement approach of the New York Convention is well highlighted in a catena of decisions across jurisdictions such as when the High Court of Hong Kong opined that

> That even if a ground of opposition is proved, there is still a residual discretion left for the enforcing court to enforce nonetheless. This shows that the grounds of opposition are not to be inflexibly applied. The residual discretion enables the enforcing court to achieve a just result in all circumstances although I accept that in many cases where a ground of opposition is established, the discretion is unlikely to be exercised in favor of enforcement...I could envisage circumstances where the court might exercise its discretion, having found the ground established, if the Court were to conclude, having seen the new material which the defendant wished to put forward, that it would not affect the outcome of the dispute.[8]

In other words, as summed by the Delhi High Court in India, the legislature left it to the court's discretion to refuse enforcement of a foreign award, depending upon the facts and circumstances of a particular case.[9] The US Court of Appeals for the Eleventh Circuit, while commenting on the nature of discretion with the enforcement courts under the Convention, stated as below:

> The contours of our obligations under the Convention that a court shall confirm an award unless it finds one of the grounds for refusal or deferral of recognition or enforcement of the award specified in the Convention...Further, the Convention provides that recognition and enforcement of an award may be refused if the defendant shows one of the defenses listed in Article V [of the] Convention.[10]

In *Dowans Holding*,[11] the English High Court acknowledged the fact that a foreign award is not automatically deprived of recognition purely on satisfying one of the subsections of Article V of the New York Convention. Pertinently, it is imperative to understand that the enforcement procedure is not an appeal process wherein the full re-examination of the award is conducted by the enforcement courts. The necessary middle path that must be adopted by the enforcement court has been laid down in *Parsons*[12] given hereinbelow,

> If the enforcing authorities were to proceed in each case with a full re-examination of such awards, the purpose of the Convention would be defeated...The Court also must remain mindful of the principle that judicial review of arbitral awards is extremely limited and that

[8] *China Nanhai Oil Joint Service Corporation Shenzhen Branch v Gee Tai Holdings Co. Ltd.* (Supreme Court Hong Kong 1994), in Yearbook Commercial Arbitration XX (1995) (Hong Kong no. 8), 671–680.

[9] *Glencore Grain Rotterdam B.V. v Shivnath Rai Harnarain (India) Co.*, (Delhi High Court 2008) (4) ARBLR 497 (Delhi).

[10] *Four Seasons Hotels and Resorts, BV (Netherlands) and others v Consorcio Barr, SA (Venezuela)* (11nd Cir. 2008), in Yearbook Commercial Arbitration XXXIII (2008) (United States no. 646), 1183–1186.

[11] *Dowans Holding S.A.* et al. *v Tanzania Electric Supply Co. Ltd* (High Court of Justice, Queen's Bench Division, Commercial Court 2011), in Yearbook Commercial Arbitration XXXVI (2011) (United Kingdom no. 93), 363–365.

[12] *Parsons & Whitemore Overseas Co. v Societe Generale de L'Industrie du Papier* 508 F. 2d 969 (2nd Cir. 1974).

> this Court does not sit to hear claims of factual or legal error by an arbitrator in the same manner that an appeals court would review the decision of a lower court.[13]

The following will examine and explain the functions of Article V. As many books have been written,[14] on this issue, this chapter will only sketch the requirements of Article V(1) in order to understand the implications of Article V(2)—the core issue of this book.

3.2 Article V(1)

3.2.1 Article V(1)(a)

> The parties to the agreement referred to in article II were, under the law applicable to them, under some incapacity, or the said agreement is not valid under the law to which the parties have subjected it or, failing any indication thereon, under the law of the country where the award was made (Article V(1)(a))

This article specifies that proof must be furnished by the party alleging incapacity in order to avoid enforcement or recognition. Proof shall be furnished if a party(s) to the agreement is under an incapacity to the arbitration agreement or the arbitration agreement is invalid under its applicable law or failing any indication under the law of the seat. In other words, Article V(1)(a) attempts to safeguard the right to access to courts of the party objecting to the enforcement of the foreign award. During the course of drafting Article V(1)(a), some delegates felt that the term "applicable

---

[13] Ibid.

[14] See generally, K.H. Bockstiegel, S. Kroll and P. Nacimiento eds, *Arbitration in Germany. The Model Law in Practice*, (Kluwer International, 2007), 1. Herbert Kronke, Patricia Nacimiento, Dirk Otto & Nicola Christine Port, *Recognition and Enforcement of Foreign Arbitral Awards: A Global Commentary on the New York Convention*, (Kluwer International, 2010).

law" should be explicitly identified[15] as lex fori[16] or that which the courts ought to determine it by utilizing the principles of conflict of laws.[17]

The two limbs in this article—in their present form—only found acceptance on the final day of the conference.[18] From a practical point of view, the first limb is rarely used and in addition has not been defined in the Convention nor in the *travaux préparatoires* but includes not only private but also public entities. In essence, any interpretation of the term must rely on the traditional understanding, namely that a person must have a legal ability to act and enter into agreements in its own name and own behalf. However, commentators agree that "the incapacity defense can cover situations in which an individual is unable to judge where its own interest lies."[19] The second limb has been used on occasions without success. Courts have followed the conflict of laws rules or by the choice of law by the parties in determining whether an arbitration agreement is valid or not.[20]

The term "incapacity" as stipulated in Article V(1)(a) has been subject to various interpretations wherein arguments have been advanced that if a party is not a party to the arbitration agreement then it should be understood that the party is under

---

[15]United Nations Economic and Social Council, "United Nations Conference on International Commercial Arbitration, Convention on the Recognition and Enforcement of Foreign Awards, Summary Record of the Eleventh Meeting", U.N. Doc. E/Conf.26/SR.11 (Sep. 12, 1958), https://newyorkconvention1958.org/index.php?lvl=notice_display&id=3403, accessed 07/05/2020.

See, (Comment of Mr. Cohn (Israel)): "As regards the validity of the arbitral agreement, the thought that any agreement which was in conformity with the law of the country in which it had been made or with the law of the State where the enforcement of the award was requested should be treated as valid; and that such a rule should be spelled out expressis verbis, instead of leaving the choice of law vague and obscure under a formula such as 'the law applicable'.",10.

[16]United Nations Economic and Social Council, "United Nations Conference on International Commercial Arbitration, Convention on the Recognition and Enforcement of Foreign Awards, Summary Record of the Twelfth Meeting", U.N. Doc. E/Conf.26./SR.12 (Sep. 12, 1958), (Comment of Mr. Rognlien (Norway)), 3, https://newyorkconvention1958.org/index.php?lvl=notice_display&id=3404, accessed 07/05/2020.

[17]United Nations Economic and Social Council, "United Nations Conference on International Commercial Arbitration, Convention on the Recognition and Enforcement of Foreign Awards, Summary Record of the Thirteenth Meeting", U.N. Doc. E/Conf.26/SR.13 (Sep. 12, 1958), (Comment of Mr. Lima (El Salvador)): "To determine which law applied, it would be necessary, if the Convention gave no indication in the matter, to apply the rules of private international law governing conflicts of legislation applicable to contracts.",4, https://newyorkconvention1958.org/index.php?lvl=notice_display&id=3405, accessed 07/05/2020.

[18]United Nations Economic and Social Council, "United Nations Conference on International Commercial Arbitration, Convention on the Recognition and Enforcement of Foreign Awards, Summary Record of the Twenty-fourth Meeting", E/CONF.26/SR.24, 7, https://newyorkconvention1958.org/index.php?lvl=notice_display&id=3416, accessed 07/05/2020.

[19]Emmanuel Gaillard & George A. Bermann, *Guide on the Convention on the Recognition and Enforcement of Foreign Arbitral Awards: New York 1958.* (BRILL, 2017)1, 144.

[20]Ibid, 150.

incapacity or as a matter of fact if incapacity is present during arbitration hearings then it should also be understood as incapacity within the confines of the term "incapacity" under Article V(1)(a). In relation to the suggestion that a party is under incapacity as it was not a party to the arbitration agreement, the judgement of the Oberlandesgericht of Hamburg is noteworthy, wherein an award was rendered in Romania against a German private company and in favour of a Romanian seller.[21] Pursuant to the passing of the award, the German company was taken over by a private businessman who resisted enforcement of the award on grounds that it was not a party to the arbitration agreement. Notwithstanding the above, enforcement was granted as according to the court in exceptional circumstances an award can be enforced against another person especially if that person is the legal successor to the party to the award.[22] Moving ahead, in the context of incapacity during the time of arbitration hearings, the US Court of Appeals for the Ninth Circuit has held that incapacity being present during arbitration hearings and not during signing of the arbitration agreement is not a legitimate defence under Article V(1)(a).[23] Lastly, it is pertinent to consider that as per established practice, courts will apply rules of conflict of laws in order to determine the applicable law to address many of the issues emanating under Article V(1)(a).[24]

3.2.2 *Article V(1)(b)*

> The party against whom the award is invoked was not given proper notice of the appointment of the arbitrator or of the arbitration proceedings or was otherwise unable to present his case. (Article V(1)(b))

This article addresses the due process-related aspects in an arbitral proceeding and notes that an award cannot be enforced or recognized if the party against whom the award is invoked proves that (1) due process not was not adhered to or (2) it was not given proper notice of the appointment of the arbitrator or of the arbitration proceedings. It is abundantly clear from a cursory reading that Article V(1)(B) revolves around the tenets of due process. However, it is unclear as to which due process applies, i.e. of the seat or where enforcement is sought?[25]

---

[21] *Rumanian Firm C v German (F.R.) party* (Oberlandesgericht Hamburg 1974), in Yearbook Commercial Arbitration II (1977) (Germany no. 10), 240–240.

[22] Ibid.

[23] *Seung Woo Lee, as Co-Receiver for Medison Co. Ltd. a Korean corporation (Korea) and others v Imaging3, Inc. and others* (9th Cir. 2008), in Yearbook Commercial Arbitration XXXIII (2008) (United States no. 645), 1180–1182.

[24] Marike R.P. Paulsson, "Chapter 6: Resisting Enforcement of Awards", in *The 1958 New York Convention in Action*, (Kluwer Law International, 2016) 1, 157–216.

[25] The delegates did not reach an agreement with respect to the law that should determine whether there has been a violation of due process. See also, Article 18 of the UNCITRAL Model Law

The procedural irregularities that were identified as the grounds for challenging enforcement of the arbitral award as noted within this article must be proven or at least raised by the party opposing recognition or enforcement of the award. Again parties have raised this issue, but in a vast majority of cases, it proved to be unsuccessful specifically as courts are not formalistic but focus on the actual facts and conduct of the parties.[26] The first point in the article mandates that a party must be able and hence must be given the opportunity to present their case. The Swiss Federal Tribunal noted that "[b]y its general wording, this provision covers any restriction, whatever its nature, of the parties' rights. It appears to contemplate, amongst others, the violation of the right to be heard."[27]

> The key term in this subsection of Article V is that "proper notice" is given. As the article is silent as to the form of notice it can be presumed that no specific form is required to be adhered to. Further the lack of "proper notice" is often a defense relied upon by the unsuccessful party to resist enforcement under Article V(1)(b). In that regard, the judgment of the Bavarian Court of Appeals[28] which refused enforcement of a default award passed in Russia on grounds of lack of notice is instructive. The court held,
>
> (A)lthough Russian arbitration law provides that a communication made to the defendant's last-known address suffices if no other address can be found after making a reasonable inquiry, there was no evidence here that any attempt had been made to find the correct address of the German buyer, which in any case had not changed since the conclusion of the contract...The principle of due process is universally recognized for all arbitration proceedings. It encompasses the timely notification of the commencement of the arbitration and the timely summons to hearings. This is why Article V(1)(b) of the Convention provides that the proven fact that one of the parties was not duly informed of the arbitral proceedings is a ground for refusing recognition.[29]

Further, in the context of "proper" notice, the Italian Supreme Court has observed that

> According to the constant jurisprudence of this Court, it is the party against which enforcement is sought that has the burden to prove that it was either not duly informed of the appointment of the arbitrators and of the arbitral proceedings, or unable to present its case, either through unsuitable means or the time limit was insufficient, or because fundamental procedural rules for the appearance of parties were not complied with...We must further notice that no objection concerning the appointment of the arbitrators and the constitution of the arbitral tribunal has been raised in the arbitral proceedings.[30]

It follows as a necessary corollary from the above that if lack of notice has not altered the conduct of arbitration and the outcome thereof, the defence of lack of

---

which provides that parties shall be treated with equality and that each party shall be given a full opportunity of presenting his case.

[26]Gaillard & Bermann, *supra* 19, 164.

[27]*Chrome Resources S.A. v Leopold Lazarus Ltd.*, Federal Tribunal, Switzerland, 8 February 1978, XI Y.B. C OM.ARB.538 (1986).

[28]*Seller v Buyer* (Court of Appeal of Bavaria 2000), in Yearbook Commercial Arbitration XXXVII (2002) (Germany no. 53), 445–450.

[29]*Seller, Supra* 29.

[30]*Conceria G. De maio & F. snc v EMAG AG* (Supreme Court 1995), in Yearbook Commercial Arbitration XXI (Italy no. 139), 602–606.

notice raised by the party resisting enforcement will not hold any ground before the enforcement court.[31]

On the contrary, the Supreme Court of Sweden has refused the enforcement of an award in a case where the notice of arbitration was sent to the former address of the defendant and was returned resulting in a situation where the defendant could not defend himself in the arbitration proceedings.[32] Similarly, the Supreme Court of Russia has opined that the burden of proving that Respondent has been duly informed of the arbitration proceedings is on the Respondent himself because "placing the burden of proving the grounds for refusal under the Convention on the applicant seeking enforcement of the award is not in accord with international treaty or procedural law."[33] The approach of enforcement courts towards defences under Article V(1)(b) has been well summed up by the US Court of Appeals for the Fifth Circuit, wherein it has been held that courts are expected to apply a narrow idea of due process under Article V(1)(b) and promote a pro-enforcement attitude encouraging arbitration and enforcing arbitration awards.[34]

Hence, a party must have knowledge of the appointment of arbitrators and the proceeding as such. As noted above, the courts will look at the facts, and as long as the conduct of the parties leads to a view that they intended to arbitrate and were aware that arbitration proceedings had commenced, it would be assumed that the party(s) were given proper notice. Notably, the approach is not formalistic, and hence if a party can show evidence that notice was given but the other party cannot show evidence to the contrary, the court assumes that proper notice has been given.[35] Simply put, form and technicality of the notice itself does not matter.[36]

3.2.3 *Article V(1)(c)*

A party preferring a challenge to the enforcement of an arbitral award must deliver proof that.

---

[31] Marike R.P. Paulsson, *Supra* 24. See also, *Guangdong New Technology Import & Export Corporation Jiangmen Branch v Chiu Shing trading as B.C. Property & Trading Company* (Supreme Court of Hong Kong, High Court 1991), in Yearbook Commercial Arbitration XVIII (1993) (Hong Kong no. 3), 385–388.

[32] *Lenmorniiproekt OAO (Russian Federation) v Arne Larsson & Partner Leasing Aktiebolag* (Sweden) (Supreme Court 2010), in Yearbook Commercial Arbitration XXXV (2010), 456–457.

[33] *Codest Engineering v OOO Grupa Most* (Presidium of the Supreme Arbitrazh Court of the Russian Federation 2005), in Yearbook Commercial Arbitration XXXIII (2008) (Russia no. 17), 666–672.

[34] *Consorcio Rive, S.A. de C.V. (Mexico) v Briggs of Cancun, Inc. (US) & David Briggs Enterprises, Inc.* (US) (5th Cir. 2003) in Yearbook Commercial Arbitration XXXI (2006) (US no. 472) at 1429–1438.

[35] *Uganda Telecom Ltd. v Hi-Tech Telecom Pty Ltd.*, Federal Court, Australia, 22 February 2011, FCA 131.

[36] *R.M.F. Global Inc.*, et al. *v Elio D. Cattan* et al., District Court, Western District of Pennsylvania, United States, 6 March 2006, 04cv0593.

> The award deals with a difference not contemplated by or not falling within the terms of the submission to arbitration, or it contains decisions on matters beyond the scope of the submission to arbitration, provided that, if the decisions on matters submitted to arbitration can be separated from those not so submitted, that part of the award which contains decisions on matters submitted to arbitration may be recognized and enforced;

The crucial wording in this article points to the issue that the arbitral award contains decisions which were "beyond the scope of the submission to arbitration", thereby indicating that the article aims to address concerns relating to transgression of mandate vested with the tribunal. The arbitration agreement is the submission to arbitrate, and hence, all decisions cannot go beyond the four corners of the agreement otherwise an award would be in breach of this subsection. A United States Court observed, "[u]nder the New York Convention, we examine whether the award exceeds the scope of the [arbitration agreement], not whether the award exceeds the scope of the parties' pleadings."[37] The Supreme Court of Italy while identifying the mandate vested with the tribunal in the context of Article V(1)(c) has held that

> We cannot review the methods followed by the arbitrators and the evidence they have considered in order to reach a conclusion against [the Italian buyer]. Our review is limited to the correspondence between the arbitral clause and the subject matter of the decision, as provided for in Article V(1)(c) of the Convention. We must stress that this issue concerns the interpretation of a contractual clause, i.e., the merits of the case.[38]

This article also makes it clear that even of matters are exceeding the scope of the arbitral agreement if it can be severed from the conforming part the remaining part will be enforced. The severability of non-confirming parts form those who are conforming is an expression of the pro-enforcement bias of the New York Convention. In that context, the Commercial Court in London while allowing the partial enforcement of an award has observed that

> The purpose of the Convention is to ensure the effective and speedy enforcement of international arbitration awards and an all or nothing approach to enforcement would be inconsistent with this purpose. Nor is there anything in the language of the Convention... which expressly prevents partial enforcement. References to the award must be read in the court's opinion as references to the award or part of it; reading them to mean the whole award and nothing but the whole award...would have absurd commercial consequences and cannot have been intended.[39]

---

[37] *The Ministry of Defense and Support for the Armed Forces of the Islamic Republic of Iran v Cubic Defense Systems, Inc.*, District Court, Southern District of California, United States of America, 8 December 1998, Civ. Case No. 98-1165-B.

[38] *Vento & C snc v E.D. & F. Man (Coffee) Limited* (Supreme Court Italy 1990), in Yearbook Commercial Arbitration XVII (1992) (Italy no. 114) at 545–550. See also, *CJSC Russian Telephone Company v OOO Sony Ericsson Mobile Communications Rus* (Supreme Court of the Russian Federation 2012), in Yearbook Commercial Arbitration XXXVIII (2013) (Russian Federation no. 35), 451–452.

[39] *Nigerian National Petroleum Corporation v IPCO (Nigeria) Limited* (Commercial Court 2008), in Yearbook Commercial Arbitration XXXIII (2008) (United Kingdom no. 82), 788–802.

3.2.4 Article V(1)(d)

This subsection mandates that an award cannot be recognized or enforced if again the party relying on this section provides proof that

> The composition of the arbitral authority or the arbitral procedure was not in accordance with the agreement of the parties, or, failing such agreement, was not in accordance with the law of the country where the arbitration took place.

The article empowers the court to refuse enforcement if the appointment of the arbitrator was not in accordance with the arbitration agreement. As a common standard of procedure, the composition of the arbitral tribunal is usually postulated in the arbitration agreement, wherein the methods of appointing the members of the tribunal along with the number of arbitrators are stipulated therein. It can be garnered from the article that the drafters of the Convention aimed to place party autonomy at the highest pedestal. In light of the same, the US Court of Appeals for the Second Circuit has held that

> Article V(1)(d) of the Convention itself suggests the importance of arbitral composition, as a failure to comport with an agreement's requirements for how arbitrators are selected is one of only seven grounds for refusing to enforce an arbitral award. As to the complaint that this result exalts form over substance, at the end of the day, we are left with the fact that the parties explicitly settled on a form and the Convention requires that their commitment be respected... While we acknowledge that there is a strong public policy in favor of arbitration, we have never held that courts must overlook agreed-upon arbitral procedure in deference to that policy...The federal policy is simply to ensure the enforceability, according to their terms, of private agreements to arbitrate.[40]

Notably, the Convention gives priority to the arbitration agreement in relation to the relevant procedures, and the second part of Article V(1)(d) that is the law of the seat only takes on a secondary role in the event the parties have not reached an express or implied agreement of the procedural points at issue.[41] It is not surprising that in the majority of cases parties failed to prove a procedural error as most arbitrations rely on institutional rules. Again, in line with all interpretations of the New York Convention, courts are not formalistic and always look for a way to keep the arbitration afloat and valid. Simply put, party autonomy in arbitration is maintained always by courts.

3.2.5 Article V(1)(e)

Recognition and enforcement may be refused if

> The award has not yet become binding on the parties, or has been set aside or suspended by a competent authority of the country in which, or under the law of which, that award was made.

---

[40] *Encyclopaedia Universalis S.A. v Encyclopaedia Britannica*, Inc (2nd Cir. 2005), in Yearbook Commercial Arbitration XXX (2005) (United States no. 520), 1136–1143.

[41] Emmanuel Gaillard & George A. Bermann, 202.

This article does not mandate that there is a need, "before a Convention award could be enforced in any other jurisdiction, for it to be shown that it has first been rendered enforceable in the jurisdiction whose law governs the arbitration."[42] The question of whether an award is binding has been resolved by most courts reference to the law of the seat.[43] However, the burden of proof whether the award has become binding has been shifted from the party seeking enforcement to the party opposing it.[44] Article V(1)(e) allows a court to refuse recognition and enforcement if the award firstly is not yet binding and secondly has been set aside or suspended by a competent court. This decision can only be made at the seat of the arbitration that is the procedural law and not by recourse to the law applicable to the merits. This is based on the wording of this article, namely "under the law *of which*, or *under the law of which* that award was made. The term "binding" as used in Article V(1)(e) has been construed to denote that the award would no longer be open to ordinary means of recourse excluding the right to challenge the award.[45]

In *SPP v Egypt*, the question regarding the "binding" nature of an award under the New York Convention was raised where SPP sought enforcement of an award in Amsterdam against Egypt. In reply, Egypt had argued that it had initiated setting aside proceedings in Paris, where the award was made, and under French law, a setting aside procedure has suspensive effect.[46] The court held

> It results from both the legislative history of the Convention and the text of Articles V(1)(e) and VI, that the mere initiation of an action for setting aside, to which the initiated *recours en annulation* must be deemed to belong, does not have as consequence that the arbitral award must be considered as not binding. An arbitral award is not binding if it is open to appeal on the merits before a judge or an appeal arbitral tribunal. If this were otherwise, the words 'has been set aside or suspended' in Article V(1)(e) to which reference is made in Article VI, would have no meaning. The drafters of the Convention chose the word 'binding' in order to abolish the requirement of the double exequatur, which was the result of the word 'final' in the Geneva Convention of 1927.

Taking cue, the Belgian Supreme Court has explained its stance on the term "binding" as quoted hereinbelow:

> It clearly appears that the Convention considers the will of the parties to be fundamental to the arbitration proceedings. Read as a whole, these provisions indicate that the award must be binding on the parties…Both [Articles V(1)](a) and (d) refer to the law of the country where the award is rendered only where an indication, of a law or agreement, by the parties is lacking…The agreement of the parties provides that the award of the arbitral tribunal

---

[42] *Dowans Holding S.A., supra* 11.

[43] Gaillard & Bermann, *supra* 19, 224.

[44] Ibid.

[45] United Nations Economic and Social Council, "United Nations Conference on International Commercial Arbitration, Convention on the Recognition and Enforcement of Foreign Awards, Summary Record of the Seventeenth Meeting", U.N. Doc. E/Conf.26/SR.17 (Sep. 12, 1958), https://newyorkconvention1958.org/index.php?lvl=notice_display&id=3409, accessed 10/08/2019, (Comment of Mr. Matteucci (Italy)), 16.

[46] *SPP (Middle East) Ltd. v The Arab Republic of Egypt* (District Court of Amsterdam 1984), in Yearbook Commercial Arbitration X (1985) (Netherlands no. 10), 487–489.

> shall be final and binding, and thus immediately enforceable upon being rendered. It does not provide for an appeal. According to the agreement of the parties, the award has become binding upon being rendered. In fact, the arbitral award states that it 'is effective as of the date hereof'. Further, the award has been neither annulled nor suspended by a competent authority of Jordan or of a country under the law of which it was made.[47]

In *Dowans Holding*, the English High Court while interpreting the term "binding" opined that

> The [van den Berg] view that there was and should be an autonomous interpretation of binding, is best analyzed by differentiating between ordinary means of recourse and extraordinary recourse. The former, which may not be permitted by the terms of the relevant agreement between the parties or the law governing the arbitration, would ordinarily be subject to a time limit, after which no such ordinary recourse (if otherwise available) would be permitted. Then there is the possibility of extraordinary recourse, which would be some limited challenge to the award in the courts of its home jurisdiction, by reference to the restrictive terms of the Convention. Once ordinary recourse is excluded, the possible availability of extraordinary recourse does not prevent an award from being, or having become binding.[48]

3.2.6 The Interplay Between Article V(I)(e) and Article VII

There is a tension between this Article and Article VII. Article VII in brief provides that a foreign award is enforceable to the full extent of the laws of the county in which enforcement is sought. Professor Davis proposed the following example to illustrate the tension or inconsistency:

> A Japanese and Columbian company enter into a contract containing an arbitration clause. The seat is Japan. The Columbian party wins the arbitration and the Japanese party applies to a Japanese court to set aside the award which is granted. Subsequently the Columbian party seeks to enforce the award in Columbia where the law notes that the award is enforceable. The problem is that the Columbian court needs to decide whether under comity the enforcement under article V(1)(e) must be refused or allow enforcement applying Columbian law and enforce the award under article VII.[49]

It appears that courts tend to follow the principle of comity unless there are domestic laws such as public policy which will trump comity.[50] Jurisprudence on this point confirms the principle of comity. On 20 July 2017, in *Thai-Lao Lignite v Lao*, the Court of Appeals for the Second Circuit affirmed the Southern District's

---

[47] *Inter-Arab Investment Guarantee Corporation v Banque Arabe et Internationale d'Investissements* (Supreme Court Belgium 1998), in Yearbook Commercial Arbitration XXIVa (1999) (Belgium no. 11), 603–614.

[48] *Dowans Holding S.A., supra* 11.

[49] K.R. Davis, "Unconventional Wisdom: A New Look at Articles V and VII of the Convention on the Recognition and Enforcement of Foreign Arbitral Awards", (2002) 37, *Texas International Law Journal*, 43, 46.

[50] *Nikolay Viktorovich Maximov v Open Joint Stock Company "Novolipetsky Metallurgichesky Kombinat.* [2017] EWHC 1911 (Comm).

refusal to enforce an award that had been annulled by a Malaysian court.[51] The facts were

> In June 2007, Petitioners initiated arbitral proceedings in Malaysia. The dispute was heard by a panel of three U.S. lawyers (the "Panel") in Kuala Lumpur in July 2009. In November 2009, the Panel issued a 48-page written award, finding for Petitioners. The Panel ruled that Petitioners' lack of success in raising funds following the Asian Financial Crisis did not put them in breach of the PDA. It further concluded that Laos breached the PDA by not properly terminating that agreement. It therefore found Laos liable to Petitioners for damages caused by the breach, and, after reviewing cost estimates submitted by all parties, concluded that Petitioners were entitled to reimbursement of $40 million in total investment costs.[52]

The interesting point to note is that after the time for challenging the award had expired the petitioner commenced enforcement proceedings against Laos in several jurisdictions which succeeded in the USA. Almost one year after the award was issued, Laos moved in Malaysia for an extension of time to file a request to set aside the award which eventually succeeded, and the award was set aside.[53] The court did order a re-arbitration. The reason given by the Malaysian court to annul the award was that "the Panel had exceeded its jurisdiction by addressing disputes arising not just under the Project Development Agreement (PDA), but under the Mining Contracts as well."[54] Laos challenged the enforcement procedure in the USA where the court relied on the Federal Rule of Civil Procedure 60(b) which provides that

> "[o]n motion and just terms, the court may relieve a party … from a final judgment" for certain specified reasons, one of which is set forth in Rule 60(b)(5): that "the judgment … is based on an earlier judgment that has been reversed or vacated."[55]

The crux of this case therefore is how "an inquiry under Rule 60(b)(5) should proceed when the judgement sought to be vacated is one confirming an arbitral award that was subsequently vacated in the primary jurisdiction."[56]

The Court of Appeal relied on Article III of the New York Convention which states as far as applicable in this context the obligation to:

> recognize arbitral awards as binding and enforce them in accordance with the rules of procedure of the territory where the award is relied upon, under the conditions laid down in the following articles.

The court also recognized that Article V(1)(e) stipulated that enforcement of an award *may* be refused but the "scope of that discretion" is "constrained by the prudential concern of international comity."[57] Carney, CJ further pointed out that Article V of the New York Convention allowed for courts to refuse enforcement in case of

---

[51] *Thai-Lao Lignite (Thailand) Co. v Lao*, No. 14-597, 2017 WL 3081817 (2d Cir. July 20, 2017).

[52] *Thai-Lao Lignite, supra* 11, 4.

[53] Ibid, 2.

[54] Ibid, 6.

[55] Ibid, 2.

[56] Ibid, 8.

[57] Ibid, 7.

breaches of public policy in the country of enforcement.[58] Laos actually acknowledges, in fact, that "Rule 60(b) is consistent with the [New York] Convention."[59] The fact is that the Convention mandated that the power and the authority of the primary jurisdiction is determinative. The court relied heavily on *Corporación Mexicana de Mantenimiento Integral, S. de R.L. de C.V. v PEP-Exploración y Producción* ("*PEP*")[60] and denied enforcement of the award.

Two possible situations are frequently litigated. First, the award has been set side, but enforcement is still sought and secondly, where the award is valid and one party wants to enforce the same. It follows therefore that the issue of refusing to enforce an annulled award is generally a question of comity. But this principle is not without exceptions and hence automatic. Courts tend to look behind the "curtain of confidentiality" and decide the issues on their merit. Three US Court decisions are noteworthy. In two cases, the courts granted comity to foreign courts annulments. A New York State appellate court denied comity to a foreign court's recognition of an annulled award and did not uphold the annulment confirming the District Courts decisions and even enjoined a party from taking steps to enforce the annulled award.[61] In effect, two methods can be observed, namely the judgement recognition approach and the denial of comity approach.

The award in question in *Getma International v Republic of Guinea*[62] had been issued in favour of Getmo International, a French cargo company, against the Republic of Guinea in 2014 by the Common Court of Justice and Arbitration ("CCJA") of the Organization for the Harmonization of Business Law in Africa ("OHADA"). The important facts relevant to this issue are as follows

> The CCJA annulled the award on the basis that the arbitrators had "breached [their] duty by deliberately ignoring the mandatory provisions" of the OHADA arbitration rules concerning the tribunal's fees, despite the [alleged] parties' agreement to a different fee arrangement.[63]

The arbitrators charged a much higher fee than allowed under the rules of CCJA and pursued the parties. Getma eventually paid however they were aware that the CCJA had made it perfectly clear that increased fees were unacceptable and gave fair notice that the arbitrators insistence of increased fees could lead to an annulment of the award.

---

[58] Ibid, 8.

[59] *Thai-Lao Lignite, Supra* 11, 9.

[60] *Corporación Mexicana de Mantenimiento Integral S. De R.L de CV v Pemex-Exploración y Producción*, No.10 Civ. 206 (AKH), 2013 WL 4,517,225, (S.D.N.Y. 27 August 2013).

[61] Debevoise & Plimpton, "U.S. Courts Confirm Judgment Recognition Approach to Annulled Awards", 24/07/2017, https://www.debevoise.com/insights/publications/2017/07/us-courts-confirm-judgment,
accessed 17/09/2020.

[62] *Getma Internationall v Republic of Guinea*, No. 16-7087, 2017 WL 2883755, (D.C. Cir. July 7, 2017), 4.

[63] Ibid. See also, Debevoise & Plimpton, *Supra* 61.

In *Citigroup v Fiorilla*,[64] the court denied comity to a French court. The creditor, John Fiorilla, obtained enforcement in France of an award that the New York State courts had previously annulled. However, Mr. Fiorilla did not let the matter rest and unsuccessfully sought to vacate the original annulment in the New York courts. To make matters worse for Mr Fiorilla, the first instance court not only refused to enforce the award but also enjoined Fiorilla from enforcing the award in France.[65] The Supreme Court of New York annulled the award because the arbitrators failed "to enforce a prior settlement agreement between the parties."[66] The French court recognized the award under French law; however, the Claimant omitted to inform the court that the award had been annulled in New York, and hence, the Respondent commenced the French proceedings in bad faith.[67]

In the case of *Chromalloy Aeroservices(Claimant) v Egypt*,[68] Claimant had entered into a contract with the Egyptian Air Force which resulted in certain disputes arising out of termination of the Contract. The disputes were referred to arbitration, and an award was passed in favour of the Claimant. Consequently, Claimant sought to enforce the award in the USA which was immediately countered by Egypt filing for setting aside of the award before the Egyptian Court of Appeal. The award was set aside by the Egyptian Court of Appeal, and Egypt resisted the enforcement of the award premising itself on the successful setting aside procedure in Egypt, i.e. Article V(1)(e). The US Court while hearing the application of Egypt resisting enforcement noted that Egypt was attempting to "repudiate its solemn promise to abide by the results of the arbitration"[69] which was invariably opposed to the public policy of USA which favours final and binding arbitration of commercial disputes. Hence, the US Courts enforced the arbitration award despite its annulment at the seat of arbitration. Per Contra, the US Court of Appeals for the Second Circuit in Baker Marine[70] issued a decision on Article V(1)(e) wherein it refused recognition of an award set aside at its seat on grounds that "it could not enforce a foreign arbitral award under the Convention when such an award has been set aside by the Nigerian Courts."[71] Notably the rationale of the court on applying Article V(1)(e) and recognizing the annulment decision was that "if a party whose arbitration award has been vacated at the site of the award can automatically obtain enforcement of the awards under the domestic laws of other nations, a losing party will have every reason to pursue its

[64] *Citigroup Global Markets, Inc. v Fiorilla*, 151 A.D.3d 665 (2017).

[65] Debevoise & Plimpton, *supra* 61.

[66] *Citigroup, supra* 64, 587.

[67] Ibid.

[68] *Chromalloy Aeroservices Inc. v The Arab Republic of Egypt* (District for Columbia 1996), in Yearbook Commercial Arbitration XXII (1997) (United States no. 230), 1001–1012.

[69] Ibid.

[70] *Baker Marine (Nig.) Limited v Chevron (Nig.) Limited, Chevron Corp., Inc. and others v Danos and Curole Marine Contractors, Inc.* (2nd Cir. 1999), in Yearbook Commercial Arbitration XXIV (1999) (United States no. 288), 909–914.

[71] Ibid.

adversary with enforcement actions from country to country until a court is found, if any, which grants the enforcement."[72]

3.2.7 *Interplay Between Article V(1)(e) and Article VII(1)—Further Explained*

The important issue which needs to be explored is the interplay between Article V(1)(e) and VII(1) of the New York Convention. Article V(1)(e) notes in the relevant parts that

> recognition and enforcement of the award may be refused...only if ...the award has been set aside or suspended by a competent authority of the country in which ... the award was made.

Applying this article in isolation suggests that Article 34 is still in command, i.e. an award which has been set aside cannot be enforced. The only issue is that the word "may" leaves the door ajar to enforce an award despite Article 34. However, in this regard, Article VII(1) needs also to be consulted.

Article VII(1) provides that the Convention shall not

> deprive any party of any right he may have to avail himself of an arbitral award in this manner and to the extent allowed by the law or treaties of the country where such an award is sought to rely on.

Article VII did—and still does—cause controversy as arguably this article, the more favourable right provision, uses the words "shall" and hence requires that when domestic law provides more favourable rights, the award, rather than the annulment, must be enforced.[73] However, opposite views are also expressed, namely that Article V only applies to the other Article V grounds for non-enforcement or Article VII does not require the imposition of more favourable rights.[74] In sum the views can best be described as either the traditional or the denationalized view.

3.2.7.1 The Traditional Versus the Denationalized View

The traditional or territorial view follows the well-tested principle that legal validity is only determinable under a system of law, i.e. the arbitrators derive their power from the legal system at the seat which includes the mandatory rules. The contract only forms the law between the parties, and the legal system gives force to that agreement—such as in this case an arbitration agreement—and also acts as gap filling system as well as enforcing mandatory rules with "trump" contractual clauses.

---

[72] *Baker Marine, supra* 70, 197.

[73] K.R. Davis, *supra* 49, 57.

[74] K.R. Davis, *supra* 49, 57.

It follows that by allocating a seat the parties subject themselves to that legal system. In brief, therefore

> An award's validity-and therefore its very existence-stem from the law of the country of origin. This view led to the requirement of double *exequatur. An* award, unless confirmed in the country of origin, had no validity and therefore another country could not enforce an award until a court in the country of origin confirmed it." A country may not enforce an annulled award, because once annulled in the country of origin, the award has ceased to exist.[75]

It follows that Article VII cannot be invoked to enforce an award which has been set aside.

The denationalized view—sometimes also referred to the delocalised approach—on the other hand does not connect the existence of an award with the law of the seat. Fouchard notes that the sources of the arbitrators' powers are derived from the international legal community.[76] In other words, tribunals and courts are detached from the controls found at the seat of arbitration. Validity of an award can only be established at the enforcement stage under the law of the country where enforcement is sought. The effect is that primacy of the law of the seat is denied and the law of the place of enforcement will determine its validity. This not only includes the *lex fori,* but may also include any procedural law they regard as appropriate.

The end result is that the "Convention strikes an uneasy compromise between the territorial view and the denationalized view. The country of origin has the power to confirm or annul awards, yet Article V grants other countries the power to enforce awards that have not been confirmed."[77]

3.2.7.2 The French View

It is of value to examine the French position as France is the best-known exponent of the denationalized view. French courts have argued that Article VII in effect authorizes the recognition of an award under French law because Article 12 of the French New Code of Civil Procedure (NCCP) mandates that a court needs to determine to what extend French law would oppose the enforcement of the award.[78] In addition, French courts have also argued that "the recognition of an award in France that had been set aside in its country of origin was not contrary to the French conception of international public policy."[79] The French position is based on the universalist conception of arbitration best explained in brief by the view that an award rendered at the seat is an international award.[80] This award is therefore "not integrated into the

[75] K.R. Davis, *supra* 49, 58.

[76] Emmanuel Gaillard and John Savage (eds), *Fouchard Gaillard Goldman on International Commercial Arbitration*, (Kluwer Law International 1999).

[77] K.R. Davis, *supra* 49, 58.

[78] Gaillard and Savage, *supra* 76, 508.

[79] Ibid, 509.

[80] *PT Putrabali Adyamulia (Indonesia) v Rena Holding,* et al. (Supreme Court France 2007), in Yearbook Commercial Arbitration XXXII (2007) (France no. 42), 299–302. See also, *Hilmarton v*

legal order of that country such that its existence continues despite its nullification and that its recognition in France is not contrary to international public policy."[81] This view can be contrasted with the argument Davis proposed, namely

> Parties to arbitration would surely prefer to submit to annulment only from the country whose law they selected. They should get what they bargained for. The international business community would undoubtedly applaud the end to a system encouraging judicial intermeddling.[82]

The French jurisprudence regarding awards annulled at the seat yet finding recognition in France is well illustrated by the case of *Hilmarton v Omnium*[83] wherein an award rendered in Switzerland was annulled by the Geneva Court of Appeal but was nonetheless enforced in France. The court applied Article VII of the Convention and relied upon Article 1502 of the France Code of Civil Procedure and further observed.

Lastly, the award rendered in Switzerland is an international award which is not integrated in the legal system of that State, so that it remains in existence even if set aside and its recognition in France is not contrary to international public policy.[84]

However, the reality is that awards which have been set aside have been enforced not only in France but also in other countries such as the United States and Belgium just to mention a few. Earlier US decisions are unfortunately inconsistent but all three[85] examined the interrelationship between Article V(I)(e) and Article VII of the New York Convention. "*Chromalloy* recognized the interrelationship between Articles V(1)(e) and VII in the New York Convention, it was the most nearly correct of the three decisions."[86]

A recent United States Court of Appeal judgement is of interest namely *Corporación Mexicana De Mantenimiento Integral, S. De R.L. De C.V., v PEP–Exploración Y Producción.*[87] The facts are unusual. Corporación Mexicana De Mantenimiento Integral, S. De R.L. De C.V. (COMMISA) prevailed in Mexico. The judgement was confirmed in the US District Court. *PEP-Exploración Y Producción (PEP)* appealed and at the same time asked for setting aside the award in the Mexican court—the seat—which was granted. On remand, the Southern District Court confirmed the arbitral award which was appealed to the Court of Appeal. Jacobs CJ opened his opinion observing that

---

Omnium de Traitement et de Valorisation (OTV) (Supreme Court 1994), in Yearbook Commercial Arbitration XX (1995) (France no. 23), 663–665.

81 Gaillard and Savage, *supra* 76, 511.

82 K.R. Davis, *supra* 49, 48.

83 *Hilmarton, supra* 80.

84 *Hilmarton, supra* 80.

85 *In re* Arbitration of Certain Controversies Between Chromalloy Aeroservices and the Arab Republic of Egypt, 939 F. Supp. 907 (D.D.C. 1996)., *Baker Marine (Nig.) Ltd. v Chevron (Nig.) Ltd.*, 191 F.3d 194 (2d Cir. 1999). And *Spier v Calzaturificio Tecnica,* S.P.A., 77 F. Supp. 2d 279 (S.D.N.Y. 1999).

86 K.R. Davis, *supra* 49, 47.

87 *Corporación Mexicana de Mantenimiento Integral, supra* 60.

> this case requires us to reconcile two settled principles that militate in favor of opposite results: a district court's discretion to confirm an arbitral award, and the comity owed to a foreign court's ruling on the validity of an arbitral award rendered in that country, here, Mexico.[88]

As the District Court denied comity to a foreign judgement, the Appeal Court reviewed the underlying conclusions of law de novo for clear error relying on *Finanz AG Zurich v Banco Economico S.A.*[89] However, in the end, the Appeal Court confirmed the decision of the District Court noting—despite the fact that the award was annulled in the seat—the New York Convention:

> affords discretion in enforcing a foreign arbitral award that has been annulled in the awarding jurisdiction, and thereby advances the Convention's pro-enforcement aim, the exercise of that discretion here is appropriate only to vindicate "fundamental notions of what is decent and just" in the United States.[90]

This approach has produced sharply different outcomes as best seen in *Nikolay Viktorovich Maximov v Open Joint Stock Company "Novolipetsky Metallurgichesky Kombinat.*[91] An award was set aside in Russia. The claimant then sought enforcement in France, the Netherlands and England. France enforced the award but England did not. In the Netherlands, an appeal is still pending.[92]

Pertinently besides the USA and French approach, there is also the Dutch approach which is referred to as the Yukos doctrine wherein Dutch courts will review the foreign annulment judgement to ascertain as to whether the recognition of the foreign annulment judgement would violate Dutch public policy. If on analysis, it is found that the public policy would be violated then the Dutch court in all likelihood will refuse to recognize the foreign judgement, thereby automatically removing the bar on the enforcement of foreign award in its territory.[93] In Yukos, awards set aside in Russia where granted enforcement by the Court of Appeal in Amsterdam on grounds that as per Dutch public policy, the recognition of the annulment judgements passed in Russia would violate its public policy. The court held as below

Whatever room the Convention otherwise leaves for granting leave for recognition of an arbitral award that has been annulled by a competent authority in the country where it was rendered, a Dutch court is not compelled to deny leave for recognition of an annulled arbitral award if the foreign decision annulling the arbitral award cannot be recognized in the Netherlands. This applies in particular if the manner in which that decision came to exist does not comply with the principles of due process and for that reason recognition of that decision is at odds with Dutch public policy. If the decisions of the Russian civil court annulling the arbitral awards cannot

[88] Ibid, 1.

[89] *Finanz AG Zurich v Banco Economico S.A.*, 192 F.3d 240, 246 (2d Cir. 1999).

[90] Ibid, 20.

[91] *Nikolay Viktorovich, supra* 50.

[92] Ibid.

[93] *OAO Rosneft v Yulos Capital s.a.r.l.*, 34 Supreme Court, First Chamber, Netherlands, Jun. 25, 2010, no. 09/02565EE.

be recognized in the Netherlands, then when deciding on the request for a leave to enforce the arbitral awards, no account is to be taken of the decisions annulling those arbitral awards.[94]

3.2.8 Summary

There is always a tension between the finality of an award and the possible challenges to it. The problem is that the annulment might not be validly judged on the relevant legal principles in the enforcement country but perfectly valid in the seat where the annulment took place. The issue is whether to follow the principle of comity or in essence use one of the enforcing countries principles such as public policy to negate the influence of the seat on the arbitral award. In other words, the principle that a valid award can be denied enforcement on grounds listed in the New York Convention by a jurisdiction other than the seat.

United States Courts have in essence followed the principle of comity and tend to respect other courts decisions. In *ThermoRio SA WSP v Electranta S.P.*[95], the court did not enforce a Columbian award which was set side even if the nullification would have been valid in the United States.[96] The enforcement action was dismissed under Article V(1)(e) of the New York Convention. Importantly, the court relied on *Scherk v Alberto–Culver Co*[97] and reiterated that the New York Convention's purpose is to "encourage the recognition and enforcement of commercial arbitration agreements in international contracts and to unify the standards by which agreements to arbitrate are observed and arbitral awards are enforced in the signatory countries."[98] In addition, the Second Circuit Court noted

> ...the Convention mandates very different regimes for the review of arbitral awards (1) in the state in which, or under the law of which, the award was made, and (2) in other states where recognition and enforcement are sought. The Convention specifically contemplates that the state in which, or under the law of which, the award is made, will be free to set aside or modify an award in accordance with its domestic arbitral law and its full panoply of express and implied grounds for relief. However, the Convention is equally clear that when an action for enforcement is brought in a foreign state, the state may refuse to enforce the award only on the grounds explicitly set forth in Article V of the Convention.[99]

---

[94] *Yukos Capital s.a.r.l. (Luxembourg) v OAO Rosneft (Russian Federation)* (Court of Appeal 2009), in Yearbook Commercial Arbitration XXXIV (Netherlands no. 31) at Pg.703–714. See also, *Northern River Shipping Lines v Kompas Overseas Inc. (District Court 2010)*, in Yearbook Commercial Arbitration XXXVI (Netherlands no. 36) and *Nikolai Viktorovich Maximov v OJSC Novolopetsky Metallurgickesky Kombinat (District Court 2011)*, in Yearbook Commercial Arbitration XXXVII (Netherlands no. 41) 274–276.

[95] *TermoRio SA WSP v Electranta S.P.*, Jr.487 F.3d 928 (D.C. Cir. 2007).

[96] Ibid, 928.

[97] *Scherk v Alberto-Culver Co.* 417 US 506 (1974).

[98] *TermoRio, supra* 95, 934.

[99] Ibid, 935.

Simply put a State in a secondary jurisdiction is not free to ignore the judgement of a competent authority in the primary State. That is equally applied to refuse enforcement of an award as well as enforce the award when it is annulled in the primary State. The issue of public policy in denying comity is an issue which needs to be looked at as well. There is at least an implied gloss that public policy is endorsed in Article V(1)(e).[100] However, it does not permit a court to revisit the reasons for the decision and second guess the outcome.

In effect two settled principles can be in play which need to be reconciled, namely the discretion of a court to confirm an arbitral award, and secondly, the comity owed to a foreign court's ruling on the validity of the arbitral award. The point is that there will always be a tension between comity and enforcing an award which has been annulled in the seat. There can never be a clear policy decision to crate certainty as in the end the facts will determine the outcome that is whether comity or enforcement will "win".

3.3 Article V(2)

3.3.1 Article V(2)(a)

This article states that recognition and enforcement may be refused if

> (a) The subject matter of the difference is not capable of settlement by arbitration under the law of that country [...].

Unlike in Article V(1) where the seat of arbitration takes a decisive role under Article V(2), it is the law of the country where enforcement is sought. However, the problem is that the "subject matter of the difference" is not defined. However,

> It is generally accepted that article V (2) (a) allows national courts to refuse to recognize and enforce an arbitral award where there is a legal impediment to the resolution of the subject matter of the underlying dispute by arbitration, i.e., where the underlying dispute is not "arbitrable.[101]

Arbitrability is to be understood as referring to the law of the country in which enforcement is sought and not the seat nor the arbitration clause. Arguably, this suggest that enforceability is only barred in a country where the issue such as family maintenance is not arbitrable but not in others where is possible to do so. If follows that commercial disputes are generally speaking arbitrable and hence Article V(2)(a) is not applicable.[102]

---

[100] Ibid, 938.

[101] Gaillard & Bermann, *supra* 19, 242.

[102] *Mitsubishi Motors Corporation v Soler Chrysler-Plymouth, Inc* (United States Supreme Court 1985), in Yearbook Commercial Arbitration XI (1986) (United States no. 59), 555–565.

The drafting history of Article V(2)(a) clearly indicates that the delegates consciously choose to have both arbitrability and public policy as grounds for denying enforcement in order to provide the courts with a separate refusal ground if the matter was not arbitrable under the *lex fori* so as to ensure that the ground of public policy was not overused by the enforcement courts. The importance of Article V(2)(a) in the context of the Convention was well highlighted by the French delegate Holleaux who concluded as below

> The judge would thus be tempted to give international application to rules, which were of exclusively domestic validity. The exception of incompatibility with public policy was quite sufficient to cover the rare cases in which the enforcement of an arbitral award might conflict with that policy.[103]

3.3.2 Article V(2)(b)

Recognition and enforcement may be refused if

> (b) The recognition or enforcement of the award would be contrary to the public policy of that country.

Public policy is not a unique concept as it includes many rules "such as the mandatory rules of the forum that override private autonomy, that allow a court to protect the integrity of the legal order to which it belongs."[104] The problem with the term public policy is that different jurisdictions define it differently and hence there is no uniform definition of public policy which will guide courts in an international sense. However, the United States Court of Appeal arguably is very useful in their comment. They noted

> [e]nforcement of foreign arbitral awards may be denied on [the basis of public policy] only where enforcement would violate the forum state's most basic notions of morality and justice.[105]

Corporaci´on Mexicana[106] is an interesting example where this issue had to be resolved. The facts—as relevant to this issue—were that *COMMISA* initiated proceedings in Mexico and obtained an award and then petitioned the United States District Court for confirmation of the award which was done. *PEP* appealed this decision and at the same time asked the Mexican court to set aside the arbitral award. Subsequently, the Mexican court set aside the award on the grounds that *PEP* is part of the Mexican government and could not be forced to arbitration. Hence, *PEP* is

---

[103] Summary Record of the Eleventh Meeting, *supra* 17, (Comment of Mr. Holleaux (France)).

[104] Gaillard & Bermann, *supra* 19, 253.

[105] Howard M. Holtzmann and Joseph Neuhaus, *A Guide to the UNCITRAL Model Law on International Commercial Arbitration: Legislative History and Commentary*, (Kluwer Law International 1989) 1, 1006–1052.

[106] *Corporación Mexicana de Mantenimiento Integral, supra* 60.

now attempting to vacate the decision of the US Court.[107] The court decided "that the Southern District properly exercised its discretion in confirming the award because giving effect to the subsequent nullification of the award in Mexico would run counter to United States public policy and would (in the operative phrasing) be 'repugnant to fundamental notions of what is decent and just' in this country."[108] In essence comity is not extended to a foreign court if it would be contrary to public policy. The court was aware that

> The public policy exception does not swallow the rule: "[t]he standard is high, and infrequently met"; "a judgment that 'tends clearly' to undermine the public interest, the public confidence in the administration of the law, or security for individual rights of personal liberty or of private property is against public policy." The exception accommodates uneasily two competing (and equally important) principles: [i] "the goals of comity and res judicata that underlie the doctrine of recognition and enforcement of foreign judgments" and [ii] "fairness to litigants."[109]

Arguably what influenced the court's decision was that the Mexican government introduced a law which had retrospective effect which is repugnant to US law and hence enlivened the public policy principle.

A French definition of public policy is also very useful. The court defined public policy as "the body of rules and values whose violation the French legal order cannot tolerate even in situations of international character."[110] Importantly, public policy is not contingent on the definition at the seat of arbitration but at the place where enforcement or recognition is sought. Arguably, the definition of public policy has moved away from the concept of national sovereignty. As an example, Indian courts for a long time held that public policy is to be defined as being contrary to "the interest of India."[111] This view has been overruled in the Indian Supreme Court in *Bharat Aluminium v Kaiser Aluminium Technical Service, Inc.*[112] The court overturned *Bhatia International v Bulk Trading S.A. & Another*[113] wherein Indian courts were allowed to annul foreign awards on grounds of public policy. The ruling now is that Indian courts cannot exercise supervisory jurisdiction and interfere in international arbitrations seated outside India.

107 Ibid, 97–98.

108 *Corporación Mexicana de Mantenimiento Integral, supra* 60, 98.

109 Ibid, 107.

110 *Agence pour la sécurité de la navigation aérienne en Afrique et à Madagascar v M. N'DOYE Issakha*, Court of Appeal of Paris, France, 16 October 1997.

111 *Renusagar Power Co. Ltd. v General Electric Company & anr.*, (India), AIR 1994 SC 860; *Penn Racquet Sports v Mayor International Ltd.*, High Court of Delhi, India, 11 January 2011; *Shri Lal Mahal Ltd. v Progetto Grano S.p.A.*, Supreme Court, India, 3 July 2013.

112 *Bharat Aluminium v Kaiser Aluminium Technical Service, Inc*, (Civil Appeal No. 7019 of 2005).

113 *Bhatia International v Bulk Trading S.A. & Anr* (2002) 4 SCC 105.

Notably, the US Courts have earmarked a distinction between national policy and public policy observing that national policy is not public policy. The same finds itself explained by the court in Cubic[114] as below

> The reference to public policy ("ordre public") should enable the courts of the enforcing country to refuse to enforce awards that are fraudulent, oppressive or scandalous.[115]

The drafting history of Article V(2)(B) highlights that the discussions between delegates essentially revolved around the terms "ordre public" and "public policy"; wherein it has agreed that the first term relates to fundamental notions of morality and justice, whereas the latter included a broader notion of governmental policy ingrained in domestic laws of the Contracting States.[116] The varied nature of public policy could oscillate from matters pertaining to antitrust to national policy on foreign affairs or tribal or religious laws.[117] It is further evident from the drafting history that the drafters were desirous of attributing the narrowest interpretation[118] to public policy often equating with "fundamental principles of law."[119] The textual interpretation of Article V(2)(b) leads to the inevitable conclusion that Article V(2)(b) depends upon the understanding of public policy of the courts enforcing the arbitral award, thereby bringing into limelight the distinction between international notions of public policy and domestic notions of public policy.[120]

The practical significance of the public policy argument raised by the party resisting enforcement is well dealt with by a judgement of the English Court of Appeal wherein the court besides acknowledging that the notion of public policy is not defined in the Convention stressed the importance of addressing public policy arguments with "extreme caution as it is never argued at all, only when all other points fail" (a so-called tool of last resort).[121] A classic example of jurisdictions

---

[114] *The Ministry of Defense and Support for the Armed Forces of the Islamic Republic of Iran v Cubic Defense Systems*, Inc (9th Cir. 2011), in Yearbook Commercial Arbitration XXXVII (2012) (United States no. 757), 350–354.

[115] U.N. Doc. E/2822/Add.4, *Supra* 4. See, Comment by Mr. Sanders (The Netherlands)).

[116] Marike R.P. Paulsson, *supra* 24, 217–232.

[117] Ibid.

[118] Note by the Secretary-General, *supra* 2.

[119] United Nations Economic and Social Council, "United Nations Conference on International Commercial Arbitration, Convention on the Recognition and Enforcement of Foreign Awards, Summary Record of the Fourteenth Meeting", U.N. Doc E/Conf.26, SR.14) (Sep. 12, 1958), https://undocs.org/E/CONF.26/SR.14, accessed 10/10/2019. See, Comment of Mr. Urabe (Japan), 7 and comment of Mr. Adamiyat (Iran), 3.

[120] Marike R.P. Paulsson, *supra* 24, 116.

[121] *Deutsche Schauchtbau-und Tiefbohrgesellschaft mbH v Ras al Khaimah National Oil Co.*, Shell International Petroleum Co. Ltd. (Court of Appeal 1987), in Yearbook Commercial Arbitration XIII (1988) (United Kingdom no. 22), 522–536. See also, *The Burton Corporation (US) v Shanghai ViQuest Precision Industries Co., Ltd* (PR China) (Southern District of New York (2010), in Yearbook Commercial Arbitration XXXV (2010) (United States no. 711), 568–570. See also, Marike R.P. Paulsson, *supra* 24.

which consistently applies a narrow interpretations of public policy is Switzerland and Spain.[122] The Swiss Federal Supreme Court has consistently held that

> In so far as the procedure is concerned, not every irregularity will automatically entail refusal of enforcement of a foreign award, even if such irregularity would entail annulment of an award rendered in Switzerland. It should rather involve a violation of fundamental principles of the Swiss legal order which hurts in an intolerable manner the notion of justice.[123]

Further, the Swiss Federal Supreme Court in another case rejected the losing party's argument that enforcement would be contrary to Swiss public policy as below:

> Public policy, being an objection, must be interpreted restrictively, especially in the context of the recognition and enforcement of foreign decisions. There is a violation of public policy where the recognition or enforcement of a foreign decision is intolerably at odds with the Swiss concept of justice. A foreign decision can be incompatible with the Swiss legal system not only because of its substantive contents, but also because of the procedure that led to it. In this respect, Swiss public policy requires compliance with the fundamental principles of procedure, as deduced from the Constitution, such as the right to a fair process and the right to be heard.[124]

The Federal Court has also defined the term public policy under the Convention as follows:

> When recognition and enforcement of a foreign decision would be unacceptably at odds with the national sense of the law because fundamental provisions of the Swiss legal system would be disregarded.[125]

The position of USA in the context of interpreting public policy vis-à-vis the New York Convention is well illustrated by the case of *Parsons & Whittemore*.[126] In that case, the American Respondent had invoked the argument of public policy during the enforcement stage of the arbitral award on grounds that US government as part of its national policy had issued instructions for US nationals not to work in Egypt. The Court of Appeals had held that

> An expansive construction of this defense would vitiate the Convention's basic effort to remove preexisting obstacles to enforcement…Enforcement of foreign arbitral awards may be denied on this basis only where enforcement would violate the forum state's most basic notions of morality and justice…In equating "national" policy with United States "public" policy, the appellant quite plainly misses the mark. To read the public policy defense as a parochial device protective of national political interests would seriously undermine the Convention's utility. This provision was not meant to enshrine the vagaries of international politics under the rubric of "public policy". Rather, a circumscribed public policy doctrine

---

[122] *Odin Shipping Co. (PTE) Ltd. v Aguas Industriales de Tarragona* (Supreme Court 1983) in Yearbook Commercial Arbitration XI (1986) (Spain no. 9), 528–529.

[123] *Chrome Resources S.A. v Leopold Lazarus Ltd.* (Supreme Court 1978), in Yearbook Commercial Arbitration XI (1986) (Switzerland no. 10), 538–542.

[124] *A SA v B Co Ltd*, CSA, Switzerland, Federal Supreme Court, Dec. 8, 2003, Yearbook Commercial Arbitration XXIX (2004), 834–842 (Switzerland no. 38), [13].

[125] *X AG v Y AS*, Switzerland, Federal Supreme Court, Oct. 4, 2010, Yearbook Commercial Arbitration XXXVI (2011), (Switzerland no. 42), 340–342.

[126] *Parsons & Whitemore, Supra* 12.

> was contemplated by the Convention's framers and every indication is that the United States, in acceding to the Convention, meant to subscribe to this supranational emphasis.[127]

Similarly, in *Ameropa*,[128] the US District Court for the Southern District of New York was presented with a case wherein the national policy mandated an embargo of trade by US persons involving goods of Iranian origin. The Swiss Company, i.e. *Ameropa* sough enforcement of the arbitral award passed in its favour in Germany in USA. The court observed that

> There is a wealth of case law that holds that the public policy exception is to be granted only where enforcement would violate the forum state's most basic notions of morality and justice. ...While there is clearly a national policy in the United States to discourage trade with Iran, public policy and national policy are not synonymous. Enforcement would therefore be granted even if some involvement of Ameropa's US subsidiary could be demonstrated...Foreign policy disputes with another country are not enough to overcome the supranational policy of providing predictable enforcement of international arbitral awards.[129]oweverArguably

The issue of public policy will be discussed at length in chapters IV and V.

3.4 Conclusion

The purpose of this chapter has been to give an overview of Article V of the New York Convention. The first point to note is that the article includes the word *may refuse* which supports the pro-arbitration stand of the New York Convention. Article V also lists the only exceptions where an arbitral award can be disturbed/set aside.

The second important point is that the difference between Articles V(1) and V(2) is noted. Article V(1) allows a court to deny enforcement or recognition of an award if the arbitral tribunal erred in their decision making on grounds of procedural shortcomings. The shortcomings are judged on the law of the seat and not on the law applicable in the enforcement jurisdictions.

Thirdly, Article V(2) allows a court to refuse recognition and enforcement of an award based on the law current in that country and not at the seat of arbitration. In effect Article V has managed to balance the legal requirement not only of the set of arbitration but also at the pace of recognition and enforcement and hence maintained as much as possible a pro-arbitration stand without jeopardizing the application of domestic jurisprudence.

---

[127]Ibid.

[128]*Ameropa AG v Havi Ocean Co. LLC* (District for the Southern District Court of New York 2011), in Yearbook Commercial Arbitration XXXVI (2011) (United States no. 731), 433–434. See also, *United The Ministry of Defense and Support for the Armed Forces of the Islamic Republic of Iran v Cubic Defense Systems, Inc* (9th Cir. 2011), in Yearbook Commercial Arbitration XXXVII (2012) (United States no. 757), 350–354.

[129]Ibid.

Chapter 4
The Public Policy Exception to Enforcement—The Origins in Private Law

Overview
This chapter analyses and explain the importance of the public policy exception as it is often resorted to and only in exceptional circumstances an argued exception is successful.

4.1 Introduction

It has been argued and this book has demonstrated it in the previous chapters that arbitration is one of the strongholds of contractual freedom.[1] It follows therefore that courts are obliged to assist the arbitral process where necessary to uphold the contractual terms of a contract. Not surprisingly international commercial arbitration has emerged over the past two decades as the preferred method for settling a growing number of trade and investment disputes involving private parties. Such choice is founded upon the unique attributes that the process holds out—flexibility, technical expertise, privacy and confidentiality.[2]

The dispute settlement process founded upon party autonomy and the binding nature of its result inform the uniqueness of this process. It is, therefore, not an overstatement to say that most awards are complied with voluntarily. The Queen Mary University, London—PriceWaterhouse Survey[3] reported that respondents indicated that the opposing party had honoured the award in full in more than 76% of cases. Only 3% reported that an award debtor had failed to comply with the award. During the interviews, corporate counsel reported that more than 90% of the awards were

[1] See, generally, Blackaby et al. [1], Pieth [2].

[2] See, generally, Rosen [3], Mattli [4].

[3] QMUL-Pricewaterhouse Survey on *International Arbitration: Corporate Attitudes and Practices, 2008* http://www.arbitration.qmul.ac.uk/research/2008/, accessed 25/2/2020.

B. Zeller et al., *Enforcement of Foreign Arbitral Awards and the Public Policy Exception*,
https://doi.org/10.1007/978-981-16-2634-0_4

honored by the non-prevailing party.[4] Despite the encouraging result issues in relation to the enforcement of awards are still producing precedential jurisprudence. The interference of courts in the arbitral process is limited as judges in signatory jurisdictions are afforded "scant discretion to deny the victor the fruits of his labours".[5] Hence "the drafters of the New York Convention intended to ensure that enforcing courts ... would not have the power to reopen cases on their merits."[6] In essence this mandate has been explained succinctly:

> We do not owe deference to the district court's legal conclusions, but we afford "maximum deference" to the arbitrators' decisions."[7] It follows that "[a]n arbitrator's erroneous interpretations or applications of law are not reversible.[8]

However, the issue that remains—and therefore needs to be analysed—is how the law related to setting aside and/or enforcing an award is still not completely settled. One of the issues is the question of public policy. Public policy is not a new phenomenon, it has been around from times immemorial. It is, probably, best described by Burrogh J in 1824 when he noted that:

> I, for one, protest... against arguing too strongly upon public policy;—it is a very unruly horse, and when once you get astride it you never know where it will carry."[9]

However, he also noted, "It may lead you from the sound law. It is never argued at all but when other points fail." However, his opinion seems far from the reality of international dispute resolution wherein public policy has and continues to play an important role in the articulation of the law.

The etymological origins of the term 'public policy' is noteworthy at this juncture before the onset of a detailed discussion regarding the varied interpretation of the term. The Black's Law Dictionary defines 'public policy' as

> 1. Broadly, principles and standards regarded by the legislature or by the courts as being of fundamental concern to the state and the whole of society. Courts sometimes use the term to justify their decisions, as when declaring a contract void because it is "contrary to public policy...
> 2. More narrowly, the principle that a person should not be allowed to do anything that would tend to injure the public at large.[10]

Further, Black's Law Dictionary also cites the definition of 'public policy' as borrowed from authoritative sources,

---

[4]See, generally, Greenberg et al. [5].

[5]Wei [6].

[6]Van den Berg [7].

[7]*EEG (Shanghai) Solar Science & Technology Co., Ltd. v LUMOS LLC n/k/a/ LUMOS Solar LLC*, the United States Court of Appeals, Tenth Circuit. 2016 WL 3909579, [3–5].

[8]Ibid.

[9]*Richardson v Mellish* (1824) 130 E.R. 294.

[10]Black's Law Dictionary (9th ed., 209).

> The policy of the law, or public policy, is a phrase of common use in estimating the validity of contracts. Its history is obscure; it is most likely that agreements which tended to restrain trade or to promote litigation were the first to elicit the principle that courts would look to the interests of the public in giving efficacy to contracts.[11]

4.2 The Articulation of Public Policy Within Private International Law

The contextualization of public policy exception within the framework of Private International law, without a doubt, owes itself to the historical treatment of foreign judgments in the common and civil law jurisdictions.[12] Pertinently, the public policy exception vis-à-vis the rules of private international law posits the protection of the "fundamental moral convictions or policies of the forum".[13] The importance of the public policy exception is well illustrated in the law governing contractual obligations in any given state wherein contracting parties, in addition to considering statutory rules governing their contract, also compulsorily have to take into consideration the public policy aspect governing their contract in order to ensure the sanctity of the executed contract.[14] As a case on point, in *Krombach v Bramberski,*[15] the court opined that resorting to public policy was a legitimate exercise, especially in a case that involved a breach of procedural justice wherein the defendant was refused to put forth his defence except in person. The general position that emanates from a perusal of the relevant literature within the sphere of private international law allows a derivation that the public policy exception serves a three-fold purpose, i.e., (i) excluding the objectionable foreign law; (ii) ensuring the proper conduct of the parties and (iii) preventing the detrimental effects of a contract.[16]

Historically, the Geneva Convention (Convention on the Execution of Foreign Arbitral Award),[17] 1927 was one of the earliest international law instruments to include provisions pertaining to public policy. Article 1(2) of the aforesaid Convention stated that "to obtain such recognition or enforcement, it shall, further be necessary…(e) That the recognition or enforcement of the award is not contrary to the public policy or the principles of the law of the country in which it is sought to be relied upon".[18] Subsequently, the draft Article IV(1)(a) of the International Chamber of Commerce (ICC) in 1953 also replaced "principles of the law" with "public

---

[11] Ibid.

[12] Born [8]. See also, Dar [9].

[13] Albert Jan Van den Berg, *supra 6.*

[14] Fentiman [10] 1, 114. See, Wasiq Abbas Dar, *supra* 12.

[15] *Krombach v Bramberski*, 2000 ECR I-1935.

[16] Richard Fentiman, *supra* 14. 114. See, Wasiq Abbas Dar, *supra* 12.

[17] Convention on the Execution of Foreign Arbitral Awards Signed at Geneva on the Twenty-Sixth Day of September, Nineteen Hundred And Twenty-Seven (Geneva Convention, 1927) https://www.arbitrationindia.com/geneva_convention_1927.html

[18] Ibid.

policy".[19] Furthermore, the Draft Convention on the Recognition and Enforcement of Foreign Arbitral Awards proposed by the United Nations Economic and Social Council (ECOSOC) in Article IV(h) used "the recognition of the award, or the subject matter thereof, would be clearly incompatible with public policy or with fundamental principles of the law ("*ordre public*") of the country in which the award is sought to be relied upon".[20] The Report of the Committee on the Enforcement of International Arbitral Awards has noted that ECOSOC deliberately attempted to use terms such as "clearly", "fundamental", etc. to ensure that public policy only applied to cases in which the recognition or enforcement of foreign arbitral awards "would be distinctly contrary to the basic principles of the legal system of the country where the award is invoked."[21]

One of the earliest expositions on the place of public policy within international dispute resolution noted within the jurisprudence of international courts has been the articulation provided by Lauterpacht J in the "*Guardianship case*".[22] He stated,

> public policy is the part and parcel of the entire doctrine of and practise of private international law almost from its very inception.... the State needs a "safety valve" so that its courts might, if thought necessary, decline to apply a particular foreign law.[23]

However, Lauterpacht J, aware of the consequences of the application of public policy by the national courts, also made a suggestion that such an application in private international law remains subject to reasonable limitations.

Silberman Abella shared an interesting observation made by a Canadian judge commenting in relation to public policy:

> For centuries, and at least from the time of Montesquieu, public policy had been in all three of the play's acts in English-speaking Western Democracies—in Act I, as Common Law; in Act 2, as Statutory Interpretation; and in Act 3, as Constitutional Review.[24]

The issue that Abella has pointed, and rightly so, is to understand the relationship between "public policy" and "judicial neutrality."[25] The argument is that public policy is a political function embedded in statutes which are formulated by the legislature. However, this does not create a conflict as judges need to interpret legislation and hence neutrality is assumed. Public policy, therefore, is presented as the philosophical blueprint for the systems and rules that regulate social and political conduct.[26]

---

[19] 9(1) ICC Bulletin 32, 35 (1998).

[20] ECOSOC's 1955 draft New York Convention, see UN Doc. E/2704 and E/AC.42/4Rev.1, Report of the Committee on the Enforcement of International Arbitral Awards, 2 (28 March 1955).

[21] Report of the Committee on the Enforcement of International Arbitral Awards, E/AC.42/4Rev.1, [49].

[22] *Netherland v Sweden.*, http://www.icj-cij.org/docket/index.php?sum=145&code=nls&p1=3&p2=3&case=33&k=37&p3=5, accessed 10/02/2020.

[23] Ibid.

[24] See, Abella [11].

[25] Ibid, 1023.

[26] Abella [12], 227.

While the concept itself has eluded a strict definitional activity, that hasn't impacted its appeal and therefore endeavours to articulate public policy are many, and coming. Notwithstanding the elusive definition, it has nevertheless had universal acceptance tempered upon each country's national needs. Some common features found within the conceptual understanding in many national jurisdictions are public good and public interest. In other words, any "given public policy stands for certain values or a code of morality with which we intend or expect most of society to abide."[27]

The International Law Association(ILA) states that the most often quoted definition of public policy is the one offered in the *Parsons and Whitemore Overseas Co. v Societe Generale de L'Industrie du Papier*,[28] where it was held that enforcement of a foreign award may be denied on public policy grounds only where enforcement would violate the State's most basic notions of morality and justice. Simply put "courts, in their relationship with public policy, are also involved in an evaluative process."[29]

There are some conceptual differences between the public policy understandings in international and domestic jurisdictions. While international public policy is a part of the country's private international law, domestic public policy's content domain area is the country's private law. In a dispute involving international public policy the decisional authority may consider other law areas' public policies for a comparative element, while in domestic public policy there is no necessity for reference to any comparative element.

While these differences are not explicit within many national jurisdictions, France offers a significant example of two distinct public policy principles—*odre public interne* and *odre public international* as noted above. There are also examples of judiciary preferring to apply international public policy over the wider domestic public policy in cases involving foreign elements.[30]

The problem is that public policy is often quoted but rarely defined. Two judges in Australia have attempted this task. Isaacs J in *Wilkinson v Osborne*[31] stated:

> In my opinion the "public policy" which a court is entitled to apply as a test of validity to a contract is in relation to some definite and governing principle which the community as a whole has already adopted either formally by law or tacitly by its general course of corporate life, and which the courts of the country can therefore recognise and enforce. The court is not a legislator: it cannot initiate the principle; it can only state or formulate it if it already exists.[32]

---

[27] Abella, *supra* 24, 1024.

[28] *Whitemore Overseas Co. v Societe Generale de L'Industrie du Papier*, 508 F. 2d 969 (2nd Cir. 1974).

[29] Abella, *supra* 24, 1025.

[30] *Scherk v Alberto-Culver Co.* 417 US 506 (1974); Also in *Renusagar Power Electric Co. v General Electric*, AIR 1994 SC 860, the court held that public policy must be construed to mean the doctrine of public policy as applied by the courts in which the foreign award is sought to be enforced.

[31] *Wilkinson v Osborne*, (1915) 21 CLR 89.

[32] Ibid., 97.

The problem is that Isaac J merely notes that public policy is a recognized principle and needs to be applied by courts but only if courts are given a definition of the principle either by implication or by legislation. The court fell short of defining the principle.

Later Jordan CJ in *Re: Jacob Morris (deceased)*[33] noted:

> The phrase "public policy" appears to mean the ideas which for the time being prevail in a community as to the conditions necessary to ensure its welfare; so that anything is treated as against public policy if it is generally regarded as injurious to the public interest…. It is well settled that a contract is not enforceable if its enforcement would be opposed to public policy... Public policy is not, however, fixed and stable. From generation to generation ideas change as to what is necessary or injurious, so that "public policy" is a variable thing. It must fluctuate with the circumstance of the time…. New heads of public policy come into being, and old heads undergo modification.[34]

Arguably, Jordan CJ observed that it is impossible to define public policy as it is tied to circumstances or ideas prevailing in the community which speak against injustice and immorality, just to mention two of the possible variables making up public policy. It follows that in a general sense there is an international public policy but not in a specific form as every community, i.e., jurisdiction would define justice and morality differently. Simply put we cannot define public policy as it is a vague and uncertain term, but we recognize when it is absent.

Interestingly Williams J observed that:

> Judges in Australia, including members of the High Court, the highest appellate court in the country, have over the past few decades made reference to public policy in justifying a change in direction and sometimes even a reversal of the common law.[35]

Arguably therefore public policy does play an important role as a general principle in international law but its application varies due to different cultural conditions.

4.3 Public Policy in International Commercial Arbitration

It has been argued that arbitration is one the strongholds of contractual freedom.[36] It follows therefore that courts are obliged to assist the arbitral process where necessary to uphold the contractual terms of a contract. To that end judges in signatory jurisdictions are afforded "scant discretion to deny the victor the fruits of his labours".[37]

However, if an award is not honoured and needs to be enforced,—or the losing party attempts to set aside an award—the avenues for such a course of action are

[33] *Re: Jacob Morris (deceased)*, (1943) S R NSW 352.

[34] Ibid., 355.

[35] Williams [13], 135, 139.

[36] M. Pieth, *supra* 1, 1375.

[37] Edward Ti Seng-wei, *supra* 5, 595.

limited. It is undisputed that "the drafters of the New York Convention intended to ensure that enforcing courts … would not have the power to reopen cases on their merits."[38] In essence this mandate has been explained succinctly:

> We do not owe deference to the district court's legal conclusions, but we afford "maximum deference" to the arbitrators' decisions."[39] It follows that "[a]n arbitrator's erroneous interpretations or applications of law are not reversible.[40]

However, a distinction is drawn by the New York Convention which is explained when viewing the difference between article V (1) and V (2).

> An important point in subsection (2) is that the grounds of non-enforcement or setting aside is that an award cannot breach public policy. As the High Court of Australia has stated a breach of—in this case—public policy is an "objective question to be determined by the competent court on the evidence and submissions before it, unaffected by the competence of an arbitral tribunal to rule on its own jurisdiction under Art 16 of the Model Law."[41] The New York Convention and the Model Law have the effect that arbitrators "cannot by their own decision … create or extend the authority conferred upon them[42]

A point which has often been either forgotten or overlooked but has been the subject of an appeal in the U.S. Court of Appeals for the Second Circuit[43] relates to the annulled awards. An arbitral award was annulled at the seat of arbitration in this case Mexico but was upheld in the District Court of New York. The court in the instant case, noted that two principles come into play in this context—a district court's discretion to confirm an arbitral award, and secondly, the comity owed to a foreign court's ruling on the validity of an arbitral award rendered in that country, which in the instant case is Mexico.[44] The court is often faced with the task of reconciling these two principles which otherwise lead to conflicting results.

> We hold that the Southern District properly exercised its discretion in confirming the award because giving effect to the subsequent nullification of the award in Mexico would run counter to United States public policy and would (in the operative phrasing) be "repugnant to fundamental notions of what is decent and just" in this country.[45]

In the *TCL Air Conditioner* case, another interesting point was argued in the High Court of Australia. The plaintiff, surprisingly, argued that the International Arbitration Act, 1974 was invalid in relation to enforce or set aside awards because it provided for the exercise of the judicial power of the Commonwealth in a manner

---

[38] A. Jan van den Berg, *supra* 6, 358.

[39] *EEG (Shanghai) Solar Science, supra* 7.

[40] Ibid.

[41] *TCL Air Conditioner (Zhongshan) Co Ltd v Judges of the Federal Court of Australia and Another* [2013] 251 CLR, *533, 548.*

[42] *Dallah Real Estate & Tourism Holding Co v Pakistan* [2011] 1 AC 763 at 810 [24].

[43] *Corporación Mexicana De Mantenimiento Integral, S. De R.L. De C.V., v PEP–Exploración Y Producción*, F.3d, 2016 WL 4087215.

[44] Ibid., Per Dennis Jacobs Circuit Judge at page 7.

[45] Ibid.

contrary to Ch III of the Constitution.[46] Furthermore to avoid contravening Ch III, courts must be able to determine whether an arbitral tribunal had applied the law correctly in reaching an award.[47] In addition the plaintiff argued that "Art 28(1) of the Model Law had the effect of confining an arbitral tribunal's authority under an arbitration agreement to deciding a dispute correctly and hence an award founded on an erroneous principle was not binding upon the parties."[48] The High Court dismissed the appeal and decided:

(1) that neither Art 28(1) of the Model Law nor an implied term of an arbitration agreement limited the authority of an arbitral tribunal to the correct application of the law. Article 28(1) was directed to the rules of law to be applied, not to the correctness of their application.

(2) that in giving the force of law in Australia to the Model Law, s 16(1) of the International Arbitration Act did not contravene Ch III of the Constitution.[49]

An important point to be noted and strictly adhered to is that "the enlistment of judicial power in enforcing an arbitral award occurs at a point in time when the obligations sought to be enforced …and they are those which are created by an award."[50] Therefore to find the correctness of the award is not a judicial function.

Public policy provisions are found postulated into almost all international treaties and agreements.[51] As already mentioned in the preceding chapters, public policy as enshrined in Article V(2)(b) is one of the most frequently asserted grounds for refusing enforcement of a foreign award[52] and finds itself posited in several arbitral legislations as "public policy", or "public policy of the state".[53] Interestingly, some statutes also refer to public policy as "international public policy",[54] "principles of international public policy",[55] "public policy as understood in private

---

[46] *TCL Air Conditioner, supra* 41, 534.

[47] Ibid.

[48] Ibid.

[49] Ibid.

[50] Ibid., 573.

[51] Albert Jan van den Berg, *supra* 6.

[52] Paulsson [14].

[53] See, English Arbitration Act, 1996, §103(3); Swiss Law on Private International Law, Art. 194 (incorporating New York Convention); German ZPO, §1061(1) (incorporating New York Convention); Belgian Judicial Code, Art. 1717(3)(b)(ii) ("award is in conflict with public policy"); Netherlands Code of Civil Procedure, Art. 1075(1) (incorporating New York Convention); Austrian ZPO, §595(1)(6) (violation of public order); Singapore International Arbitration Act, §31(4)(b); Hong Kong Arbitration Ordinance, §89(3)(b); Australian International Arbitration Act, §8(7)(b); Danish Arbitration Act, §39(1)(2)(b); Japanese Arbitration Law, Art. 45(2)(ix); Indian Arbitration and Conciliation Act, §57(1)(e); New Zealand Arbitration Act, Schedule 1, Art. 36(1)(b)(ii); Norwegian Arbitration Act, Art. 46(2)(b); Scottish Arbitration Act, Art. 20(4)(b); Guatemalan Decree No. 67-95, Art. 47(b)(ii); Egyptian Arbitration Law, Art. 58(2)(b); Maltese Arbitration Act, Art. 36(1)(b)(ii); Ukrainian Civil Code, Art. 228.

[54] French Code of Civil Procedure, Art. 1520(5); Lebanese Code of Civil Procedure, Art. 814.

[55] Portuguese Code of Civil Procedure, Art. 1096(f); Algerian Code of Civil and Administrative Procedure, Art. 458 bis 23(h).

international law",[56] "public interest" or "good morals".[57] In line with the above, some courts have opined that public policy should not be premised upon "general considerations of supposed public interests", but rather should be premised upon "laws and legal precedents".[58] Accordingly, in some jurisdictions it is well settled that public policy is not be to invoked by the court on a subjective assessment or political prejudices and must be applied on the basis of articulated, fundamental policies that find support in the constitutional, legislative or judicial authority.[59]

The New York Convention, 1958[60] and the UNCITRAL Model Law have brought in the much-needed streamlining of the arbitration law in many jurisdictions by ensuring that there is crystallization of principles governing recognition and enforcement of foreign arbitral awards within the territorial jurisdiction of the signatories. It is necessary that we recall here the provisions of the Convention and the provisions of the Model Law that emphasize upon the enforcement of foreign arbitral awards. The New York Convention, 1958, stated

> Each Contracting State shall recognize arbitral awards as binding and enforce them in accordance with the rules of procedure of the territory where the award is relied upon, under the conditions laid down in the following articles. There shall not be imposed substantially more onerous conditions or higher fees or charges on the recognition or enforcement of arbitral awards to which this Convention applies than are imposed on the recognition or enforcement of domestic arbitral awards.[61]

The above-mentioned provision has two significant features to it. It asks the contracting parties to ensure foreign arbitral awards as final and binding within their territories. It states further, and more significantly, an obligation upon the contracting parties to ensure that enforcement of foreign awards is not subjected to any disadvantage through rules and conditions that are not visited upon in case of domestic arbitral awards. To put it more succinctly, the Convention calls upon member parties to desist from having standards of difficulty that are not applicable to the domestic arbitral

---

[56]Romanian Law 105/1992 on the Settlement of Private International Law Relations, Arts. 168(2), 174.

[57]See, Chinese Civil Procedure Law, Art. 160 ("the social and public interest of the country"); Japanese Arbitration Law, Art. 45(2)(ix) ("public policy or good morals of Japan"); Libyan Code of Civil and Commercial Procedure, Arts. 407(4), 408; Omani Arbitration Law, Art. 53 ("contrary to public order"); Qatari Code of Civil and Commercial Procedure, Art. 380(4) ("does not breach the rules of public order and good morals"); Syrian Arbitration Act, Art. 56(2)(b) (breach of "public order in the Syrian Arab Republic").

[58]*WR Grace & Co. v Local Union* 749, 461 U.S. 757, 767 (U.S. S.Ct. 1983). See also, *United Paperworkers Int'l Union v Misco Inc.*, 484 U.S. 29, 43 (U.S. S.Ct. 1987) (citing *Muschany v U.S.*, 324 U.S. 49, 66, 65 (U.S. S.Ct. 1945)); *Indus Risk Insurers v M.A.N. Gutehoffnungshütte GmbH, 141* F.3d 1434, 1445 (11th Cir. 1998); *Asignacion v Rickmers Genoa Schifffahrtsgesellschaft mbH & Cie KG*, 783 F.3d 1010, 1016 (5th Cir. 2015); *Hardy Exploration & Prod. (India), Inc. v India, Ministry of Petroleum & Natural Gas*, 314 F.Supp.3d 95, 109 (D.D.C. 2018).

[59]Born [15].

[60]Convention on the Enforcement of Foreign Arbitral Awards, 1958; see for further information and research materials related to the Convention at https://newyorkconvention1958.org/, accessed 10/09/2019.

[61]Article III, New York Convention, Ibid.

awards. While similar standards have not been expressly emphasized upon within the language of the Article III of the Convention standards of extra difficulty have been expressly discouraged. Under this Convention recognition and enforcement of the award may be refused, at the request of the party against whom it is invoked only if that party furnishes to the competent authority where the enforcement is sought, sufficient proof that, amongst other grounds, the recognition or enforcement of the award would be contrary to the public policy of that country.

A perusal of the draft proposals indicates that at the fourteenth meeting on 29.05.1958, the majority of the delegates suggested keeping the wording used in the Geneva Convention and the UN ECOSOC's draft.[62] Similarly, the seventeenth ECOSOC meeting on 03.06.1958 records that it was decided by the Working Group that the provisions relating to refusal of enforcement of arbitral awards on grounds of public policy should be interpreted narrowly and should not be given a broad scope of application.[63] Pursuant to detailed discussions as already enumerated in the above chapters, the Drafting Committee adopted the current text of Article V(2)(b) on 06.06.1958 which states that 'Recognition and enforcement of an arbitral award may also be refused if the competent authority in the country where recognition and enforcement is sought finds that:… (b) the recognition or enforcement of the award would be contrary to the public policy of that country.'

There has been a diversity of opinion on the content of the words public policy as applied to the enforcement of foreign arbitral awards. The commonly held opinion is that the standards of public policy should be contoured on international standards, rather than extrapolating its meaning in domestic circumstances to international arbitration.[64]

While there is an expansive meaning of public policy in terms of litigation and also by logical extension to arbitration, it is unclear whether the same standard of public good and welfare could be extrapolated to international arbitration. It is necessary to recall the scholarly statement of Fouchard et al. on the import of the words public policy–

> The provision certainly refers to international public policy, and not domestic public policy. Not every breach of a mandatory rule of the host country could justify refusing recognition or enforcement of a foreign award. Such refusal is only justified where the award contravenes principles which are considered in the host country as reflecting its fundamental convictions, or as having an absolute, universal value.[65]

Scholarly opinion on the standards of public policy has been categorized under two theoretical constructs. The Organisation for Economic Co-operation and Development (OECD), an inter-governmental organization of 37 member-States founded

---

[62]Examples include Iran (UN Doc. E/CONF.26/SR.14, p. 3), Israel (UN Doc. E/CONF.26/SR.14, p. 5), and Peru (with suggested deletion of the word 'clearly': UN Doc. E/CONF.26/SR.14, p. 9).

[63]Mr de Sydow, Chairperson of the Working Group, UN Doc. E/CONF.26/SR. 17, p. 3 (12 September 1958); See also, Chen [16].

[64]Hanotiau and Caprasse [17].

[65]Gaillard and Savage [18], [1711–1712].

in 1961, prepared a document[66] on the hearings in arbitration and mediation specifically in competition law issues provides interesting insights into these theoretical constructs that have been used to categorize the deployment of public policy exception. Though it is a statement founded upon research into competition law, generality could be attributed to the principles of public policy discussed in the document. According to the document, there are two doctrinal and jurisprudential approaches which have been adopted, the maximalist and the minimalist approach.

Under the maximalist approach, national courts are required to carry out an in-depth review of arbitral awards when they are challenged, or when enforcement is required. This involves a full review of the entire case and all the evidence associated with it. The rationale for this approach is to avoid the risk that arbitration will be used to circumvent the basic law of the land concerning the subject-matter of the dispute submitted for arbitration. Courts can therefore consider in detail whether a specific law has been applied 'correctly'. Thus, it can be said the maximalist approach towards public policy is largely addressed towards a greater emphasis on the need of enforcing the law on any specific issue that was otherwise submitted to arbitration. In *Mitsubishi Motors Corp. v Soler Chrysler-Plymouth, Inc.*,[67] the American court held that public policy could be a method to cast a second look at the award for being in larger compliance with the law and policy of the land and ensuring that there is nothing in the award that is against the law of enforcing country.

Under the minimalist approach no special treatment is given for awards raising specific legal issues or a review based upon the merits of the award, and emphasis remains on taking the case outside of the courts and settling it via arbitrators. The rationale for this approach is that if a full review of the award is carried out, this arguably defeats the purpose of going into arbitration in the first place and undermines the trust afforded to arbitrators and the institution of arbitration. Courts should therefore only overturn awards where there is a fundamental breach of public policy.[68]

The UNCITRAL Model Law[69] states that an arbitral award, irrespective of the country in which it is made shall be recognized as binding and upon an application to the competent court shall be enforced subject to the provisions of Articles 35 and 36.[70]

Such recognition may be refused, amongst other grounds, on the ground that

(b) if the court finds that:

> (i) the subject-matter of the dispute is not capable of settlement by arbitration under the law of this State; or

---

[66]OECD Hearings–Arbitration and Competition 2010 http://www.oecd.org/competition/abuse/49294392.pdf, accessed 08/07/2020.

[67]*Mitsubishi Motors Corp. v Soler Chrysler-Plymouth, Inc.* 723 F.2d 155 (1983), cert. granted, 105 S. Ct.291 (1984).

[68]OECD Hearings, *supra* 66.

[69]The UNCITRAL Model Law, 1985 (Amended in 2006) ("The Model Law).

[70]Ibid., Article 35(1).

(ii) the recognition or enforcement of the award would be contrary to the public policy of this State.[71]

Justice French in his 2016 Goff lecture at the City University of Hong Kong pointed to the most important issue underpinning the public policy issue in arbitration,

> the external public policy environment which underpins and informs the legal regimes which govern arbitration and the internal public policy constraints expressly and impliedly embedded in the legal criteria for setting aside and refusing recognition and enforcement of awards.[72]

The external public policy environment allows courts to provide recognition and enforcement of awards which is a judicial function derived from public law which is explained in the judgment in *Westport Insurance Corp v Gordian Runoff Ltd*[73] where the court noted:

> That statutory regime involves the exercise of public authority, whether by force of the statute itself or by enlistment of the jurisdiction of the Supreme Court. It also … displays a legislative concern that the jurisdictions of the courts to develop commercial law not be restricted by the complete insulation of private commercial arbitration.[74]

In essence "Enforcement [does] not…involve the enforcement of the rights and liabilities which were the subject of the dispute submitted to arbitration."[75] What it does do is that it gives legal effect to the parties' agreement to binding arbitration.

There is general consensus that in the absence of the public policy ground in the New York Convention the success of the Convention would be severely impacted. Hence, it follows that the ambiguity and uncertainty of public policy follows closely associated with the overall success of the Convention.[76] The supposed 'back door' of public policy has often become a 'gateway for undesirable obstructions' in recent times whereby Contracting States refuse recognition and enforcement of foreign arbitral awards thereby impeding the pro-enforcement policy of the New York Convention.[77] The friction between the appropriate use of public policy as a 'safety valve' and avoidance of its abuse as an obstruction to New York Convention's pro-enforcement policy seems 'unlikely to be ever fully resolved'.[78] However, it is noteworthy that ILA's Final Report on public policy states that public policy 'has not given rise to any serious mischief and attempts to resist enforcement on grounds of public policy have rarely been successful', uncertainty and inconsistency in the interpretation and application of public policy have 'encouraged losing parties to rely on public policy to resist, or at least delay, enforcement'.[79]

---

[71] Ibid., Article 36(1)(b)(i) and (ii).

[72] French [19].

[73] *Westport Insurance Corp v Gordian Runoff Ltd*, (2011) 244 CLR 239.

[74] Ibid., 261 [19].

[75] French, *supra* 72, 10.

[76] Wolff [20].

[77] Ibid.

[78] Ibid.

[79] Mayer and Shepard [21] ("ILA's Final Report").

As far as internal public policy is concerned, Articles 34 and 36 of the Model law and Article V of the New York Convention govern this issue. Public policy is not defined in either international instrument because—as noted above already—the definition of public policy is a matter for each jurisdiction to determine and hence there is no international definition possible. The question which needs to be asked is whether the public policy criteria is to be applied restrictively or expansively. The International Bar Association (IBA) released a report in 2015 where they found that only in very few exceptions such as in Australia and the United Arab Emirates public policy was statutorily defined.[80]

The Australian International Arbitration Act, 1974 (Cth) provides the best example where Section 8(&A) provides that:

> To avoid doubt and without limiting paragraph (7)(b)[which makes the violation of public policy a ground for refusing to enforce a foreign award], the enforcement of a foreign award would be contrary to public policy if: (a) the making of the award was induced or affected by fraud or corruption; or (b) a breach of the rules of natural justice occurred in connection with the making of the award.[81]

Unfortunately, the lack of a concise definition of public policy is not the only problem as in some countries a distinction is drawn between domestic and international public policy which is, in some jurisdictions, mandated by the local arbitration law.[82]

The IBA came to the conclusion that:

> In the vast majority of jurisdictions covered by this report, a violation of public policy implies a violation of fundamental or basic principles. These principles seem, however, to be differently expressed by courts (and scholars) depending on whether they are in civil law or common law jurisdictions. In the first group, the definitions of public policy generally refer to the basic principles or values upon which the foundation of society rests, without precisely naming them. In the second group, on the other hand, the definition often refers to more precisely identified, yet very broad, values, such as justice, fairness or morality.[83]

It appears that as the IBA noted "many courts stress that public policy is an ever-evolving concept"[84] hence making it even more difficult to ascertain what it actually

---

[80]See International Bar Association Subcommittee on Recognition and Enforcement of Arbitral Awards, 'Report of the Public Policy Exception in the New York Convention' (October 2015) http://www.ibanet.org/LPD/Dispute_Resolution_Section/Arbitration/Recogntn_Enfrcemnt_Arbitl_Awrd/publicpolicy15.aspz ("the IBA Report"), accessed 10/10/2019.

[81]The International Arbitration Act 1974 (Cth) (IAA) governs international commercial arbitrations in Australia. Part II sets out Australia's accession to, and implementation of, the UN Convention on the Recognition and Enforcement of Foreign Arbitral Awards adopted in 1958 (New York Convention) (*Section 8, IAA*). Part III of the IAA provides that the UNCITRAL Model Law on International Commercial Arbitration 1985 (with the amendments adopted in 2006) (Model Law) has force in Australia (see *Section 16(1), IAA*); See, for the text of the legislation—https://www.legislation.gov.au/Details/C2011C00342.

[82]IBA Report, *supra* 80, 4–5.

[83]Ibid., 6.

[84]Ibid., 10.

means. It appears that in Australia the term embraces nations of unfairness, fraud and corruption which has been given effect in article 18 of the Model law.

Unfairness under Article 18 does involve the hearing and the bias rule. French J explained it briefly in the following terms:

> The hearing rule requires that the arbitrator hears from a party before making a decision on an issue affecting that party's interests. There may be a question whether it imports a requirement of diligent attention to all the claims made and material advanced by each party. The hearing rule cannot be invoked as a means of revisiting the factual merits of an arbitration decision. And the bias rule requires that the arbitrator be impartial as between the parties. It is also important that arbitral tribunals not conduct themselves so as to compromise the appearance of neutrality.[85]

4.4 The Public Policy Limitation as Envisaged in New York Convention and UNCITRAL Model Law

Article V (2) of the New York Convention states:

> 2, Recognition and enforcement of an arbitral award may also be refused if the competent authority in the country where recognition and enforcement is sought finds that:
>
> (b) The recognition or enforcement of the award would be contrary to the public policy of that country.[86]

The UNCITRAL Model law also included public policy as a reason for the arbitral award to be set aside. The Model Law which has been the interpretative force in Australia notes in Article 34(2)(b)(ii) that an award can be set aside on reasons on public policy. Further, Article 36 of the Model Law in effect reiterates Article V of the NYC of non-enforcement and in essence operates in harmony with the NYC. Importantly the NYC uses the words '*that country*' and the Model law public policy of '*this State*'. This can be interpreted as a clear indicator of the fact that the drafters deemed it imperative to respect the public policy recognised by every Contracting State and allowing the Contracting state to interpret the meaning of public policy themselves.

It is obvious that public policy issues change or are not the same in every country. It is well established that the:

> public policy exception is … useful and necessary because of its ability to place limitations on … globalizing tendencies to the extent private contracting parties overstep fundamental public policy limits.[87]

It is thus obvious that outcomes can be different depending on the public policy of the chosen jurisdiction. It also stands to reason that the outcomes can also be different

---

[85] French, *supra* 72, 14.

[86] Model Law, *supra* 69, Article 36 is much similar to Article V of the New York Convention.

[87] Gibson [22], 1240.

if the setting aside and enforcement processes are taking place in two different jurisdictions. Simply put an attempt at setting aside an award might fail but the award still cannot be enforced, as in the enforcing jurisdiction the public policy is defined differently. The wording of the two instruments is clear on this point. The New York Convention used the word "that country" which is the enforcing country whereas the Model Law uses the word "this country" which is the country where the attempt is made set aside an award.

It is therefore important to note that the choice related to the seat of arbitration shall be informed by, apart from other reasons, also with the enforcement issue in mind. The seat of arbitration holds exclusive jurisdiction over arbitral proceedings which include the challenges to an award.[88] However, the application for enforcement of an award obviously can be instituted in any jurisdiction, practically, where the assets are located. If both are in the same jurisdiction the same public policy considerations will be considered in either the enforcing or setting aside proceedings. However, courts generally have noted that it would be appropriate to enforce an award which was unsuccessfully challenged at the seat of arbitration.[89]

A good example to the contrary (until recently) was the problem of enforcing an arbitral award in India. The Indian Supreme court in *Bharat Aluminium v Kaiser Aluminium Technical Service, Inc*[90] (*BALCO*) overturned *Bhatia*[91] wherein Indian courts were allowed to order interim relief in foreign-seated arbitrations. The legacy of *Bhatia* continued and further expanded to obliterate the distinction between domestic and international arbitrations, which was a part of the legislative scheme of the Indian Arbitration Act, 1996, and this impacted the enforcement of awards.[92] The law now, following the ruling in *BALCO* is that Indian courts cannot exercise supervisory jurisdiction and interfere in international arbitrations seated outside India.

The High Court of England and Wales in *IPCO (Nigeria) Ltd v Nigerian National Petroleum Corp.*[93] noted that:

> Pro-enforcement assumptions are sometimes outweighed by the respect due to the courts exercising jurisdiction in the country of origin—the venue chosen by the parties for their arbitration.[94]

---

[88]*C v D* [2007] EWHC 1541, [52].

[89]*Gujarat NRE Coke Limited v Coeclerici Asia (Pty) Ltd* [2013] FCAFC 109, [55]–[68].

[90]*Bharat Aluminium v Kaiser Aluminium Technical Service, Inc.*, (Civil Appeal No. 7019 of 2005).

[91]*Bhatia International v Bulk Trading S.A. & Anr* (2002) 4 SCC 105.

[92]See, *Venture Global Engineering v Satyam Computer Services Ltd. and Ors*, AIR 2008 SC 1061 and *McDermott International Inc. v Burn Standard Co. Ltd. and Ors.*, (2006) 11 SCC 181. Also see, Nariman [23].

[93]*IPCO (Nigeria) Ltd v Nigerian National Petroleum Corp.*, [2005] EWHC 726.

[94]Ibid., [14].

4.5 Public Policy and Natural Justice—Two Constructs, but Symbiotic?

A significant concern that remains pertinent here is that public policy and natural justice are not terms which are definable as they are depending on the cultural norms of a country as well as the facts of each case. There is no debate that natural justice and public policy are linked due to statutory regulations in many countries. As far as the legislation in Australia is concerned Section 19 of the enabling legislation removes any doubt that natural justice is linked to public policy. It notes:

> Without limiting the generality of Articles 17I(1)(b)(ii), 34(2)(b)(ii) and 36(1)(b)(ii) of the Model Law, it is declared, for the avoidance of any doubt, that, for the purposes of those Articles, an interim measure or award is in conflict with, or is contrary to, the public policy of Australia if:
>
> (b) a breach of the rules of natural justice occurred in connection with the making of the interim measure or award.[95]

Section 19's effect is such that it really does not matter whether an award is set aside or enforcement is sought in Australia under the Model law. Natural justice is applicable in both situations. Section 19 also has the effect that public policy does not need to be defined because as soon as a breach of natural justice is proven it automatically equates to a breach of public policy.

A breach of natural justice—simply put—triggers automatically the public policy exception in the Model Law as well as in the New York Convention. However it must be always remain noted that "the extent to which a Court will intervene in the arbitral process depends on how widely or narrowly the Courts interpret these provisions and it is in the interpretation, rather than the provisions themselves, that the problem lies."[96] A breach of natural justice triggering the public policy exemption is not to be confused as simply revisiting the facts as viewed by the losing party.

Lord Mustill explained the issue succinctly in *Pupuke Service Stations Ltd v Caltex Oil (NZ Ltd.*[97] He noted:

> Having agreed at the outset to take his dispute away from the Court the losing party may afterwards be tempted to think better of it, and ask the Court to interfere because the arbitrator has misunderstood the issues, believing an unconvincing witness, decided against the weight of evidence or otherwise arrived at the wrong conclusion. All developed systems of arbitration have in principle set their face against accommodation such a change of mind. ... the findings of the arbitrator are impregnable.[98]

Lord Mustill further opined,

> At the other extreme are complaints that the decision has been reached by methods which are unfair, contrary to natural justice, in breach of due process, or whatever other term is

---

[95]International Arbitration Act 1974, Act No. 136 of 1974 (as amended).

[96]Megens and Cubitt [24], 127.

[97]*Pupuke Service Stations Ltd v Caltex Oil (NZ Ltd.*, [2003] 3 NZLR 338 (PC).

[98]Ibid. 338–339.

preferred. With very few exceptions all systems of law permit the injured party some means of recourse.[99]

The pertinent issue therefore that needs to be identified and addressed is about the constituent elements of a claim asserting a breach of natural justice in contrast to the tribunal making a finding based on how they interpreted the submitted evidence.[100]

Jurisprudential insights on public policy from States indicate that national courts have addressed issues and concerns of breaches related to obligations of natural justice within their articulation of the content of public policy. Jurisprudence from Australia seems to be emblematic of such discussion. In *Emerald Grain Australia Pty Ltd v Agrocorp International Pte Ltd*[101] the court had to decide whether the breach of the rules on evidence and the rule related to hearing constituted a breach of natural justice. Agrocorp claimed demurrage, dead freight as the agreed additional freight was not loaded as well as the loss of profit from the shortfall. The tribunal found substantially on all accounts in favour of Agrocorp.

The Counsel for the plaintiff contended that there was no evidence before the tribunal to permit it to make certain findings and therefore presented before the court the no-evidence claim. Such claim refers to contention that the tribunal had founded its order/decision upon no available evidence before it. Furthermore because the tribunal made the findings based on its own opinion without given the plaintiff adequate notice was stated as a ground for the no hearing claim.[102] They based their claim on Article 34(2)(b) of the Model Law and Section 19 of the International Arbitration Act 1994 (Cth).

The preliminary issue to be noted here is that decisions founded upon no probative evidence are considered as decisions without evidence. It is pertinent to recall here, for purposes of articulation and reiteration, the view expressed by Spiegelman CJ that in assessing claims of breach of natural justice, courts take note of "acting without probative evidence is the equivalent of acting without evidence."[103] A pertinent question in this context therefore refers to whether the tribunal relied on the probative evidence as argued by the parties? In addition it needs to be understood that, "it is not to an applicant's ability to rely upon grounds not expressly stated but the continuing power of a court to determine for itself that an award offends public policy."[104]

It needs to be noted here that Article 34, Model Law does not require the courts to inquire into matters that the parties did not, though they could have, raised during the hearing before the tribunal. Simply put, pursuant to the Model Law, a party cannot challenge an arbitral award on the facts, even if not presented and pleaded before the tribunal. Therefore, courts are precluded from examining the facts afresh as noted above. An award is only set aside if the court finds that the award is against public

[99]Ibid.

[100]Model Law, *supra* 69, Article 34(2)(a)(ii).

[101]*Emerald Grain Australia Pty Ltd v Agrocorp International Pte Ltd*, [2014] FCA 414: Pagone J, 30 April 2014.

[102]Ibid., [5].

[103]*Skiwing Pty Ltd v Trust Company of Australia* [2006] NSWCA 276 [52].

[104]*Emerald Grains, supra* 101, [9].

policy. Doug Jones observed that Article 34(2)(b) needs to be considered by the court on its own motion without affecting the applicant's burden of proof.[105] As Pagone J. noted,

> The Court's task in the application of the kind brought by [the applicant] is not to consider the correctness of the facts found by the tribunal but to determine whether the tribunal in finding the facts did so in breach of the rules of natural justice.[106]

As noted above, the burden of proof to establish that there was a breach of natural justice therefore is vested in the applicant alleging such breach. The plaintiff has to unequivocally prove that the tribunal reached their decision going beyond the probative evidence and hence were found in breach of natural justice and not how the permissible facts were applied. The real challenge for the plaintiff is to identify, with precision, the alleged breach factually and then adapt it to a legitimate claim of a breach of the "no evidence" rule.[107] The challenge for the court is to ascertain the content of the rules of natural justice. As Tucker LJ noted,

The requirements of natural justice must depend upon the circumstances of the case, the nature of the inquiry, the rules under which the tribunal is acting, the subject matter that is being dealt with, and so forth.[108]

Considering the above, it could be argued that natural justice in many cases is not a precise science but rather a determination of instances which arguably are "feeling not right" or offend fundamental notions of justice and fairness.[109] Arguably, therefore, it is not easy for the plaintiff to establish a breach of the probative evidence rule. One point to note is that not all evidence is probative and hence does not contribute to a breach of natural justice. The conclusion to be drawn is that a judicial review is only possible if a tribunal does not take the probative evidence into consideration when making a decision. However courts have established that want of logic is not synonymous with error of law as long as the interference appears to have been drawn as a result of illogical reasoning based on the probative evidence.[110] There is a fine line between illogical reasoning but made on probative evidence and a decision based on completely distorted facts as argued in the Regional Court of Cologne wherein the court decided that the award be set aside.[111] It was argued therein that reliance on pleadings that invoked breach of public policy owing to the award allegedly founded upon illogical probative evidence is incorrect.

It could therefore be concluded that the plaintiff has to establish that the outcome of the award has no basis at all on the evidence presented i.e., the tribunal has not taken the probative evidence into consideration. In other words, the decision reached by the tribunal does not have a connection to the available material. Simply put,

---

[105] Jones [25].

[106] *Emerald Grains, supra* 101, [10].

[107] Ibid., [11].

[108] *Russell v Duke of Norfolk* [1949] 1 All ER 109, at 118.

[109] *Emerald Grain, supra* 101, [13].

[110] *Reg v The District Court; Ex parte White* (1966) 116 CLR 644, 654.

[111] Binder [26].

arriving at an illogical conclusion that is based on probative evidence is not to be perceived as a breach of natural justice.

In addition, a plaintiff must also understand that the reasoning of arbitrators need not essentially be equated to be at the same level as that of a court and the tribunal cannot be faulted solely on the basis of absence of detailed findings and extensive reasons.[112] Such challenges fail when the the plaintiff is unable to show that the tribunal had no probative evidence on which they based their decision and instead only managed to show that the tribunal misconstrued the evidence. This was exactly the scenario in *Emerald Grain*. The court therefore rejected the claim of the plaintiff.

Arguably therefore the issue of natural justice i.e., making a decision without the availability of probative evidence only can be accommodated in the application of the Model Law. This is strengthened by Article 18 of the Model Law.

Article 18. Equal treatment of parties

> The parties shall be treated with equality and each party shall be given full opportunity of presenting his case.

Material insights for operationalizing this provision are available from primary and secondary sources that have extensively commented upon natural justice issues in international arbitration. In the context of equal treatment of parties within the tribunal's proceedings, the UNCITRAL recorded extensive discussion.[113] The draft Article 19(3) which is the precursor to above-stated Article 18 was concerned with reconciling the parties' freedom to set out arbitral procedure and the tribunal's authority to determine such procedure where the parties had not, as well as further determine the admissibility, relevance and materiality of evidence.[114] The Official Commentary of the UNCITRAL noted the mandatory nature of the draft article 19 and described it as the "magna carta of arbitral procedure.[115] Furthermore many countries such as Australia, New Zealand and Singapore clarified the issue further by introducing enabling legislation when adopting the model law.

4.6 Public Policy—The Law and Its Praxis

A significant number of nations have adopted both the New York Convention as well as the Model Law, underscoring the importance of harmonised legal platforms and the need to ensure uniformity in the national laws. It is widely debated that public policy in the context of Article V(2)(b) should be treated as international public policy which can be broadly categorised into three different approaches.[116] The first

[112] *Emerald Grain, supra* 101, [16].

[113] See, generally, UNCITRAL, Analytical Commentary on the Draft Text of the Model Law, UN Doc. A/ CN.9/264 (25 March 1985) (UNCITRAL Analytical Commentary), chapter 5—Conduct of Arbitral Proceedings, 44–58.

[114] Bantekas et al. [27].

[115] UNCITRAL Analytical Commentary, *supra* 113, 44.

[116] Born [28].

approach entails understanding the meaning of international public policy through the lens of international law which is equivalent to 'transnational public policy' or 'truly international public policy'.[117] The second approach contemplates that international public policy be regarded as the public policy of the country where enforcement is sought and only be relied upon by Court where such public policy is consistent with important public policies postulated by international principles.[118] The third and the last approach has been advocated by Albert Jan van den Berg, according to which it is pertinent to ascertain the enforcement State's legislative purpose and intent rather than directly exploring international sources of law for ascertaining public policy.[119]

It follows from the above mentioned that, the first two approaches are clearly targeted at achieving uniformity in application of public policy on an international as well as domestic level whereas the third approach operates as an 'escape mechanism' whereby the enforcement court is empowered to apply and enforce its local laws in exception circumstances.[120] The distinction drawn by commentators between international public policy and national public policy is a redundant one because Article V(2)(b) of the New York Convention does not expressly make the differentiation. Notably, the New York Convention acknowledges the freedom of Contracting States to shape their own public policy reflecting their own national requirements thereby implying that Contracting States can either apply the same or devise a different standard(s) for the treatment of international and domestic arbitral awards.[121]

4.6.1 International Standard of Public Policy

With respect to the interpretation of public policy, Albert Jan van den Berg has noted that,

> It may suffice to draw the attention to the important *distinction between domestic and international public policy*... According to this distinction what is considered to pertain to public policy in domestic relations does not necessarily pertain to public policy in international relations. It means that the number of matters considered to fall under public policy in international cases is smaller than that in domestic cases. The distinction is justified by the differing purposes of domestic and international relations.
>
> [....]
>
> It may be added that certain French and Swiss authors maintain that there also exists a third category of public policy, the so-called truly international public policy' (*'ordre public reellement international'*). The rules of this public policy would comprise fundamental rules of natural law, the principles of universal justice, *jus cogens* in public international law and the general principles of morality accepted by what is referred to as 'civilized nations.[122]

[117] Lalive [29]; ILA's Final Report, *supra* 79, 251–252.

[118] Sheppard [21]; ILA's Final Report, *supra* 79.

[119] Van den Berg [30].

[120] Gary B. Born, *supra* 116, 3657; Reinmar Wolff, *supra* 76.

[121] Ibid.

[122] Albert Jan van den Berg, *supra* 6, 360–361.

Despite the stated intention of uniformity of application of arbitral legislation, the issue of public policy as first introduced into the New York Convention suffers from the same problem as many other international conventions in private law, namely, how to marry both common law and civil law meanings into one cohesive approach. The common law principle of public policy has its counterpart in the notion of "ordre public." Both terms do have in common that they touch on the basic rules of law of a nation and are sometimes linked to morality. Van den Berg noted that the civil law notion of public policy has a wider meaning than the common law and, arguably though, includes principles of procedural justice.[123] He also sounded a note of caution in operationalizing public policy—while attempting to understand it in a broad sense, public policy should not be interpreted with domestic connotations in mind.[124]

It seems that the New York Convention within its English version uses the term 'public policy' while the French version uses '*ordre public*'. Thus, at first reading, it is safe to presume that the drafters of the New York Convention desired of attributing public policy the same meaning across translations.[125] The above view is endorsed by Albert Jan van den Berg in his seminal work on the Convention, 'The New York Convention of 1958—Towards a Uniform Judicial Interpretation, wherein he observed that it is common understanding that '*ordre public*' in civil law has a wider scope of application than that of its common law counterpart 'public policy'; yet both are used interchangeably and should therefore be understood as having the same meaning in the context of Article V.[126] The same view finds adopted in the Interim and Final Report of the ILA.[127]

A further issue is that Article V(2)(b) of the New York Convention states "of that country" and in the model law "this country" which suggests strongly that it is a geographical reference where enforcement takes place i.e., domestic law is applied. The danger is that courts, given the domestic mandate, will ignore or at least not take sufficient notice of the international standards pertaining to public policy and follow the homeward trend whereby the enforcement court will prioritize its own public policy as a result completely excluding the international principles regarding public policy. The point is that deep-seated—or arguably what can be termed mandatory notions—are taken note of and hence a truly uniform interpretation is never possible, but it should be the exception rather than the rule. The Indian experience as noted above is a good example where domestic interpretation has now attempted to gain insights from an international perspective as well. However, the term "international origin" does not suggest that there must be absolute uniformity in applying the term of public policy on the contrary as noted by the Model Law and the NYC.

[123] Ibid., 359.

[124] Albert Jan van den Berg, *supra* 6, 361–362.

[125] Helena Hsi-Chia Chen, *supra* 63, 11–26.

[126] Albert Jan van den Berg, *supra* 6.

[127] ILA's Final Report, *supra* 79.

> ... only the State courts can be the sole decider of whether an act, conduct or event contravenes public policy as it is the State's public policy, which is sought to be protected, and not just some abstract notion of international public policy.[128]

Additionally, within national legislations concerning public policy it can be seen that there has been a varied approach. Some national legislations, without referring to public policy, stipulate that recognition and enforcement of foreign arbitral awards be governed by the New York Convention.[129] Examples include the United States (US) Code: Title 9—Arbitration § 201,[130] German Code of Civil Procedure Article 1061(1),[131] English Arbitration Act 1996 Section 100,[132] Korean Arbitration Act Article 39(1)[133] and the Chinese Civil Procedure Law Article 269.[134] The term 'this country' as discussed above finds itself enshrined in Article 36 of the Russian Federation on International Commercial Arbitration[135] which states:

> Recognition or enforcement of an arbitral award, irrespective of the country in which it was made, may be refused only...(2) if the court finds that:... the recognition or enforcement of the award would be contrary to the public policy of the Russian Federation.

Alternatively, there are national legislations which do not incorporate the term 'this country' as is Article 1721(1) of the Belgian Judicial Code which postulates 'public policy' without expressly stipulating public policy of 'this country'[136]: 'The Court of First Instance may only refuse to recognize or enforce an arbitral award, irrespective of the country in which it was made, in the following circumstances:... (b) if the Court of First Instance finds that... the recognition or enforcement of the award would be contrary to public policy.'

---

128 Nicholas [31].

129 Helena Hsi-Chia Chen, *supra* 63, 11–26.

130 9 U.S.C. § 201 states: 'The Convention on the Recognition and Enforcement of Foreign Arbitral Awards of June 10, 1958, shall be enforced in United States courts in accordance with this chapter'.

131 The Tenth Book of the German Code of Civil Procedure contains provisions relating to arbitration.

132 English Arbitration Act 1996 s. 100.

133 Korean Arbitration Act, Act No. 10207 (revised on 31 March 2010). Article 39(1) stipulates: 'Recognition or enforcement of a foreign award which is subject to the Convention on the Recognition and Enforcement of Foreign Arbitral Awards, shall be governed by that Convention'.

134 Chinese Civil Procedure Law Art. 269 provides: 'If an award made by a foreign arbitration agency requires the recognition and enforcement by a people's court of the People's Republic of China, the party concerned shall directly apply to the intermediate people's court in the place where the party subject to execution has its domicile or where its property is located. The people's court shall deal with the matter in accordance with the relevant provisions of the international treaties concluded or acceded to by the People's Republic of China or on the principle of reciprocity.' English translation from the website of the Supreme People's Court of the People's Republic of China, http://en.chinacourt.org/public/detail.php?id=2694(accessed 20 February 2021).

135 International Commercial Arbitration Court at the Chamber of Commerce and Industry of the Russian Federation (ICAC), https://mkas.tpprf.ru/en/documents/, (accessed 20 February 2021).

136 The Belgian Centre for Arbitration and Mediation, http://www.cepani.be/en/arbitration/belgian-judicial-code-provisions (accessed 20 February 2021).

Interestingly, there are few national legislations such as Article 1502(5) of the French Code of Civil Procedure which differentiates between domestic and international public policy by expressly stipulating that one of the grounds for refusal of a foreign arbitral award is 'where the recognition or enforcement is contrary to international public policy'.[137]. The same finds judicial backing by the French Court of Appeal which in the case of *Intrafor Cofor v Gagnant*[138] observed that international public policy and domestic public policy are two different concepts and clarified that violation of domestic public policy did not constitute a ground for appealing against the foreign arbitral award in France, because Article 1502(5) stipulates that 'the recognition or enforcement is contrary to international public policy' (and not domestic public policy).[139] Likewise, Article 56 of Portuguese Law on Voluntary Arbitration Law (which became effective in 2012) provides[140]: 'Recognition or enforcement of an arbitral award made in a foreign country may be refused only:... (b) if the court finds that:... (ii) The recognition or enforcement of the award would lead to a result incompatible with the international public policy of the Portuguese State.'

In Japan, public policy is often read together with 'good morals'. Article 45 paragraph 2 of the Japanese Arbitration Law states that Article 45 paragraph 1 relating to arbitral awards having the same effect as judgments will not apply if 'the content of the arbitral award would be contrary to the public policy or good morals of Japan'.[141] Similarly, Article 235(2) of the UAE Civil Procedure Code stipulates[142]: 'Execution may not be ordered unless the following was verified:...(e) It... does not include any violation of public policy or *bonos mores* as understood in the UAE.' Article 49 paragraph 1 of Taiwan's Arbitration Law also enumerates the above approach[143]: which reads as 'The court shall issue a dismissal with respect to an application submitted by a party for recognition of a foreign arbitral award,... Where the recognition or enforcement of the arbitral award is contrary to the public order or good morals' of Taiwan'.

Article 55 of the Swedish Arbitration Law provides[144]: 'Recognition and enforcement of a foreign award shall also be refused where a court finds:... (2) that it would be clearly incompatible with the basic principles of the Swedish legal system to recognize and enforce the award.' Another example is Article 39 paragraph 2 of

---

[137]See the website of the Government of France, http://www.legifrance.gouv.fr/affichCode.do?cidTexte=LEGITEXT000006070716&dateTexte=20050514(accessed 20 February 2021)

[138]*Intrafor Cofor v Gagnant*, 1985 Rev. Arb. 299, 12 March 1985.

[139]Helena Hsi-Chia Chen, *supra* 63, 11–26.

[140]Portuguese Law on Voluntary Arbitration, Law No. 63/2011 of 14 December 2012 (effective from 14 March 2012).

[141]Japanese Arbitration Law, Law No. 138 of 2003 (promulgated on 1 August 2003, effective from 1 March 2004).

[142]The UAE Civil Procedure Code, Federal Law No. 11 of 1992.

[143]Revision dated 2 December 2015. English translation from the Taiwan Laws & Regulations Database, http://law.moj.gov.tw/Eng/LawClass/LawAll.aspx?PCode=I0020001, accessed 20 February 2021.

[144]Swedish Arbitration Law (SFS 1999:116).

Korean Arbitration Law, which, by reference to Article 217 of Korean Civil Procedure Law, provides that in terms of an arbitral award not subject to the New York Convention, one of the conditions to recognise such award is that the award 'does not violate good morals and other social order of the Republic of Korea'.[145]

4.6.2 *Public Policy—The Praxis: Jurisprudential Insights*

The following narrative attempts to understand the articulation of public policy within the jurisprudence of Contracting States to the New York Convention. The research would attempt to identify through the jurisprudence if public policy was explained with domestic content or was it laced with an international law perspective. To present the context, the narrative begins with a reference to the Model Law.

The notion of "public policy" was introduced into the Model Law in Articles 34 and 36. The similarities between the New York Convention and the Model Law are obvious. However, it took some debate to work out the content of Articles 34 and 36 of the Model Law as documented in the *travaux preparatoires*.[146] The Commission stated:

> It is understood that the term "public policy" which was used in the 1958 New York Convention and many other treaties, covered fundamental principles of law and justice in substantive as well as procedural respects. Thus, instances such as corruption, bribery or fraud and similar serious cases would constitute a ground for setting aside. It was noted, in that connection, that the wording "the award is in conflict with the public policy of this State" was not to be intended as excluding instances or events in relation to the manner in which an award was arrived at.[147]

4.6.2.1 Jurisprudential Insights

A number of Asian countries, subscribing to the New York Convention and the UNCITRAL Model Law have adopted a narrow view of the public policy within their arbitration laws, thus giving limited scope for the judicial forums to initiate a review of the arbitral award.[148]

In *PT Asuransi Jasa Indonesia (Persero) v Dexia Bank SA,*[149] the Singapore Court of Appeal reflected upon the reasons for favouring this narrow approach in the

[145] Article 217 of Korean Civil Procedure Law, Act No. 10373 (revision dated 23 July 2010) provides: 'A final and conclusive judgment by a foreign court shall be acknowledged to be valid, only upon the entire fulfillment of the following requirements:... 3. That such judgment does not violate good morals and other social order of the Republic of Korea.' In contrast, Art. 39 para. 1 of Korea's Arbitration Law expressly stipulates that recognition and enforcement of arbitral awards which are subject to the New York Convention are governed by the New York Convention.

[146] Holzmann and Neuhaus [32].

[147] Ibid., 914.

[148] Greenberg et al., *supra* 4, 462.

[149] *PT Asuransi Jasa Indonesia (Persero) v Dexia Bank SA*, [2006] 1 SLR 507 [59].

following words—Although the concept of public policy of the State is not defined in the Singapore International Arbitration Act or the Model Law, the general consensus of judicial and expert opinion is that public policy under the act encompasses a narrow scope. "In our view, it should only operate in instances where the upholding of an arbitral award would 'shock the conscience'... or is 'clearly injurious to the public good or...wholly offensive to the ordinary, reasonable and fully informed member of the public'...or where it violates the forum's most basic notion of morality and justice..."

A perusal of court decisions of other Asia-Pacific jurisdictions indicates that often courts have adopted a parochial view when it comes to the application of the public policy exception under Article V(2)'(b). As a case on point, in *Hebei Import & Export Corp v Polytek Engineering Co Ltd (No.2),*[150] the Hong Kong Court opined that for the public policy exception to come into the play it is imperative to prove there was substantial injustice which as a result has the potential to shock the conscience of the enforcement court. In addition to the abovementioned, in a situation where the court relies upon inadmissible evidence it can also be said that it is 'repugnant to fairness and justice'[151] and violates the basic notions of public policy. In the words of the District Court of Yokohama in Japan for the application of public policy exemption the alleged contravention 'should be such that it foul of basic principles or rules of the Japanese judicial order'.[152]

Similarly, in the case of *J.J.Agro Industries (P) Ltd v Texuna International Ltd.,*[153] the Hong Kong High Court held that if the affidavit of evidence submitted before it by Respondent's witness was obtained by kidnapping and putting the witness under distress then it would be clearly contrary to the public policy of Hong Kong if the court were to enforce the award.

Another feature of the public provisions finding place in the national legislations with much detail is that there have been different standards of public policy understandings with regard to setting aside proceedings and enforcement proceedings. For example, the Malaysian Arbitration Act 2005 and the Singapore International Arbitration Act (Original Enactment: Act 23 of 1994, Revised Edition 2002) are particular because their setting aside provisions expressly include fraud and corruption as forming part of public policy but no such elaboration of public policy is contained within the law on enforcement of arbitral awards.

Singapore's courts have been known for their persistent non-interventionist and pro-arbitration stance which has been reaffirmed in few recent judgments.[154] However, in 2010, in what was perceived as a deviation from the above position, the

---

[150] *Hebei Import & Export Corp v Polytek Engineering Co Ltd (No.2),* [1998] 1 HKC 192; and A v R [2009] HKCU 632 (High Court), 30 April 2009, [23].

[151] Greenberg et al., *supra* 4, 464.

[152] *Zhong Guo Hua Gong Jian Sh Quig Dao Gong v Color Chemical Industry KK,* (Dist. Court Yokohama), 25 August 1999, (2002).

[153] J. J. Agro Industries (P) Ltd v Texuna International Ltd. (1992).

[154] Megans and Stauber [33], 226.

High Court for the first time set aside an award in *AJT v AJU*[155] which subsequently was reversed on appeal.[156] The court did give some guidance in relation to setting aside an award. It can only apply to findings of law made by the tribunal to the exclusion of finding of facts and in this case the finding that the agreement was illegal is a factual one.[157]

That said, the object has always been to give effect to the Model Law as noted above. However, the application of the natural justice principle shows that there is no recognition of the no evidence rule as being part of the natural justice principle. The court in *Kempinski Hotels SA v PT Prima International Development*[158] stated:

> As is well known, the concept of natural justice comprises two rules. The first is that the adjudicator must be disinterested and unbiased and the second is that the parties must be given adequate notice and opportunity to be heard.[159]

Later in *TMM Division Maritima SA de CV v Pacific Richfield Marine Pte Ltd.*[160] Justice Chan confirmed that the "no evidence rule" has not yet been accepted in Singapore as part of the rules of natural justice.[161] However he observed that in line with international interpretations the real task for the court is to separate the genuine challenge from those which are in fact appeals on the merits of the case.[162] Furthermore, the application of public policy exception either in the case of award vacating processes or in the context of enforcement requires the establishment of a "…real and substantial concern should be demonstrably clear on the face of the record without the need to pore over thousands of pages of facts and submissions."[163]

Justice Chan's articulation, in *PT Asuransi Jasa Indonesia (Persero) v Dexia Bank SA*[164] seems to be the best possible approximation of what amounts to a breach of public policy. The following extract from the decision articulates the judicial angst that could trigger an order of breach of public policy. He opined,

> [a breach of public policy] should only operate in instances where the upholding of an arbitral award would "shock the conscience", or is "clearly injurious to the public good or … wholly offensive to the ordinary reasonable and fully informed member of the public," or where it violates the forum's most basic notion of morality and justice … this would be consistent with the concept of public policy that can be ascertained from the preparatory materials to the Model Law.[165]

---

155 *AJT v AJU*, [2010] 4 SLR 649.

156 Ibid. 739.

157 Nicholas Poon, *supra* 128, at 186.

158 *Kempinski Hotels SA v PT Prima International Development*, [2011] 4 SLR 633.

159 Ibid. [65].

160 TMM Division Maritima SA de CV v Pacific Richfield Marine Pte Ltd., [2013] SGHC 186.

161 Ibid. [119–120].

162 *TMM Division Maritima SA, supra* 160, [2].

163 Ibid. [125].

164 *PT Asuransi Jasa Indonesia (Persero), supra* 149.

165 Ibid. [59].

Singapore's courts emphasise on the adherence t a balance between finality and interference. The Court in *CRW Joint Operation v PT Perusahaan Gas Negara (Persero) TBK*[166] noted,

> This policy of minimal curial intervention by respecting finality in the arbitral process acknowledges the primacy which ought to be given to the dispute resolution mechanism that the parties have expressly chosen.[167]

However at the same time minimal intervention does not equate to no intervention at all.[168]

The court did make what appears to be a less than pro-arbitration statement regarding annulment of an award where one or more of the grounds specified in Art 34(2) of the Model Law potentially apply. The court noted that the existence of any of these grounds is "sufficiently serious [for] annulment of the award [to] be virtually automatic."[169] It can therefore be assumed, given Singapore's reputation as an arbitration-friendly jurisdiction, that a breach must be serious and unfair and not merely a technical breach of the rules of natural justice. Affirmation of this assumption is found in *Soh Beng Tee & Co. Pty Ltd v Fairmont Development Pty Ltd*[170] where the rationale for minimal interference was summarized,

> Curial intervention is underpinned by two principal considerations. First, there is a need to recognise the autonomy of the arbitral process by encouraging finality...Second, having opted for arbitration, parties must have acknowledged and accepted the attendant risks of having only a very limited right of recourse to the courts.[171]

Hong Kong's courts have expressed similar articulation regarding breaches that could possibly entail an application of the public policy exception. The ratio in *Hebei Import & Export Corp v Polytek Engineering Co Ltd*[172] has been considered to be the leading authority on which subsequent decisions are based. Justice Bokhary PJ stated that:

> before a Convention jurisdiction can ... refuse enforcement of a Convention award on public policy grounds, the award must be so fundamentally offensive to that jurisdiction's notions of justice that, despite its being a party to the Convention, it cannot reasonably be expected to overlook the objection.[173]

Notably therefore Bokhary J and Sir Anthony Mason expressed the correct approach to Article V(2)(b),

---

[166] *CRW Joint Operation v PT Perusahaan Gas Negara (Persero) TBK*, [2011] SGCA 33.

[167] Ibid. [25].

[168] Nicholas Poon, *supra* 128, 188.

[169] *CRW Joint Operation*, *supra* 166, 97.

[170] *Soh Beng Tee & Co. Pty Ltd v Fairmont Development Pty Ltd*, [2007] 3 SLR(R) 86.

[171] Ibid., 65.

[172] *Hebei Import & Export Corp*, *supra* 150.

[173] Ibid., [30].

> In my view, there must be compelling reasons before enforcement of a Convention award can be refused on public policy grounds…[the reasons do not need to be extreme] … But the reasons must go beyond the minimum which would justify setting aside a domestic judgment or award.[174]

Simply put due to concerns of international comity and predictability in global commerce public policy should not be judged on domestic standards only and hence a refusal to enforce an award due to public policy must be the exception rather than the rule. Sir Anthony Mason echoed the concern,

> … the object of the Convention was to encourage the recognition and enforcement of commercial arbitration agreements in international contracts and to unify the standards by which agreements to arbitrate are observed and arbitral awards are enforced.[175]

This approach totally ignores the object of the Convention which is an international instrument and not a domestic legislation hence ethnocentric interpretation is simply not in line with the expectations of the drafters of the instrument.

In Hong Kong, the jurisprudence on international arbitration demonstrates a reassurance to the disputant parties that public policy exception could be a hindrance to enforcement of an award only where it would be contrary to fundamental concepts of morality and fairness of Hong Kong.[176]

However the mandate of uniformity and harmonisation of international arbitration outcomes has not always been heard or applied. As an example, in *Corvetina Technology Ltd v Clough Engineering Ltd*[177] wherein the court stated,

> The very point of provisions such as s 8(7)(b) is to preserve to the court in which enforcement is sought, the right to apply its own standards of public policy in respect of the award. But I do not think that it can be said that the court should forfeit the exercise of the discretion, which is expressly referred to it, simply because of some "signal" that this might send to people who engage in arbitrations under the Act. There is, as the cases have recognised, a balancing consideration. On the one hand, it is necessary to ensure that the mechanism for enforcement of international arbitral awards under the New York Convention is not frustrated. But, on the other hand, it is necessary for the court to be master of its own processes and to apply its own public policy.[178]

4.7 Ensuring Uniformity Within the Application of the Public Policy Exception

Much has been said about the public policy exemption in enforcing or setting aside arbitral awards as not only noted in the New York Convention but also in the Model

[174] *Hebei Import & Export Corp*, *supra* 150, 11.

[175] Ibid., 41.

[176] Smith [34], 163.

[177] *Corvetina Technology Ltd v Clough Engineering Ltd,* (2004) 183 FLR 317.

[178] Ibid., 18.

Law. It is only a reiteration that a uniform application and understanding of public policy is most desirable as arbitration is as close as it gets to an international dispute resolution process. It is not true to argue that there is an overuse of the NYC and therefore "perceived uncertainty and inconsistency concerning the interpretation and application of public policy by State courts has encouraged losing parties to rely on public policy to resist, or at least delay, enforcement."[179]

Given that the arbitral jurisprudence from jurisdictions that have adapted the UNCITRAL Model Law, the judiciary should continue to conscientiously support and promote arbitration".[180] Foster J in *Traxys Europe SA v Balaji Coke Industry Pvt Ltd and Another (No 2)*[181] succinctly stated the position:

> [Public policy] should not be used to give effect to parochial and idiosyncratic tendencies of the courts of the enforcement state. This view is consistent with the language of s 8(7), the terms of s 8(7A), the text of Art V(2) of the Convention, the fundamental objects of the Convention and the objects of the IAA. This approach also ensures that due respect is given to Convention-based awards as an aspect of international comity in our interconnected and globalised world which, after all, are the product of freely negotiated arbitration agreements entered into between relatively sophisticated parties.[182]

However it has also been argued that enforcement of awards is going "two steps forward and one step back" as not all Convention countries are equal in their approach.[183] However, on a positive note, case law indicates first that a pro-arbitration and pro-international approach has been established internationally and secondly a coherent and consistent application of public policy has been applied by courts. Although, it can be argued that the legal interpretation of 'public policy' is shrouded with uncertainty, internationally there is substantial consensus on the fundamentals of public policy in Article V(2)(b) of the New York Convention as is well illustrated from the drafting process of international conventions, case law and discussions amongst scholars.[184] The above detailed discussion regarding public policy can be therefore summed up as below[185]:

(1) The international consensus is that 'public policy' as stipulated in Article V(2)(b) of the New York Convention is the public policy of the 'enforcement State'.
(2) However, another international consensus is that 'public policy' as stipulated in Article V(2)(b) of the New York Convention is still limited by the requirement of 'internationality'.
(3) The enforcement courts may jointly consider the merits of the parties' claims and the arbitral tribunal's decisions rather than confining to the content of remedies granted by the arbitral tribunal.

---

179 ILA Final Report, *supra* 79, 254.

180 Warren [35], 7.

181 *Traxys Europe SA v Balaji Coke Industry Pvt Ltd* (No 2) [2012] FCA 27.

182 Ibid. [105].

183 Megans and Stauber, *supra* 154, 243.

184 Helena Hsi-Chia Chen, *supra* 63, 187–192.

185 Ibid.

(4) 'Public policy' as stipulated in Article V(2)(b) of the New York Convention applies in exceptional circumstances only.
(5) With respect to procedural violations, applying Article V(1)(b) or (d) of the New York Convention should suffice, rather than interpreting 'public policy' in Article V(2)(b) as including 'procedural public policy'.

The next chapter continues the discussion on public policy, and tries to examine the jurisprudence specifically from the jurisdictions of South Asia, which have adopted a vacillating posture on this exception—the pendulum oscillating between a narrow construction of the exception, under the influence of a pro-arbitration position, and a broad-based construction allowing for judicial intervention. Both these positions were largely necessitated by local concerns, thus keeping open the issue of contouring public policy alive.

References

1. Blackaby, N., Partasides, C., Redfern, A., & Hunter, M. (2015). In *Redfern and hunter on international arbitration*, OUP.
2. Pieth, M. (2011). Contractual freedom v public policy considerations in arbitration. In A. Buchler & N. Muller-Chen (Eds.), *Private Law, national—global—comparative, Festschrift fur Ingeborg Schwenzer* zum 60 (Vol. 1, pp. 1375), Geburtstag. Stampfli Verlag Bern.
3. Rosen, J. A. (1993) Arbitration under private international law: The doctrines of separability and competence de la competence. *Fordham International Law Review, 17*(3), 598.
4. Mattli, W. (2001). Private justice in a global economy: From litigation to arbitration. *International Organization, 55*(4), 919.
5. Greenberg, S., Kee, C., Romesh Weeramantry, J. (2011). In *International commercial arbitration—An Asia-Pacific perspective*, CUP.
6. Wei, E. T. S. (2009). Why egregious errors of law may yet justify a refusal of enforcement under the new york convention. *Singapore Journal of Legal Studies, 592*, 595.
7. van den Berg, A. J. (1981). In *The New York arbitration convention of 1958: Towards a uniform judicial interpretation* (Vol. 1, pp. 358), Kluwer Law.
8. Born, G. B. (2009). In *International commercial arbitration* (Vol. 2, pp. 2828), Kluwer Law International.
9. Dar, W.A. (2015). Understanding public policy as an exception to the enforcement of foreign arbitral awards. *European Journal of Comparative Law and Governance*, 316–350.
10. Fentiman, R. (2010). In *International commercial litigation* (Vol. 1, pp. 114), OUP.
11. Silberman Abella, R. (1989). Public policy and the judicial role. *McGill Law Journal, 34*, 1021–1022.
12. Abella, R. S. (1986). Public policy and Canada's judges: The impact of the charter of rights and freedoms. *Law Society Gazette, 20*, 217.
13. Williams, J. G. (2005). Importance of public policy considerations in judicial decision-making. *International Legal Practice*, 25, 134.
14. Paulsson, J. (1996). The New York convention in international practice: Problems of assimilation. In M. Blessing (Ed.), *The New York convention of 1958: A collection of reports and materials delivered at the ASA conference held in Zurich on 2 February 1996* (ASA Special Series No 9), (Vol. 100, pp. 113).
15. Born, G. B. (2021). International commercial arbitration, (3rd edn., pp. 3691–4098), Kluwer Law International.

16. Chen, H. H.-C. (2017). In *Predictability of 'Public Policy' in article V of the New York convention under mainland China's judicial practice* (pp. 11–26), Kluwer Law International.
17. Hanotiau, B., Caprasse, O. (2008). Public policy in international commercial arbitration. In E. Gaillard, & D. Di Pietro (Eds.), *Enforcement of arbitration agreements and international arbitral awards* (Vol. 1, pp. 787), London.
18. Gaillard, E., & Savage, J. (Eds.).(1999). *Fouchard, gaillard, goldman on international commercial arbitration,* (pp. 996–997), Kluwer.
19. French, R. (2016). Arbitration and public policy. *Asia Pacific Law Review, 24*(1), 1.
20. Wolff, R. (Ed.) (2012). *The New York convention: Convention on the recognition and enforcement of foreign arbitral awards of 10 June 1958–Commentary.* (Vol. 1, pp. 406), Beck, Hart & Nomos.
21. Sheppard, A. (2003) Interim ILA report on public policy as a bar to enforcement of international arbitral awards. *Arbitration International, 19*(2), 217.
22. Gibson, C. S. (2009). Arbitration civilization and public policy: Seeking counterpoise between arbitral autonomy and the public policy defence in view of foreign mandatory public law. *Penn State Law Review, 113*(4), 1227.
23. Nariman, F. (2011). Ten steps to salvage arbitration in India: The first LGIA-India arbitration lecture. *Arbitration International, 27*(2), 115–128.
24. Megens, P., & Cubitt, B. (2009). Meeting disputants' needs in the current climate: What has gone wrong with arbitration and how can we repair it?"*The Arbitrator and Mediator, 28,* 115.
25. Jones, D. (2011). In *Commercial arbitration in Australia,* (Vol. 1, pp. 450), Thompson Reuters Australia.
26. Binder, P. (2010). In *International commercial arbitration and conciliation in UNCITRAL model law jurisdictions* , (Vol. 1, pp. 402), London:Sweet and Maxwell.
27. Bantekas, I., Ortolani, P., Ali, S., Gomez, M., & Polkinghorne, M. (2020). In *UNCITRAL model law on international commercial arbitration: A commentary* (CUP:2020), (Vol.1, pp. 524).
28. Born, G. B. (2014). In *International commercial arbitration* (Vol. 1, 2nd ed., pp. 3657), Kluwer Law International.
29. Lalive, P. (1987). Transnational (or Truly International) public policy and international arbitration. In P. Sanders (Ed.), *Comparative arbitration practice and public policy in arbitration* (Vol. 1, pp. 257), Kluwer Law International.
30. van den Berg, A. J. (2005). Why are some awards not enforceable?. In A. J. van den Berg (Ed.), *New horizons in international commercial arbitration and beyond* (Vol. 1, pp. 309), Kluwer Law International.
31. Poon, N. (2012). Striking a balance between public policy and arbitration policy in international commercial arbitration: AJU v. AJT. *Singapore Journal of Legal Studies, 185,* 189.
32. Holzmann, H., & Neuhaus, J. (1995) *A guide to the UNCITRAL model law on international commercial arbitration: Legislative history and commentary, 1,* 911 Kluwer Law.
33. Megans, P., & Stauber, A. (2015). Recent trends in the enforcement of awards in the South-East Asian region. *International Trade and Business Law Review, 18* , 204.
34. Smith, J. (2014). The enforcement of arbitral awards in the Asia-Pacific region: A comparative study of the recent cases. *Building and Construction Law, 30,* 148.
35. Warren, M. (2012). The evolving 'Australian' brand of arbitration. *Australian Construction Law Newsletter, 145,* 6.

Chapter 5
The Law on the Public Policy Exception in International Arbitration—State Practice in South Asia

Overview
Definitional clarity on the boundaries of the public policy exception in the context of international arbitration has been limited, and the exception therefore continues to be explained in a varied manner by national courts as they rely on domestic policies. It is therefore important to understand how various jurisdictions have approached this issue in order to understand the underlying problem and also importance of this exception. Curiously enough, within South Asian jurisdictions there are some interesting, and often self-contradicting, content/policy reasons that have been attributed to this exception in the context of enforcement of arbitral awards. This chapter proposes to parse the legal regime—normative and jurisprudential—on the articulation of this important ground for refusing recognition and enforcement to a foreign arbitral award within the jurisdictions of India, Bangladesh, Sri Lanka, Pakistan and Nepal.

5.1 Public Policy Exception—Theorization—Instances of Normative Delimitation Through Legislative Activity

While there is no strict definitional activity attached to this concept, public policy has nevertheless had an all-embracing presence and approval that is hinged upon each country's national needs. Notable features of this protean concept, found in many jurisdictions, include public good and public interest, and notions of justice. As explained by the court in *Parsons and Whitemore Overseas Co. v Societe Generale de L'Industrie du Papier*,[1] enforcement of a foreign award may be refused for reasons related to public policy only if such enforcement impinged upon the State's most basic notions of morality and justice.

[1] *Parsons and Whitemore Overseas Co. v Societe Generale de L'Industrie du Papier*, 508 F. 2d 969 (2nd Cir. 1974). See, generally, Greenberg et al. [1]; Mattli [2].

B. Zeller et al., *Enforcement of Foreign Arbitral Awards and the Public Policy Exception*,
https://doi.org/10.1007/978-981-16-2634-0_5

Staying with the notion of diversity in the conception of the public policy exception within the various jurisdictions, diversity seems to be further infused with different normative content made applicable for domestic and international arbitrations. While international public policy is a part of the country's Private International Law, the content of domestic public policy is located within the jurisdiction's private law applicable to the enforcement of contracts and arbitration. In a dispute involving a challenge to enforcement of a foreign arbitral award for concerns related to public policy, the courts may draw inspiration from comparative law experiences in deploying public policy considerations, while in the context of domestic arbitral awards, references to comparative law and practice are not necessary.

Interestingly, this tendency to have dual versions of the public policy construct is prevalent within the statutory law on arbitration as well as in the jurisprudence on the same, within South Asian jurisdictions, to which this chapter will presently revert to. However, there are examples of similar legal provisions in jurisdictions that have robust arbitration regimes like France, where two distinct public policy principles exist—*ordre public interne* and *ordre public international*. Judicial opinion in a few jurisdictions evidences preference for international public policy over the wider domestic public policy in cases involving foreign elements.[2]

Scholarship on international arbitration suggested hinging the standards of public policy on international standards, rather than extrapolating its meaning in domestic circumstances to international arbitration.[3] Recalling the scholarly statement of Fouchard et al.,

> The provision certainly refers to international public policy, and not domestic public policy. Not every breach of a mandatory rule of the host country could justify refusing recognition or enforcement of a foreign award. Such refusal is only justified where the award contravenes principles which are considered in the host country as reflecting its fundamental convictions, or as having an absolute, universal value.[4]

It needs to be remembered—as noted in previous chapters—that the New York Convention[5] and the UNCITRAL Model Law[6] have steered a structured legal regime for international arbitration towards an effective and efficient management of the regulatory and the business needs. The New York Convention, 1958, with 159 signatories at the last count[7] stated

---

[2] *Scherk v Alberto-Culver Co.* 417 US 506 (1974); Also in *Renusagar Power Electric Co. v General Electric* AIR 1994 SC 860, the court had held that public policy must be construed to mean the doctrine of public policy as applied by the courts in which the foreign award is sought to be enforced.

[3] See generally, Hanotiau and Caprasse [3].

[4] Gaillard and Savage [4], [1711] [1712].

[5] Convention on the Enforcement of Foreign Arbitral Awards, 1958, https://www.newyorkconvention.org/english, accessed 23/02/2021 ("New York Convention").

[6] UNCITRAL Model Law on International Commercial Arbitration (amended in 2006). https://uncitral.un.org/sites/uncitral.un.org/files/media-documents/uncitral/en/19-09955_e_ebook.pdf, accessed 23/02/2021. ("Model Law").

[7] The UNCITRAL database on the New York Convention reported that there are 166 signatories https://uncitral.un.org/en/texts/arbitration/conventions/foreign_arbitral_awards/status2, accessed 23/02/2021.

> Each Contracting State shall recognize arbitral awards as binding and enforce them in accordance with the rules of procedure of the territory where the award is relied upon, under the conditions laid down in the following articles. There shall not be imposed substantially more onerous conditions or higher fees or charges on the recognition or enforcement of arbitral awards to which this Convention applies than are imposed on the recognition or enforcement of domestic arbitral awards.[8]

Recognition and enforcement *may* (emphasis supplied by the authors) be refused, if the court hearing an enforcement application finds that such enforcement is against the public policy; while there is no express statement on the allocation of burden of proof, jurisprudence points out that the party opposing recognition and enforcement have the onus to prove the grounds for denying the enforcement.[9]

The UNCITRAL Model Law specified that arbitral awards, irrespective of their country of origin, be recognized as binding and enforceable subject to the provisions of Articles 35 and 36[10] except

> [...]
>
> *(b)* if the court finds that:
>
> (i) the subject-matter of the dispute is not capable of settlement by arbitration under the law of this State; or
>
> (ii) the recognition or enforcement of the award would be contrary to the public policy of this State.[11]

However, neither did the Convention nor the Model Law, explicitly, articulated upon the content of public policy that could result in a refusal of enforcement of a foreign arbitral award. State parties could therefore interpret it within their legal systems and apply such understanding to international commercial arbitration.

The Report submitted to the 18th Session of the UNCITRAL[12] however, included a lucid expression on public policy in the context of international arbitration

> [..] It was understood that the term "public policy", which was used in the 1958 New York Convention and many other treaties, covered fundamental principles of law and justice in substantive as well as procedural respects. Thus instances such as corruption, bribery and fraud and similar serious cases would constitute a ground for setting aside an award.[13]

The report reiterated that the Convention itself did not consider the prospect of arbitral awards set aside for reasons of arbitrability or public policy as having an *erga omnes* impact.[14]

---

[8]Article III of the New York Convention on Recognition and Enforcement of Foreign Arbitral Awards, 1958, ("New York Convention").

[9]See, for instance, *Licensee v Licensor*, Düsseldorf Court of Appeal (Germany), 21 July 2004, XXXII Yrbk Com. Arb. 315 (2007); *Gater Assets Ltd v Nak Naftogaz Ukrainiy*, Court of Appeal (England and Wales), 17 October 2007, [2007] EWCA Civ 988.

[10]Ibid., Article 35(1).

[11]Ibid., Article 36(1)(b).

[12]UNCITRAL Report on the work of its 18th session, UN Doc: A/40/17, June 3–21, 1985, ("UNCITRAL Report") https://undocs.org/en/a/40/17(supp), accessed 26/03/2021.

[13]Ibid., [297].

[14]Ibid., [291].

The OECD attempted at arranging the doctrinal and the jurisprudential developments concerning public policy under two broadly construed constructs—a maximalist approach and a minimalist approach.[15] The maximalist approach relates to the practice of national courts engaging in a compendious scrutiny of the award, irrespective of the nature of the application to the court—challenge or enforcement. It entails a detailed perusal of the dispute and the evidence appraised by the tribunal and is founded upon the preponderant idea of risk avoidance. In *Mitsubishi Motors Corp. v Soler Chrysler-Plymouth, Inc.*,[16] the court opined that the public policy construct could be the methodology for revisiting the award for ensuring compliance with the law and policy of the land and ensuring that there is nothing in the award that is against the law of enforcing country. The minimalist approach desists from extensive parsing of the case and the evidence, and, as per the OECD Report, courts shall only (emphasis supplied by the authors) overturn awards where there is a fundamental breach of public policy.[17]

One of the earliest and often quoted judicial statements on public policy is from the English case of *Holman v Johnson*.[18] Lord Mansfield, speaking for the court, observed

> the principle of public policy is this. *Ex Dolo malo moritur non actio.* No court will lend its aid to a man who founds his cause of action on an illegal or an immoral act.[19]

While the *Holman* ratio was an interesting observation, the decision in *Egerton v Brownlaw*[20] gave further guidance on the possible contours of public policy. The court explained that the concept requires that members of a legal community should desist from acting for causes that bear a propensity to be pernicious to the public or against public good. While this seems to be a highly inclusive statement, it does offer a level of guidance in understanding public policy—to consider public policy in terms of public good.

---

[15] OECD Hearings—Arbitration and Competition 2010 http://www.oecd.org/competition/abuse/49294392.pdf, accessed 01/02/2021.

[16] *Mitsubishi Motors Corp. v Soler Chrysler-Plymouth, Inc.* 723 F.2d 155 (1983), cert. granted, 105 S. Ct.291 (1984).

[17] OECD Report, *supra* 15, 14.

[18] *Holman v Johnson*, (1775) Cowp, 341, https://www.trans-lex.org/301700/_/holmann-v-johnson-%5B1775%5D-98-engl-rep-1120-/, accessed 26/02/2021; see, generally, John Tarlinton, *International commercial arbitration and public policy: with principal reference to the laws of Australia, France, Switzerland, the United Kingdom and the United States* (doctoral thesis) http://epress.lib.uts.edu.au/research/handle/2100/624, accessed on 03/08/2020.

[19] Ibid., 344.

[20] *Egerton v Brownlow* (1853) 4 HLC 1.

5.2 Derivations from the Jurisprudence of National Courts—A Shift Towards Localization in International Public Policy

An arbitral award is final and binding, within the legal regime of its origin and in jurisdictions that hear applications for enforcement; therefore, a review on merits is not possible, except that merits maybe a part of the conception of public policy and *ultra petita.*

In *Deutsche Schachtbau-und Tiefbohrges v Ras Al Khaimah National Oil Co. and Shell International Petroleum Co. Ltd.,*[21] the court articulated the scope of public policy as below:

> It has to be shown that there is some element of illegality or that the enforcement would be clearly injurious to public good or, possibly, that enforcement would be wholly offensive to ordinary reasonably and fully informed member of the public on whose behalf the powers of the State are being exercised.[22]

In *Soleimany v Soleimany,*[23] the English court refused to enforce an award on grounds of public policy, for reasons that the contract involved tax evasion as per Iranian law.

In *Allsop Automatic Inc. v Tecnoski snc,*[24] the Court of Appeal in Milan sketched public policy as a collection of pervasive principles common to jurisdictions that share similar legal systems and its content is oriented towards guarding the fundamental human freedoms as specified in international declarations or Conventions.

It is pertinent to recall the words of Lauterpacht J in the *Case Concerning application of the Convention of 1902 Governing the Guardianship of Infants* (The Netherlands v. Sweden).[25] He observed—"the recognition of the part of *odre public* must be regarded as the general principle of the private international law."[26]

The French Law on Arbitration, contained in Book II of *Nouveau Code de Procedure Civile* (Code of Civil Procedure), specified that the execution of arbitral awards may be refused if such award was found antithetical to international public policy (*odre public international*).[27]

---

[21] *Deutsche Schachtbau-und Tiefbohrges v Ras Al Khaimah National Oil Co. and Shell International Petroleum Co. Ltd*, [1987] 3 WLR 1023.

[22] Ibid., 1035.

[23] *Soleimany v Soleimany* [1998] APP.L.R. 02/19.

[24] Italy No. 143, *Allsop Automatic Inc. v Tecnoski snc*, Corte di Appello [Court of Appeal], Milan, Not Indicated, 4 December 1992', in Van den Berg [5].

[25] Application of the Convention of 1902 Governing the Guardianship of Infants (Netherlands v. Sweden) https://www.icj-cij.org/en/case/33, accessed 20/01/2021.

[26] Ibid., 92. separate opinion of Judge H Lauterpacht https://www.icj-cij.org/public/files/case-related/33/033-19581128-JUD-01-02-EN.pdf, accessed 20/01/2021.

[27] Article 1514—An arbitral award shall be recognized or enforced in France if the party relying on it can prove its existence and if such recognition or enforcement is not manifestly contrary to international public policy https://www.iaa-network.com/wp-content/uploads/2016/10/French-Arbitration-Law.pdf, accessed 21/01/2021.

The content of international public policy embraces the primordial values derived from natural law and universal justice, *jus cogens* in the law of nations, basic human rights and the beliefs that form morality. For example, the Canadian court in *Attorney General for Canada v SD Myers Inc.*[28] held that the conclusions of an arbitral tribunal could be contrary to public policy if such conclusions were "patently unreasonable," "clearly irrational" and "totally lacking in reality." Having found no trace of such concern, the court concluded that no aspect of the tribunal's decisions subject to judicial review "is contrary to the public policy of Canada."[29]

The International Law Association's Committee on international commercial arbitration made the following recommendation on public policy.

> *Recommendation 1(d)*
>
> The international public policy of any State includes: (i) fundamental principles, pertaining to justice or morality, that the State wishes to protect even when it is not directly concerned; (ii) rules designed to serve the essential political, social or economic interests of the State, these being known as "lois de police" or "public policy rules"; and (iii) the duty of the State to respect its obligations towards other States or international organisations.[30]

5.2.1 *More Theorization on Public Policy—The Arena of Local Interpretations*

Unusual though, but the history of theorization on public policy also points to jurisdictions that seem less enamoured with international considerations, and on rare occasions when there was a dalliance towards international jurisprudence, the inspiration did not come across in a consistent manner.[31] Notions of public interest, public morality and public security, all understood in terms of sovereign territorial definition, have been infused into public policy articulation.[32] Early examples of such localized interpretations are evident within the jurisprudence of the English courts. In *Mitchel v Reynolds*,[33] the court deployed the concept of public policy to invalidate agreements that resulted in restraint of trade. The court opined that contracting to acquire the right to commercial activity to the exclusion of every other similar business across England is in violation of public policy, "because it is a monopoly, and

[28] *Attorney General for Canada v SD Myers Inc.*, 2004 FC 38.

[29] Ibid., [56]. https://reports.fja.gc.ca/fja-cmf/j/fr/item/330850/index.do, accessed 27/03/2021.

[30] International Law Association, Final Report on Public Policy as a bar to the Enforcement of International Arbitral Awards, Report of the Committee on International Commercial Arbitration, 2002. https://www.academia.edu/18312524/ILA_FINAL_REPORT_ON_PUBLIC_POLICY_AS_A_BAR_TO_ENFORCEMENT_OF_INTERNATIONAL_ARBITRAL_AWARDS_NEW_DELHI_2002_, accessed 27/03/2021.

[31] See, generally, Moses [6].

[32] See, generally, Ghodoosi [7]; Maniruzzaman and Chisti [8].

[33] *Mitchel v Reynolds*, (1711) 24 Eng. Rep. 347 (Q.B.). http://www.commonlii.org/uk/cases/EngR/1711/38.pdf, accessed 29/03/2021.

against the policy of common law [..]."[34] Thus, public policy seemed to be deployed by courts to address concerns arising from local contractual causes, as well as a methodology to prevent "violations of communal values and mores."[35]

The jurisprudence from the Indian courts vouches for the assertion that they have denied enforcement of a foreign award on reasons of public policy essentially because of concerns with an arbitrator's interpretation or for support of Indian law.[36] Further, courts have characterized foreign awards that seemed inconsistent with *their* (emphasis supplied by the authors) understanding of the Indian law, as "patently illegal" and therefore against public policy.[37] These have, in effect, been decisions on the merits, disguised as violations of public policy.[38]

In more recent times, India's Parliament has amended its Arbitration Act in ways that positively impact enforcement of foreign arbitral awards,[39] and its courts have delivered several pro-arbitration decisions.[40] It helped restore a distinction between treatment of foreign and domestic arbitration awards and make it less likely for Indian courts to negate the execution of a foreign award for reasons of "patent illegality."[41] The discussion that follows in the next few pages would attempt to map this feature within India's tryst with public policy in international arbitration.

5.3 South Asian Jurisdictions and International Arbitration—Is the Public Policy Exception Leading to Enforcement Concerns?

The law on arbitration in the South Asian region is an interesting mix of colonial law(s) that persist to this day, and attempts, albeit tentative in some jurisdictions, towards law reform based on international law. The discussion in this part would map the law in the countries belonging to the Indian subcontinent, India, Pakistan, Bangladesh, who are impacted by a shared history of the arbitration law, and Nepal and Sri Lanka. The discussion here would also include a brief statement of the

[34] Ibid., 348.

[35] Maniruzzaman and Chisti, *supra* 32, at 185.

[36] See, *Oil and Natural Gas Corporation v Saw pipes, Ltd.*, (2003) 5 SCC 705; *Venture Global Engineering v Satyam Computer Services*, AIR 2008 SC 1061; *Phulchand Exports Ltd v OOO Patriot* (2011), 10 SCC 300.

[37] See, Kumar et al. [9]. See also, Sattar [10].

[38] Margaret Moses, *supra* 31.

[39] Arbitration and Conciliation Amendment Act (2015); and further in 2018, and the recent ordinance. Can you revise this note with exact details of the amendment.

[40] See, *Shri Lal Mahal Ltd. v Progretto Grano SpA* (2014), 2 SCC 433; *Penn Racquet Sports v Mayor International Ltd.* (2011) (122) DRJ 117; *Bharat Aluminium Co v Kaiser Aluminum Technological Services*, (2012) 9 SCC 552; *Bharat Aluminium Co v Kaiser Aluminum Technological Services,)* Civ. App 3678 of 2007 4 SCC 126 (28 January 2016); *Union of India v Reliance Industries Limited and others*, 2015, (1) SCALE 149.

[41] See, Aragaki [11].

law on international arbitration in these jurisdictions. It may be noted here that these jurisdictions have, specifically, made a place for their local law within their articulation of the content of public policy.

The Bengal Regulation of 1772 ushered the first known law on arbitration in colonial India.[42] Several regulations followed resulting in much modification to this regulation, to ensure its extension to other regions as and when the East India Company's regime applied to that region and further when the transfer of power to the Crown in 1857 occurred.[43] Further the Act VIII of 1857 codified the procedure of Civil Courts except those established by the charter (which gave the power to the company in the eighteenth century), which contained Sections 312 to 325 concerned with arbitration in suits. Sections 326 and 327 are provided for arbitration without the intervention of the court.

In 1899, the Indian Arbitration Act, which was largely inspired by the English law,[44] was enacted within the Presidency towns of Bombay, Madras and Calcutta.[45] Arbitration found place within the Civil Procedure Code in 1908.[46] The Arbitration Act, 1940, replaced the 1899 Act as well as the arbitration-related features within the CPC, counted amongst its notable features substantial judicial intervention in arbitral process. As was later seen in the jurisprudence under the legislation,[47] while it was enacted to regulate domestic arbitration; however, it was applied to foreign arbitral awards when

(a) An award based upon an arbitration agreement between parties one of whom is not a citizen/corporate of India may provide for an arbitration in India to be governed by the Arbitration Act, 1940.[48]

---

[42]Steinbruck [12].

[43]The British rule, by the early nineteenth century extended to almost all of the Indian subcontinent, or the territories of India, Pakistan and Bangladesh, as known today. The law for a major part of the 200 years of colonial rule that ended in 1947 was a mix of colonial law in public law, commercial and civil matters, whereas the personal laws are applied to matters related to family, inheritance and succession. The Presidency courts were termed as such because they were ruled directly under a charter of the British Parliament to the East India Company, and the territories outside these towns were called as mofussil areas and were administered the local law by the local rulers and administrators under a feudatory from the East India Company. See, generally, Rankin [13]. Rankin was of the view that English law became *ipso jure* the *lex loci* in India as soon as the country became a possession of the British Crown. See, further, Rao [14]; Garimella [15].

[44]English Arbitration Act, 1899.

[45]This was the first exclusive law on arbitration in this region. See, generally, K. Jayachandra Reddy, Alternate Dispute Resolution, in P.C. Rao and William Sheffield (eds.), *Alternative Dispute Resolution: What it is and How it Works*, (Delhi: Universal Law Publishing, 1997) 1, 79.

[46]Arbitration has been placed in Section 89 and Schedule II of the Code of Civil Procedure, 1908, and extended to other territories of British India which were otherwise not covered by Arbitration Act, 1899.

[47]See generally, Sai Ramani Garimella and Gautam Mohanty, 'The Faux Pas of the Automatic Stay Under the Indian Arbitration Act, 1996—The HCC Dictum, Two Cherry Doctrine, and Beyond (2021) 21 *Pepperdine Dispute Resolution Law Journal* 195–256.

[48]See, *Michel Golodetz v Serajuddin & Co.*, A.I.R. 1959 Cal.603; *W. Woods & Son Ltd. v Bengal Corporation*, A.I.R. 1959 Cal. 8.

(b) An award resulting from a reference to arbitration in a dispute involving a foreign element could still be decided as per the Arbitration Act, 1940, as reference to arbitration by the trial court was based on the said legislation and its validity was not open to any objections.[49]

Further, The Arbitration (Protocol and Convention) Act 1937 ushered the (Geneva Protocol) 1923—PROTOCOL ON ARBITRATION CLAUSES related to recognition and enforcement of the arbitration compromis/clause related to existing and/or future differences in commercial matters and the Convention on the Execution of Foreign Awards of 1927 (Geneva Convention) into the Indian law.

Thus as of 1947 when new independent states emerged within the Indian subcontinent the law on arbitration was as follows.

i. The Indian Arbitration Act, 1940 ("Act, 1940") and
ii. The Arbitration (Protocol and Convention) Act 1937.

5.3.1 India—Public Policy—Is There a Settled Law, Now?

Independent India inherited the above mentioned regulatory regime and signed up for the New York Convention on 10 June 1958. The Parliament of India ratified the accession on 13 July 1960 following which the Convention entered into force on 11 October 1960. The instrument of ratification was in the form of a new legislation—Foreign Awards (Recognition and Enforcement) Act, 1961.

The Arbitration and Conciliation Act, 1996,[50] guided by the UNCITRAL Model Law, 1983, aimed at a reformed legal regime ensuring speedy and efficacious dispute resolution through arbitration. Towards this, the dual regime that existed since independence was repealed and replaced with a uniform and exclusive law on normative regime on recognition and enforcement of foreign arbitral awards. Courts continued to have a role in facilitating arbitration through assisting in taking evidence, and such, but importantly under the Act, 1996, the arbitral award is now treated as a decree, and enforceable as such, unlike the Act, 1940, that required an arbitral award to be decreed by the court as final and binding. The legislation is structured into two parts—Part I contains the definitions, including the definition of an international commercial arbitration,[51] and the law regulating domestic arbitration, while Part II,

---

[49]See, *Nachiappa Chettiar v Subramaniam Chettiar* AIR 1960 SC 307.

[50]Act 26 of 1996—16 August 1996. A uniform legislation that regulates arbitrations seated in India and regulating parties that are Indian resident, and arbitrations seated in India for international parties, and for recognition and enforcement of arbitral awards from foreign-seated arbitrations. ("Act, 1996). https://www.indiacode.nic.in/bitstream/123456789/11799/1/the_arbitration_and_conciliation_act%2C_1996.pdf, accessed 01/07/2020.

[51]Ibid., Section 2 (1) (f) defines International Commercial Arbitration as under:

"an arbitration relating to disputes arising out of legal relationships, whether contractual or not, considered as commercial law in force in India and where at least one party is:

(a) An individual who is a national of, or habitually resident in, any country other than India

(b) A body corporate which is incorporated in any country other than India alone, is applied to the execution of certain foreign arbitral awards.[52] However, it needs to be noted that courts in India[53] shall be approached for and shall hear applications regarding reference of parties to arbitration,[54] certain orders related to interim

(c) A company or an association or a body of individuals whose central management and control is exercised in any country other than India

(d) The government of a foreign country.

[52] *Bharat Aluminium Co v Kaiser Aluminum Technological Services*, (2012) 9 SCC 552.

[53] Act, 1996, *supra* 51, Section 2 (1) (e) [...].

"Court" means the principal Civil Court of original jurisdiction in a district and includes the High Court in exercise of its ordinary original civil jurisdiction, having, jurisdiction to decide the questions forming the subject-matter of the arbitration if the same had been the subject-matter of a suit, but does not include any civil court of a grade inferior to such principal Civil Court, or any Court of Small Causes.

[54] Act, 1996, *supra* 51, section 8 (1) substituted by the Arbitration & Conciliation (Amendment) Act, 2015 (Act 3 of 2016, w. e. f. 23-10-2015).

8. Power to refer parties to arbitration where there is an arbitration agreement.

(1) A judicial authority, before which an action is brought in a matter which is the subject of an arbitration agreement shall, if a party to the arbitration agreement or any person claiming through or under him, so applies not later than the date of submitting his first statement on the substance of the dispute, then, notwithstanding any judgment, decree or order of the Supreme Court or any court, refer the parties to arbitration unless it finds that prima facie no valid arbitration agreement exists.

(2) The application referred to in sub-section (1) shall not be entertained unless it is accompanied by the original arbitration agreement or a duly certified copy thereof. Provided that where the original arbitration agreement or a certified copy thereof is not available with the party applying for reference to arbitration under sub-section (1) and the said agreement or certified copy is retained by the other party to that agreement, then, the party so applying shall file such application along with a copy of the arbitration agreement and a petition praying the court to call upon the other party to produce the original arbitration agreement or its duly certified copy before that court.

(3) Notwithstanding that an application has been made under sub-section (1) and that the issue is pending before the judicial authority, arbitration may be commenced or continued and an arbitral award made.

relief (Section 9), and appointment of arbitrators.[55] The law was amended in 2015 to lend clarity on assistance of courts in foreign-seated arbitrations.[56]

The narrative about India's tryst with articulating a normative content to the public policy exception in international arbitration is just not limited to operationalizing its New York Convention-related commitments. The Arbitration and Conciliation Act, 1996, did not define "public policy." It however legislated upon public policy matching the content of Article 34 of the UNCITRAL Model Law.[57] Briefly stated, a domestic award in India can be set aside if it is found to be conflict with public policy or vitiated by patent illegality. Additionally, other grounds for setting aside awards include lack of jurisdiction, non-arbitrability and illegal composition of the tribunal. Further, Section 5 exemplifies the pro-party autonomy[58] and pro-enforcement philosophy of the legislation. Section 5 limits the ambit of judicial intervention to only Part I of the legislation.[59]

The articulation of public policy content in India, inspired by common law methodology as discussed earlier, is intrinsically linked with the notion of arbitrability of the dispute. The concept has been used to explain that certain matters could be decided only by national courts and not be subjected to arbitration.[60] As

[55]The Arbitration and Conciliation (Amendment) Act, 2019, amended Section 11 to update the law as follows: "The appointment shall be made, on an application of the party, by the arbitral institution designated by the Supreme Court, in case of international commercial arbitration, or by the High Court, in case of arbitrations other than international commercial arbitration, as the case may be." http://www.egazette.nic.in/WriteReadData/2019/210414.pdf, accessed 18/02/2021.

[56]An extract of the Section 2(2) with amendment is given herein below:

"This Part shall apply where the place of arbitration is in India.

Provided that subject to an agreement to the contrary, the provisions of Sections 9, 27, and clause (a) of sub-section (1) and sub-section (3) of Section 37 shall also apply to international commercial arbitration, even if the place of arbitration is outside India, and an arbitral award made or to be made in such place is enforceable and recognized under the provisions of Part II of this Amendment." http://www.prsindia.org/uploads/media/Arbitration/Arbitration%20and%20Conciliation%20Act,%202015.pdf, accessed 12/02/2021.

[57]When originally enacted in 1996, Section 34 of the 1996 Arbitration Act was almost identical to Section 34 of the UNCITRAL Model Law. Amendments enacted with effect from 23 October 2015 introduced subsection (2A), (5) and (6) and a second explanation to Section 34(2)(b). The first explanation to Section 34(2)(b) was also replaced to narrowly restrict the scope of review on the ground of conflict with public policy. See also, Khambata [16].

[58]The Working Group that drafted the Model Law observed that "Probably the most important principle on which the Model Law should be based is the freedom of the parties in order to facilitate the proper functioning of international commercial arbitrations according to their expectations". See, Yearbook of the United Nations Commission on International Trade Law, 1981, Volume XII, 'Report of the Secretary-General: possible features of a model law on international commercial arbitration, A/CN.9/207', [17] https://undocs.org/pdf?symbol=en/A/CN.9/207, accessed 20/10/2020. ("Yearbook of the UNCITRAL").

[59]Act, 1996, *supra* 51, section 5: "Extent of judicial intervention.—Notwithstanding anything contained in any other law for the time being in force, in matters governed by this Part, no judicial authority shall intervene except where so provided in this Part.".

[60]See, generally, Rab [17].

a common understanding of the law on international arbitration, a dispute is arbitrable if it concerns a subject-matter "capable of settlement by arbitration."[61] The Supreme Court of India in *Booz Allen and Hamilton Inc. v SBI Home Finance Ltd.*,[62] opined that "arbitrability" relates to the subject-matter itself being arbitrable. This explains the possibility of either an arbitral tribunal adjudicating over the dispute or the dispute is such that it ought to be addressed by courts alone.

The intrinsic linkages between arbitrability and public policy become more evident within the Indian law, also because of the fact that both these concepts have not been articulated exhaustively within the statutory law,[63] and their content is only a jurisprudential derivation. While the content of international law and the enforcing instrument in India[64] have made place for these concepts to exist as two separate grounds, decisions relating to public policy are often hinged upon arbitrability as it may not be in public interest that certain matters are arbitrated, as they are impacted by national security, sovereignty, social objectives, etc.[65] Note therefore that this linkage entails a fertile space to read a localized understanding into international public policy.

The questions related to arbitrability could arise at any time—when courts are approached with a Section 8[66] or Section 45[67] application; during the arbitration, as part of the jurisdictional discussion under the *kompetenz-kompetenz* principle, when courts hear applications for vacating/set aside [of] arbitral awards[68]; and, during enforcement proceedings.[69]

The reasons for disregarding an arbitration *compromis*, as discussed by Gary Born,[70] include public interest, public policy and the need for judicial protection. Courts, though, need to avoid generic and casual interpretation of the ousting of

---

[61] Articles II (1) and V (2) (a), The New York Convention, 1958, 330 U.N.T.S. 38; see, generally, Arfazadeh [18].

[62] See, *Booz Allen and Hamilton Inc. v SBI Home Finance Ltd.* (2011) 5 SCC 532.

[63] Arbitration and Conciliation Act, 1996, Section 2(3) "This Part shall not affect any other law for the time being in force by virtue of which certain disputes may not be submitted to arbitration." There is therefore no exhaustive list of subject-matters wherein the disputes shall be non-arbitrable. See, *A Ayyasamy v A Paramasivam* (2016) 10 SCC 386; *Aftab Singh v Emaar MGF Land Limited* 2017 SCC Online 1614.

[64] Act, 1996, *supra* 51, sections 34 (2) (b) and 48 (2).

[65] Ajar Rab, *supra* 60, at 162.

[66] Application before the designated court for reference to arbitration in a domestic arbitration matter.

[67] Application before the designated court for reference to arbitration in an international commercial arbitration.

[68] Act, 1996, *supra* 51, section 34 (2) (b)—The Court finds that—(i) The subject-matter of the dispute is not capable of settlement by arbitration under the law for the time being in force, …

[69] Ibid., Section 48 (2)—Enforcement of an arbitral award may also be refused if the court finds that—(a) The subject-matter of the difference is not capable of settlement by arbitration under the law of India.

[70] See, Born [19]. See also, Ajar Rab, *supra* 60, at 162.

jurisdiction for reasons of non-arbitrability, limiting to a set of subject-matters that are "clearly non-arbitrable."[71]

The *Booz Allen* ratio is the watermark for arbitrability and its contextualization with public policy. A brief statement of the above-said ratio is presented here. The court was hearing pleadings related to an arbitration clause in a bank mortgage agreement. While much of the factual position in the dispute related to actions/obligations *inter partes*,[72] the court engaged with the issues of arbitrability by framing it as a specific issue for clarification.

> On the contentions urged the following questions arise for our consideration:
>
> […]
>
> (iv) Whether the subject matter of the suit is 'arbitrable', that is capable of being adjudicated by a private forum (arbitral tribunal); and whether the High Court ought to have referred the parties to the suit to arbitration under section 8 of the Act?[73]

While agreeing that arbitration is a private form of dispute resolution, founded upon parties' choice, the court also averred that all disputes, civil or otherwise, are capable of arbitration, unless barred from doing so, either expressly or by necessary implication.[74] Following this, the court made its first reference to public policy in the matters related to or arising out of arbitrability. It said

> Adjudication of certain categories of proceedings are reserved by the Legislature exclusively for public fora as a matter of public policy. Certain other categories of cases, though not expressly reserved for adjudication by a public fora (courts and Tribunals), may by necessary implication stand excluded from the purview of private fora. Consequently, where the cause/dispute is inarbitrable, the court where a suit is pending, will refuse to refer the parties to arbitration, under section 8 of the Act, even if the parties might have agreed upon arbitration as the forum for settlement of such disputes. The well recognized examples of non-arbitrable disputes are: (i) disputes relating to rights and liabilities which give rise to or arise out of criminal offences; (ii) matrimonial disputes relating to divorce, judicial separation, restitution of conjugal rights, child custody; (iii) guardianship matters; (iv) insolvency and winding up matters; (v) testamentary matters (grant of probate, letters of administration and succession certificate); and (vi) eviction or tenancy matters governed by special statutes where the tenant enjoys statutory protection against eviction and only the specified courts are conferred jurisdiction to grant eviction or decide the disputes.[75]

The court found the path for public policy articulation via the nature of the rights involved in the subject-matter agreed for arbitration—*in personam* and *in rem*—while still engaged with the decision upon the arbitability of any subject-matter. It, however, advised against adopting this distinction in a rigid manner.

> Generally and traditionally all disputes relating to rights in personam are considered to be amenable to arbitration; and all disputes relating to rights in rem are required to be adjudicated

---

[71] See, Ajar Rab, *supra* 60, at 163, referring to *Eros International Media Ltd. v Telemax Links India Pvt Ltd.* 2016 SCCOnline Bom 2179.

[72] *Booz Allen, supra* 62, 539–541.

[73] Ibid., 543.

[74] Ibid., 547.

[75] Ibid., 547–548.

by courts and public tribunals, being unsuited for private arbitration. This is not however a rigid or inflexible rule. Disputes relating to sub-ordinate rights in personam arising from rights in rem have always been considered to be arbitrable.[76]

Booz Allen ratio found that the subject-matter of the dispute, a mortgage suit for sale, being an action *in rem*, was not arbitrable. The decision, in effect, explained that allowing an ouster clause that tied the dispute to arbitration would impact the rights of the third parties in an extinguishing manner and that is impermissible on grounds of public policy.[77]

> Many commentaries treat it as axiomatic that 'real' rights, that is rights which are valid as against the whole world, cannot be the subject of private arbitration, although some acknowledge that subordinate rights in personam derived from the real rights may be ruled upon by arbitrators. The conventional view is thus that, for example, rights under a patent licence may be arbitrated, but the validity of the underlying patent may not.....An arbitrator whose powers are derived from a private agreement between A and B plainly has no jurisdiction to bind anyone else by a decision on whether a patent is valid, for no-one else has mandated him to make such a decision, and a decision which attempted to do so would be useless.[78]

Before the impact of *Booz Allen* ratio on the development of public policy is gauged, it is necessary to understand the localized content of public policy in the arbitration law in India. The absence of statutory articulation of the concept necessitates the parsing of the jurisprudence. Recent scholarship in India on the subject characterized this construct as inherently imperfect.[79] It is shaped in a transitory manner with the shifts in the doctrinal underpinnings explained by the "vicissitudes of time and changing notions of morality and justice",[80] thus leading to an understanding that the shifts have been largely localized to the specific geographies and the prevailing public interest therein. Within the law on contracts, public policy was legislated into Section 23 of the Indian Contract Act, 1872. The expression "opposed to public policy" has been construed in a local context, and the jurisprudence indicates that the idea of immorality was related to the object of the contract,[81] leading to a derivation that immorality was meant to be understood in the context of the public-at-large in that society. Indian courts initially favoured a restrictive interpretation of public policy, with much jurisprudence ruling against an expansion of the themes of public policy that adversely impacted the freedom of the contract, which was

[76]Ibid., 548.

[77]Ibid., 548, citing Mustil and Boyd [20].

[78]Ibid., 549.

[79]See, generally, Hariani [21].

[80]Ibid., at 161.

[81]See, for instance, *Chandra Sreenivasa Rao v Korrapati Raja Rama Mohana Rao* AIR 1952 Mad 579; *Gherulal Parakh v Mahadeodas Maiya & Ors.* AIR 1959 SC 781.

considered as the paramount principle.[82] In *State of Rajasthan v Basant Nahata,*[83] the court has noted the absence of definitional clarity regarding the concept of public policy and the impossibility of achieving that as well. It observed that the phraseology "opposed to public policy" may be applied to acts that are likely to deprave, corrupt or are injurious to public morality. Noting the importance of time and change to the ideas of public good and public interest the court in *Murlidhar Aggarwal & Anr v State of Uttar Pradesh &Ors.*,[84] called for examining the rules, the factual evidence as to their probable effect(s), and the social consequences that could result from the operationalization of such rules. The court observed

> Public policy does not remain static in any given community. It may vary from generation to generation and even in the same generation. Public policy would be almost useless if it were to remain in fixed moulds for all time.[85]

Scholarship has commented that Indian courts have viewed public policy construct as an arena for their control of the narrative through interpretation, albeit acknowledging the inherent dangers of paying heed to the concept of public policy for nullifying commercial transactions.[86] In *Rattan Chand Hira Chand v Aksar Nawaz Jung,*[87] it was held that courts are obliged to engage in the exercise, free of past precedent, of ascertaining public policy reflecting the Indian scenario at any given moment. While recognizing its difficulty in making an accurate interpretation, the court observed that the judiciary is comparatively better positioned to interpret public policy than any other forum. Examples of the contents of public policy as identified by the courts include principles of law that pertain to justice, fair play, transparency are all included within the term public policy.[88]

A paradigm shift towards widening the narrative of public policy, beyond the precedent, happened in the decision in *Central Inland Water Transport Corporation & another v Brojo Nath Ganguly & another*,[89] wherein the Supreme Court found disfavour with the specific service rules because there existed an unequal bargaining position in the contract involving an employee and the organization (a government corporation, in the instant case), thus leading to an unfair contract. The offending

[82] See, for instance, *Govind v Pacheco* (1902) 4 Bom LR 948; *Bhagwan Dei v Murari Lal & Ors* (1916) 36 Ind Cas 259; *Kamala Devi v Gur Dial* (1916) 36 Ind Cas 319; *Shrinivasdas Lakshminarayan v Ramchandra Ramrattandas* AIR 1920 Bom 251; *Dhirendra Kumar Bose v Chandra Kanta Roy & Ors* AIR 1923 Cal 154; *Dharwar Bank Ltd v Mahomed Hayat* AIR 1931 Bom 269; *Bhagwant Genuji Girme v Gangabisan Ramgopal* AIR 1940 Bom 369.

[83] *State of Rajasthan v Basant Nahata* (2005) 12 SCC 77, [44].

[84] See *Murlidhar Aggarwal & Anr v State of Uttar Pradesh &Ors.* (1974) 2 SCC 472 [32].

[85] Ibid., [31].

[86] See, generally, Khambata [22].

[87] *Rattan Chand Hira Chand v Aksar Nawaz Jung* (1991) 3 SCC 67, [19].

[88] See, *Board of Control for Cricket in India v Cricket Association of Bihar* (2015) 3 SCC 251, [96]. The Supreme Court held that any rule, contract or arrangement that defeated or tended to defeat the "high ideals of fairness and objectivity in the discharge of public functions no matter by a private non-governmental body will be opposed to public policy".

[89] *Central Inland Water Transport Corporation & another v Brojo Nath Ganguly & another*, (1986) 3 SCC 156.

portion of the said service rules was held as opposed to public policy and violative of the constitutional rights of equality because of being arbitrary. Notably, the decision created the precedent for future modifications and additions to the concept of public policy, if public interest explained such action.[90]

> It is thus clear that the principles governing public policy must be and are capable on proper occasion, of expansion or modification. Practices which were considered perfectly normal at one time have today become obnoxious and oppressive to public conscience. If there is no head of public policy which covers a case, then the court must in consonance with public conscience and in keeping with public good and public interest declares such practice to be opposed to public policy. Above all, in deciding any case which may not be covered by authority Indian Courts have before them the beacon light of the Preamble to the Constitution. Lacking precedent, the Court can always be guided by that light and the principles underlying the Fundamental Rights and the Directive Principles enshrined in our Constitution.[91]

The above-mentioned ratio was reiterated by the court in *Delhi Transport Corporation v DTC Mazdoor Congress & others.*[92] It noted that the courts must, in consonance with public conscience and in keeping with public good and public interest, invent new public policy and declare such practice or rules that are derogatory to the constitution to be opposed to public policy.[93]

Thus, it remained firmly established that courts in India bear a responsibility to adapt, modify and add content to public policy, given that it is a requirement of public interest and public conscience. This could be perceived as reinforcing the observation that the content of public policy in India is founded upon local reasons and the judiciary shall endeavour to articulate it with a local flavour, albeit in public interest.

The *Renusagar*[94] ratio was the first important statement on the contours of public policy in international commercial arbitration. Hearing an application challenging the execution of a foreign award under the Foreign Awards (Recognition and Enforcement) Act, 1961 the court opined

> [...] This would mean that 'public policy' in section 7 (1)(b)(ii) has been used in narrower sense and in order to attract the bar of public policy the enforcement of the award must invoke something more than the violation of law of India . . . Applying the said criteria it must be held that the enforcement of a foreign award would be refused on the ground that it is contrary to public policy if such enforcement would be contrary to

(a) fundamental policy of Indian law; or
(b) the interests of India; or
(c) justice or morality."[95]

The court noted the absence of the words "law of India" within the text of Section 7(1) (b) (ii), nevertheless, held that the provision did not seem to depart

[90]Ibid., [91].

[91]Ibid., [92].

[92]*Delhi Transport Corporation v DTC Mazdoor Congress & others*, (1991) Supp (1) SCC 600.

[93]Ibid., [292].

[94]*Renusagar Power Plant Co. v General Electric Corporation* (1994) Supp (1) SCC 644.

[95]Ibid., [66].

from the regime on public policy as understood within the Arbitration (Protocol and Convention) Act, 1937. The court reinforced its articulation by drawing support from the English Common Law and its commentaries that seemed to State that public policy within Section 5(3) of the Arbitration Act, 1975 referred to "English public policy" only.[96] The decision identified these three heads, nevertheless left them undefined and for future subjective interpretation.

However, it could be argued that the reference to "interests of India," necessarily, may not conform with the approach of the *Renusagar* that constructed a narrow public policy exception to enforcement of foreign arbitral awards. Rather, it could be interpreted by the courts as enabling them with discretion to refuse enforcement. The jurisprudence that followed *Renusagar* lends force to the aforesaid argument, as shown in the following narrative.

The *Oil and Natural Gas Corporation Ltd. v Saw Pipes Ltd.,*[97] decision is an important example in the context of public policy in domestic arbitration; however, the import of this decision continued to affect the enforcement of foreign arbitral awards till recently. The *Renusagar* ratio was discussed for modification and expansion of the content of public policy articulated therein. Such expansion was based on local content. Hearing an application for vacating the award, the court held that an award would be antithetical to public policy if it was "patently illegal"—a new feature added into Section 34 that crystallized the public policy exception. In the Supreme Court's words, "if the award is contrary to the substantive provisions of law or the provisions of the Act or against the terms of the contract, it would be patently illegal, which could be interfered under Section 34"[98] [of the Arbitration and Conciliation Act, 1996], that applies to domestic arbitration, or for arbitrations seated in India. The *Saw Pipes* ratio was critiqued[99] and faulted for creating the path for courts to examine the merits of an award and because (if accepted) the decision effectively adds another setting aside ground to Section 34. The importance of this ratio in the context of public policy in international commercial arbitration is because of another interesting decision that preceded it, and for more than a decade impacted India's regulatory regime and structure for international arbitration. In the year 2002, in *Bhatia International v Bulk Trading SA & Another*[100] the Supreme Court of India had held that that the provisions of Part I (including Section 34; "Application for setting aside arbitral award") are applicable to foreign-seated arbitrations as well.[101]

---

[96] Ibid., [44].

[97] *ONGC v Saw Pipes,* (2003) 5 SCC 705.

[98] Ibid., [15].

[99] See, for instance, Nariman [23].

[100] *Bhatia International v Bulk Trading SA & Another*, (2002) 4 SCC 105.

[101] The court specified that that the language of s. 2(2) of the 1996 Act, which provided that "This Part shall apply where the place of arbitration is in India" was inclusive and clarificatory because it omitted the word "only" which found place in the corresponding Article 1(2) of the UNCITRAL Model Law. *Bhatia* and the judgements that followed it until the *BALCO (I)* ratio repudiated the *Bhatia* in 2012, received significant criticism from the Indian and international arbitration community, for judicial overreach and for creating significant uncertainty and delay in foreign-seated arbitrations involving Indian parties or laws. See, Mathew [24].

The *Saw Pipes* ratio noted that it could exercise jurisdiction in proceedings challenging an award if the award was patently illegal, or was against the legislative content of the Arbitration and Conciliation Act, 1996, or was against any other substantive law governing the parties or is against the terms of the contract. It, however, clarified that the illegality must go to the root of the matter and must shock the conscience of the court; an illegality which was trivial would not vitiate the award on ground of conflict with public policy.[102]

In *McDermott International Inc. v Burn Standard Co Ltd. and Others,*[103] the court demonstrated deference to the precedent in *Saw Pipes*, while also explaining that the 1996 Act envisaged the intervention of the court in a few circumstances like in cases of fraud or arbitrator bias, concerns related to natural justice and such. It observed

> […] patent illegality, however, must go to the root of the matter. The public policy violation, indisputably, should be so unfair and unreasonable as to shock the conscience of the court.[104]

The *Saw Pipes* precedent was applied in *Centotrade Minerals and Metals Inc. v Hindustan Copper Limited*[105] as well. It is interesting to note that the *Saw Pipes* ratio violated the doctrine of precedent by attempting to modify and expand the content of the public policy as laid down in *Renusagar*, which was delivered by a larger bench, nevertheless, it continued to impact the content of public policy.[106]

In *Venture Global Engineering v Satyam Computer Services,*[107] the court, following the *Saw Pipes* ratio, held that section 34 (of part I of the 1996 Act) could be applied to challenges related to enforcement of foreign awards.

In *Phulchand Exports v OOO Patriot,*[108] the court found agreement with the Appellant's contention that the *Saw Pipes* precedent be applied to international arbitrations and enforcement of foreign arbitral awards, thus allowing challenges to enforcement of a foreign arbitral award on grounds of patent illegality. The court overlooked the specific distinction made in the *Saw Pipes* ratio between a foreign award that has attained finality and thus is executable as such and a domestic award that is yet to attain finality as per section 34, not to mention the disregard of the precedent in *Renusagar*.

The decision in *Bharat Aluminium Company v Kaiser Aluminium Technical Services, Inc.*[109] overruled the decision in *Bhatia International* and limited the role of the Indian courts in foreign-seated arbitrations. Part II would be the only legislative content that would apply to international arbitrations; foreign awards enforcement will be subject to the provisions and standards specified in Part II alone. No suit shall

---

[102] *Saw Pipes, supra* 97, [31].

[103] *McDermott International Inc. v Burn Standard Co Ltd*, (2006) 11 SCC 181, [52].

[104] Ibid., [59].

[105] *Centotrade Minerals and Metals Inc. v Hindustan Copper Limited*, (2006) 11 SCC 245.

[106] Hariani, *supra* 79, 178.

[107] *Venture Global Engineering, supra* 36.

[108] *Phulchand Exports, supra* 36.

[109] *Bharat Aluminium Company, supra* 52, [195]–[197].

lie for interim injunctions under Section 9 of the act in cases of international arbitration. Indian courts no longer have the power to vacate an international commercial award made outside India. Section 48(1) of Part II applies to foreign arbitral awards and is meant only for the purpose of enforcement.

BALCO was followed by another important development in arbitration law, explaining the contours of the public policy as applicable in arbitrations that have the seat outside the country. In *Shri Lal Mahal,* the court overruled the precedent in *Phulchand* and restored the content of public policy stated position in *Renusagar*[110] for reasons that it was a decision of a larger bench as compared to *Phulchand* and further, specified that section 48(2) of the (in Part II of the 1996 Act) does not allow for parsing the dispute and the findings thereof within the foreign award by the court hearing an execution application and its challenge. The dispute concerned an award of the Grain and Feed Trade Association ("GAFTA") tribunal seated at London. The award's history included a challenge application before the London court which was rejected, hearing the challenge to the enforcement by the Appellants (seller) the court held that unlike the set aside proceedings wherein the award is not yet final and executable, the awards that are sought to be enforced are final and binding. As such, the court found favour with the argument that public policy in the context of execution applications is distinct from the construct as understood in the set aside proceedings. Refusing to allow a challenge for reasons of "patent illegality," the court reiterated that section 48(2)(b)(ii) does not permit a path for reappraising the award and its record of evidence. It can thus be stated that this decision has been a significant step towards determining the province of judicial challenge against enforcement of foreign awards on grounds of public policy.

The *Shri Lal Mahal* ratio is an important precedent[111] especially for those seeking execution of foreign arbitral awards in India. The overruling of *Phulchand* meant that Indian courts would adopt a restrictive approach and refrain from interfering with the merits of foreign awards in enforcement proceedings. The court thus returned to the idea of "different thresholds" for domestic and international arbitrations[112] and importantly set the precedent clearly against the review of a foreign award on grounds of patent illegality.[113]

Two decisions, *Oil & Natural Gas Corpn.Ltd v Western Geco International Ltd.,*[114] and *Associated Builders v Delhi Development Authority,*[115] attempted to move away from the course correction adopted in *Shri Lal Mahal* and carve an expansive arena for public policy. In the *Western Geco,* the Supreme Court attempted an extensive explanation to the expression "fundamental policy of Indian law" (the first

[110] *Shri Lal Mahal, supra* 40, [47].

[111] The precedent of *Shri Lal Mahal* has been followed in *Perma Container (UK) Line Limited v Perma Container Line (India) Pvt Ltd*, 2014 SCC OnLine Bom 575 wherein the court observed that the content of public policy in foreign-seated arbitration is restricted to section 48(2)(b).

[112] See, generally, Garimella [25].

[113] See, generally, Sattar [26].

[114] *Oil & Natural Gas Corpn.Ltd v Western Geco International Ltd,* (2014) 9 SCC 263.

[115] *Associated Builders v Delhi Development Authority*, (2015) 3 SCC 49.

head in *Renusagar*). It said that the expression encompasses three distinct but non-exhaustive juristic principles—(1) the duty to adopt a judicial approach, (2) compliance with the principles of natural justice, particularly the application of mind and recording of reasons[116] and (3) that the decision is not so perverse or irrational that no rational person would arrive at it, i.e. the *Wednesbury* principle of unreasonableness.[117] The Law Commission of India in its supplementary report[118] cautioned that the *Western Geco* decision hurts the fundamental premise of the 1996 Act—minimal judicial intervention in arbitration. The expression related to unreasonableness, the Commission felt, could open a path for a reappraisal of the merits of the award on the basis of it violating public policy.[119]

Following immediately after the *Western Geco*, the *Associated Builders* decision, summarized herein below, reiterated the former and further explained and consolidated the law on public policy.

1. 'Fundamental policy of Indian law'—the expression shall include provisions of the substantive law and the orders of superior courts in India. Perversity or irrationality would occur if the arbitral tribunal arrived at a finding without evidence or relied upon irrelevant evidence, or ignored evidence pertinently important to reach a conclusion. The court, however, reiterated that in decisions related to public policy it doesn't function as an appellate court, thereby stating that errors of fact, or opinion of an arbitrator regarding the dispute, cannot be corrected.
2. 'Interests of India'—The court held that this head would need to be evolved on a case to case basis, thus stating that courts can adapt, modify and add to its content.
3. 'Justice'—an award could be against the notions of justice were it to come off as shocking the conscience of the court.
4. 'Morality': adopting the understanding available from section 23 of the Contract Act, as applied to an arbitral award it would mean the enforcement of an immoral award, that is likely to shock the conscience of the court.

---

[116]The case, a contract between the appellant and the respondent, was related to technical upgradation of the appellant's seismic survey vessel. Following return of the vessel to the appellant, the appellant failed on the agreed payments to the respondent, deducting various amounts under different heads. It led to an arbitration which eventually resulted in an award in the respondent's favour. The appellant unsuccessfully challenged the award before the single judge of the High Court, however, in appeal the division bench set aside the award only insofar as it granted interest *pendente lite* in future interest. Eventually, the Supreme Court modified the award permitting some deductions which in its view were justified. See, Hariani, *supra* 79, at 182, and note 106. Also see, Arthad Kurlekar, 'ONGC v. Western GECO—A New Impediment in Indian Arbitration', Kluwer Arbitration Blog (7 Jan. 2015), http://arbitrationblog.kluwerarbitration.com/2015/01/07/ongc-v-western-geco-a-new-impediment-in-indi, accessed 03/01/2021. 'The decision may plummet Indian seated arbitration into a sea of uncertainty and unpredictability being forced into the rigours of the Courts'.

[117]Derived from the ratio in *Associated Provincial Picture Houses Ltd v Wednesbury Corpn*, (1947) 2 All ER 680 (CA).

[118]Law Commission of India, Supplementary to Report No. 246 on Amendments to the Arbitration and Conciliation Act, 1996, at 18. http://lawcommissionofindia.nic.in/reports/Supplementary_to_Report_No._246.pdf, Accessed 25/01/2021.

[119]Ibid., 17.

5. 'Patent illegality': Relying on previous decisions, the court approved three sub-heads to this head, viz., (a) contravention of the substantive law of India, (b) contravention of the 1996 Act itself, and (c) contravention of section 28(3) of the 1996 Act specifically; would each be regarded as patently illegal.[120]

The Arbitration and Conciliation (Amendment) Act, 2015, ("Amendment Act, 2015") specified that as per section 48 an award would be in conflict with public policy in India only if such award was impacted by fraud or corruption, or is against the fundamental policy of India, violated the provisions of confidentiality or admissibility of evidence related to conciliation proceedings, or is pernicious to the most basic notions of morality or justice. The Amendment clarified through an explanation that inquiries related to contravention of the fundamental policy of India shall not indulge in an examination of the merits of the dispute.[121]

In the light of the maze-like situation created by the 2015 Amendment and the conflicting jurisprudence on the subject, the Supreme Court once again attempted to provide a consolidated explanation to public policy exception in *Ssangyong Engg & Construction Co Ltd v National Highways Authority of India,*[122] summarized herein below.

1. 'fundamental policy of Indian law'—in Sections 34 and 48 of the 1996 Act—reset to the *Renusagar* position.
2. *Western Geco*'s enumeration—failure to adopt a judicial approach, as part of the fundamental policy of Indian law—is in conflict with the Amendment Act, 2015 and hence deleted, also because it could be construed as allowing a reappraisal of the record of the award.
3. the failure to comply with principles of natural justice as specified within sections 18 and 34(2)(a)(iii) of the 1996 Act would remain within the armoury for challenging the award;
4. the ground 'interest of India' is now removed;
5. the 'justice and morality' ground would now mean a conflict with the 'most basic notions of morality or justice'; i.e. only such arbitral awards that shock the conscience of the court that could be set aside on this ground;

---

[120] *Associated Builders v Delhi Development Authority*, supra 115, [17]–[19] and [27]–[42]. See also, Hariani, *supra* 79, 183–184.

[121] Arbitration and Conciliation (Amendment) Act, 2015,—In Section 48 of the principal Act, for the explanation to sub-section (2) the following explanations shall be substituted, namely—"Explanation 1.—For the avoidance of any doubt, it is clarified that an award is in conflict with the public policy of India, only if— (i) the making of the award was induced or affected by fraud or corruption or was in violation of section 75 or section 81; or (ii) it is in contravention with the fundamental policy of Indian law; or (iii) it is in conflict with the most basic notions of morality or justice. Explanation 2.—For the avoidance of doubt, the test as to whether there is a contravention with the fundamental policy of Indian law shall not entail a review on the merits of the dispute." https://lawmin.gov.in/sites/default/files/ArbitrationandConciliation.pdf, accessed 27/03/2021.

[122] *Ssangyong Engg & Construction Co Ltd v National Highways Authority of India*, (2019) 15 SCC 131.

6. Given the addition of Explanation 2 to the said sections on public policy in domestic as well as international arbitrations, the *Wednesbury* principle of *Western Geco* is no longer applicable.
7. Patent illegality, however, remains as part of the public policy exception applicable to arbitrations seated in India.

Despite the clarification on the law given in *Ssangyong,* it seems that the Indian law on public policy has to cover much terrain to ensure it meets its vision of an arbitration-friendly jurisdiction. The following concerns with regard to the articulation of the public policy exception remain.

(A) The expression "fundamental policy of Indian law" is subjective and lacks clarity—an award could be denied enforcement if it goes against a statute linked to a national or a public interest. Curiously, the terms national and public interest are undefined terms and thus complicate the already unclear situation.

(B) The above-said expression is applicable to international arbitrations as well. Its operationalization in the context of enforcement of foreign arbitral awards and India-seated international arbitrations could only render the regime to much scrutiny and disfavour from international business community when India is on the quest towards an arbitration-friendly jurisdiction.

Two recent decisions of the Supreme Court of India engaged with the expression "fundamental policy of Indian law" but differed on what constitutes the meaning of that expression, thereby exposing the flaw in persisting with the architecture of a localized explanation of public policy exception. In *Vijay Karia & Others v Prysmian Cavi E Sistemi SRL & Others,*[123] the court held that a foreign award, which is in violation of a mandatory provision of the Foreign Exchange Management Act, 1999, would not be in violation of the fundamental policy of Indian law.[124] This ratio is a rare instance, within India's arbitration jurisprudence, of the court noting the need to move beyond articulating a localized content to public policy.

In *National Agricultural Co-operative Marketing Federation of India v Alimenta SA,*[125] the court refused to enforce a foreign award that granted damages for breach of contract holding that supply of commodities under the said contract would be

---

[123] *Vijay Karia & Others v Prysmian Cavi E Sistemi SRL & Others,* 2020 SCC Online SC 177.

[124] Articulating upon the wording of Section 48 of the Arbitration and Conciliation 1996, the Court said that the grounds for challenges to the enforcement of a foreign arbitral award could be categorised as follows—(a) grounds that affect the jurisdiction of the arbitration proceedings, no discretion vests with the courts and they shall refuse enforcement, (b) grounds that impact party interest alone, wherein the courts possess a discretion to refuse enforcement though not bound to do the same, and (c) grounds that address the public policy of India—no discretion exists with the courts, and they shall refuse enforcement. In the instant case, concerning the violation of a mandatory provision of a foreign exchange related law, the court noted that a rectifiable breach could never be a violation of the fundamental policy of Indian law, and that 'fundamental policy' refers to the core values of India's public policy as expressed in statutory law as well as conventional practice, and hence cherished by the courts of law.

[125] *National Agricultural Co-operative Marketing Federation of India v Alimenta SA,* 2020 SCC Online SC 381. The award related to a contract for shipment of certain commodities in which there

in breach of the export control policy—a constituent of the "fundamental policy of Indian law."

The above two decisions exemplify the concerns arising from the localization of the content of public policy exception in the form of divergent opinion, thus also coming into conflict with the stated vision of the national law and international law as well.

5.3.2 Bangladesh—The Tata Power *Decision—Ushering a Pro-enforcement Regime for Foreign Arbitral Awards*

Bangladesh (formerly East Pakistan), following independence in 1971, inherited the then existing colonial law on arbitration—the Arbitration (Protocol and Convention) Act 1937 ("APC Act, 1937") and the Arbitration Act 1940 ("AA, 1940"), apart from the Indian Contract Act, 1872, which were all made applicable within the combined Pakistan *vide* the Adoption of Central Acts and Ordinances Order, 1949.[126] The 1937 Act dealt with foreign awards while the 1940 Act regulated the conduct of domestic arbitrations (arbitrations seated in Bangladesh and in between parties who were residents of Bangladesh). These legislations believed that arbitrations were linked to the territoriality of the place of arbitration (as in, the seat of arbitration) and thus placed them within the supervisory role of the law and the courts.[127] Bangladesh, upon independence in 1971, adopted these laws through its own adoption ordinance.[128]

In spite of accession to the New York Convention on Recognition and Enforcement of Foreign Arbitral Awards on 6 May 1992,[129] Bangladesh persisted with the law and jurisprudence on arbitration as per the existing legal regime, the 1940 Act and the 1937 Act. This ensured that the arbitration scenario was not impacted by the accession to the New York Convention, and the concerns related to judicialization of arbitration persisted.[130] In 2001, inspired by the UNCITRAL Model Law and the British and

---

was a partial performance by the appellant. Upon denial of the permission by the Government of India for carrying forward the supply to the following year, the appellant failed to supply the goods. Consequently, the respondent initiated arbitration at the FOFSA, London in 1981. The 1989 award in favour of the respondent granted damages to them and the same was applied for enforcement in India under the Foreign Awards Act, 1993. The Delhi High Court heard the appellant twice but turned down their appeal, hence the appeal before the Supreme Court.

[126] Adaptation of Central Acts and Ordinances Order, 1949 (G.G.O. 4 of 1949).

[127] See, for example, Sections 15 and 16 of the 1940 Act.

[128] National Legislative Bodies/National Authorities, *Bangladesh: Bangladesh (Adaptation of Existing Laws) Order, 1972*, 26 March 1971, https://www.refworld.org/docid/3ae6b51c2c.html, accessed 20/02/2021.

[129] The Convention entered into force on 4 August 1992. Interestingly, Bangladesh did not make any declarations, related to reciprocity or commercial relationship, within Article I of the NYC.

See, https://uncitral.un.org/en/texts/arbitration/conventions/foreign_arbitral_awards/status2. accessed 01/02/2021.

[130] See, generally, Maniruzzaman [27]; See, also, Khan [28].

Indian legislations on arbitration, a new legislation, the Arbitration Act 2001 ("the AA, 2001"), was adopted.[131] The obligations related to the New York Convention were inserted into Chapter X of the AA 2001. The courts have held that the New York Convention had no legal force in Bangladesh, prior to this legislation.[132] At the apex of the judicial structure in Bangladesh is the Supreme Court of Bangladesh with its two divisions—the Appellate Division (AD) and the High Court Division (HCD). The AD would hear appeals from the HCD which exercises ordinary as well as constitutional jurisdiction. Its ordinary jurisdiction includes original, appellate, revisionary and reference jurisdiction, while its constitutional jurisdiction allows it to as a court of writs and for transfer of cases. Lower to the HCD in the hierarchy are the District Courts, civil and criminal. The jurisdiction in respect of international commercial arbitrations is vested in the HCD.

Aimed at efficacious and expeditious handling of all matters concerning arbitration, the AA, 2001 specified that national courts shall consider the awards similar to a decree[133] subject to the provisions identified within Section 46. The procedure for enforcement of an award is the same as provided within the Code of Civil Procedure 1908 ("CPC") and is similar to a court's decree.[134]

On lines similar to the source of inspiration, the NYC and the UNCITRAL ML, the AA, 2001 restricted the grounds for challenging the enforcement of a foreign award, however, it is possible that the courts could indulge in expansive interpretations of these grounds on which a foreign arbitral award can be denied enforcement.[135] Following the enactment of the AA 2001, the judiciary has been demonstrating a pro-enforcement approach towards foreign awards.

In *Uzbekistan Airways and another v Air Spain Ltd,*[136] the HCD ruled that foreign arbitral awards are enforceable in Bangladesh, as per sections 45–47 read with Section 3(2), AA 2001. The HCD held in favour of the above-stated position in *Smith Co-Generation (BD) Pvt Ltd v Bangladesh Power Development Board*[137] while holding that the provisions for seeking a remedy against the execution of the award have been specified within the said legislative provisions alone. It stated its commitment to operationalize the normative content in Article V of the New York Convention as by law established in Bangladesh. The ratio of these decisions indicates minimal intervention by Bangladesh's courts in arbitration.

[131] Maimul Ahsan Khan, *supra* 130, 287.

[132] See, for instance, *M/s.Haji Azam v Singleton Binda & Co. Ltd.* [1975] 27 DLR 583.

[133] AA 2001, section 45.

[134] Ibid., section 45(1)(b). see, *Canada Shipping and Trading SAv TT Katikaayu and another* (2002) 54 DLR (HCD) 93 [7].

[135] Ibid., s 46—The grounds stated therein are similar to the content of Article 36, UNCITRAL Model Law and of Article V, New York Convention.

[136] *Uzbekistan Airways and another v Air Spain Ltd* [2005] 10 BLC 614, [5].

[137] *Smith Co-Generation (BD) Pvt Ltd v Bangladesh Power Development Board*, (2010)15 BLC (HCD) 704, [24].

5.3.2.1 Foreign Arbitral Awards—The Legal Regime in Bangladesh

The law related to execution of foreign arbitral awards in Bangladesh is located in Chapter X of the AA, 2001. An award, holding the status of a decree of a court, is enforceable per se and would not require an exequatur. The court in *Canada Shipping and Trading SA v TT Katikaayu and another (Admiralty Jurisdiction)*[138] clarified the same in the following words:

> Once an arbitration proceeding in a foreign country is completed, the Arbitral Award, on an application by any party, will be enforced by a court of this country under the Code of Civil Procedure in the same manner as if it were a decree of the court.[139]

The judgement in the *Goenka Impex S.A. v Tallu Spinning Mills Ltd,*[140] demonstrated a pro-arbitration approach from the Bangladesh higher judiciary. An application for attachment of award-debtor's properties located outside Dhaka was filed before the District Judge of Dhaka, pending the execution application. The District Judge, following a hearing, denied the attachment application, for absence of jurisdiction (the properties were outside the territorial jurisdiction of the court). It held that being a transferee court cannot order outside their territorial jurisdiction, as per section 46, Code of Civil Procedure. Hearing the award-holder's Revision Application the HCD parsed the legislative intent explaining section 45(b) and found that the law allowed the jurisdiction of the district courts to participate in the execution of foreign arbitral awards, by treating such award similar as its decree. The HCD found no favour with the averments that characterized the district court as a transferee court and therefore found its order erroneous for denial of the application for attachment as being contrary to the law on enforcement proceedings.[141]

An award, in proceedings as per an arbitration agreement, shall be considered as a foreign award, if it is made in pursuance of such agreement, in any territory other than Bangladesh.[142] However, awards made in the territory of a specified State are not considered to be foreign awards capable of enforcement under this legislation.[143] The "specified state" feature of the legislation is a curios inclusion in the law, given that Bangladesh has not contracted any reservations to the New York Convention upon accession in 1992. Such legislative features could act as a restriction upon the enforcement of foreign awards in Bangladesh.

---

[138] *Canada Shipping and Trading SA v TT Katikaayu and another (Admiralty Jurisdiction),* 54 DLR [2002] 93.

[139] Ibid., 94.

[140] *Goenka Impex S.A. v Tallu Spinning Mills Ltd,* [2013] 33 BLD 340.

[141] Ibid., [15]–[16].

[142] AA, 2001, s 2(k); see, Maniruzzaman [29].

[143] Ibid., s 47—Power of Government to declare specified state—For the purposes of this chapter, the Government may, by notification in the official Gazette, declare a state as a specified state.

Interestingly, despite accession to the New York Convention in 1992, owing to the absence of an enabling statute, the courts were reluctant to apply the Convention.[144] When the law was enacted in the form of The Arbitration Act, 2001, the inspiration of the New York Convention was evident within the content of section 46.[145]

The jurisprudence from Bangladesh's courts allows a derivation that the courts were invested in identifying the four corners of their intervention in foreign-seated arbitrations. Speaking in the context of interim relief, the HCD in *STX Corporation Ltd v Meghna Group of Industries Ltd. &Ors.,*[146] observed that given the clear and unambiguous language of Section 3(1), AA 2001 courts in Bangladesh could be approached only (emphasis supplied) if the seat of arbitration is in Bangladesh.[147] It

---

[144]See, *Bangladesh Air Service (PVT) v British Airways PLC* 49 DLR 187(AD) (1997); also see, Bangladesh No. 1, *Bangladesh Air Service (Pvt) Ltd. v British Airways PLC*, Appellate Division, 8 May 1997', in Van den Berg [30].

[145]s 46. Grounds for refusing recognition or execution of foreign arbitral awards.-(1) Recognition or execution of foreign arbitral award may be refused only on the following grounds, namely

(a) if the party against whom it is invoked furnishes proof to the Court that

(i) a party to the arbitration agreement was under some incapacity;

(ii) the arbitration agreement is not valid under the law to which the parties have subjected it;

(iii) the party against whom the award is invoked was not given proper notice of the appointment of the arbitrator or of the arbitral proceedings or was otherwise unable due to some reasonable causes to present his case; or

(iv) the concerned foreign arbitral award contains decisions on matters beyond the scope of the submission to arbitration; Provided that, if the decisions on matters submitted to arbitration can be separated from those not so submitted, that part of the award which contains decisions on matters submitted to arbitration may be recognised and enforced;

(v) the composition of the arbitral tribunal or the arbitral procedure was not in accordance with the agreement of the parties or, in absence of such agreement was not in accordance with the law of the country where the arbitration took place;

(vi) the award has not yet become binding on the parties, or has been set aside or suspended by a competent authority of the country in which, or under the law of which, that award was made; or

(b) the court in which recognition or execution of the foreign arbitral award is sought, finds that—

(i) the subject matter of the dispute is not capable of settlement by arbitration under the law for the time being in force in Bangladesh; or

(ii) the recognition and execution of the foreign arbitral award is in conflict with the public policy of Bangladesh.

(2) If an application for setting aside or suspension of the enforcement of the foreign arbitral award has been made to a competent authority referred to in sub-clause (v) of clause (a) of sub-section (1) the Court may, if it considers it proper, adjourn the decision on the enforcement of the foreign arbitral award and may also, on the application of the party claiming enforcement of the foreign award, order the other party to give suitable security.

[146]*STX Corporation Ltd v Meghna Group of Industries Ltd. &Ors.* [2012] 32BLD 400.

[147]Ibid., [28]. In this context, the Court referred to a contrarian position adopted in *HRC Shipping v M.V. X-Press Manaslu & Others* [2007] 12 MLR 265. It also extensively cited the prevailing arbitral regime in India and the scholarship on the subject of interim relief and Indian courts.

applied the precedent set by the AD in *Unicol Bangladesh v Maxwell*[148] wherein it was explained that pursuant to sections 3(1) and 3(4) read with 3(2) the power of the court to grant interim relief under the legislation is restricted to arbitrations seated in Bangladesh. The HCD in *STX Corporation* holding similarly cited the constitutional provision on the binding precedent, as per Article 111 of the Constitution of the People's Republic of Bangladesh.[149]

The decision in *Egyptian Fertilizer Trading Limited v East West Property Development (Private) Limited,*[150] was on similar lines wherein another bench of the HCD narrowly interpreted the provisions of sections 3(1) and (4) read with the almost exclusive legal regime placed within section 3(2) in the context of foreign awards, to restrict the usage of the law on interim relief under the AA, 2001 to arbitrations seated within Bangladesh.

In *Tata Power Company Ltd. v M/S Dynamic Construction,*[151] the Supreme Court reiterated the legislative intent against a judicial review of the arbitral award that would go against the purpose of the legislation—an efficacious and expeditious resolution of disputes. The ambit of judicial intervention is much limited,[152] in matters related to gross illegality. The AD explained such illegality in terms *only* (emphasis supplied by authors) of inconsistency with the law of the land.

> [..] The factual and contractual positions are matters for decision of the Arbitrator and as such, unless there appears to be gross illegality, neither the High Court Division nor this Division would enter into the merit of such arguments.[153]

The court explained the content of public policy exception as follows:

> We also feel that a definition of public policy would make it easier to decide what would be considered as being in conflict with public policy. In the absence of such definition, we are to rely upon the usual meaning of the phrase 'public policy' which according to Black's Law Dictionary, 18th Edition is: "Broadly, principles and standards regarded by the legislature or by the courts as being of fundamental concern to the state and the whole of society". It could be said, for example, that if the decision of the learned Arbitrator would have a negative impact on the future of international agreements by foreign companies investing in Bangladesh, then such a decision could be terms as being in conflict with public policy. However, in the facts of the instant case we do not consider that the contract entered into by the parties or the award made by the learned Arbitrator has any impact on the state and the whole of society. We also cannot agree with the submission of the learned Counsel for the appellant that a decision contrary to the law of the country is necessarily in conflict with public policy an envisaged by the Act, 2001. That would be an illegality pure and simple. It would be giving too broad a meaning to the phrase 'in conflict with public policy' to include decisions which are contrary to law, or where the learned Arbitrator has traveled beyond the terms of his reference, or has misinterpreted a principle of law or precedent, or for misreading or non-consideration of evidence. These matters can be considered as matters

[148] *Unicol Bangladesh v Maxwell*, 56 DLR (AD) (2004).

[149] *STX Corporation Ltd, supra* 146, [29]–[34] 7 [39].

[150] *Egyptian Fertilizer Trading Limited (Egyptian Fertilizer) v East West Property Development (Private) Ltd* (Arbitration Application No. 11 of 2010, 10 June 2014).

[151] *Tata Power Company Ltd. v M/S Dynamic Construction* 2 SCOB [2015] AD 1.

[152] Ibid., [21].

[153] Ibid., [24].

relating to propriety, *but are not*, in our view, *matters relating to public policy.*[154] (emphasis supplied by the authors)

Arbitral awards contrary to the law, necessarily, do not seem to be in conflict with public policy as per the legislation, terming that any such interpretations would allow a much broader meaning to the expression "in conflict with public policy" and is not envisaged under the AA, 2001. Arbitral awards that seem contrary to law, or are beyond the scope of arbitral reference, or involve a misinterpretation of the law or the precedent, or a misconstruction of evidence do not seem to be matters relating to public policy.[155] The *Tata Power* ratio is important for identifying a few elements that need not be viewed as being "in conflict with public policy."[156]

Bangladesh seems to present an interesting scenario on public policy—a narrow, albeit, localized content, similar to its subcontinental neighbourhood.

5.3.3 Pakistan—Public Policy—A Mixed Bag of Jurisprudential Insights

Pakistan is still on a quest to achieve a robust arbitration regime founded upon its commitment to the New York Convention. The existing content of the law is primitive and could be traced to its colonial connection. Following independence from the British India in 1947, the Government of Pakistan ordered adopted certain specific laws of the pre-independence era, including in the context of arbitration. It inherited the Indian Contract Act, 1872, the Arbitration Act, 1940 and the Arbitration (Protocol and Convention) Act, 1937, vide an executive order in 1949.[157] Pakistan became a signatory to the New York Convention in 1958; however, it was made applicable for the first time in 2005 through an ordinance[158]—the Recognition and Enforcement (Arbitration Agreements and Foreign Arbitral Awards) Ordinance, 2005 ("the REAO")[159] to replace the Arbitration (Protocol and Convention) Act 1937. While domestic arbitration continues to be administered under the Arbitration Act, 1940, the Recognition and Enforcement (Arbitration Agreements and Foreign Arbitral Awards)

[154] Ibid., [27].

[155] Ibid.

[156] Ibid., [27].

[157] Adaptation of Central Acts and Ordinances Order, 1949 (G.G.O. 4 of 1949).

[158] It is of interest to note that Pakistan signed the NYC on 30 December 1958, but ratified it on 14 July 2005 http://www.newyorkconvention.org/countries, accessed 28/01/2021.

[159] Ordinance No. VIII of 2005; Ordinance for ratification and implementation of the New York Convention in Pakistan. It was re-promulgated eight times (as per Pakistan's constitution the ordinance (an executive order) could remain in force for 120 days only, and has to be either approved in the form of a law or repromulgated. http://pakistancode.gov.pk/english/UY2FqaJw1-apaUY2Fqa-apaUY2FuaJ4%3D-sg-jjjjjjjjjjjj, accessed 21/07/2020.

Act of 2011 ("the REA Act, 2011")[160] deals with foreign arbitration agreements and awards.[161] The draft law aimed at consolidating these two regimes, modelled on the UNCITRAL Model Law, is yet to be approved by the national legislature and enacted.[162]

Section 7 of the APC Act, 1937 specified that a foreign award could be denied enforcement for reasons of invalidity of the arbitration agreement, due process concerns, award being beyond the scope of arbitral reference, the tribunal not being constituted in accordance with the arbitration compromis, award being set aside, or for reasons of conflicting with public policy.[163]

The content of public policy construct has been derived from the contracts law—section 23 called upon the courts to declare contracts violative of the law or are otherwise tainted by fraud, likely to cause injury to person or property, immoral or opposed to public policy, as nullity. Improper procurement of the award and misconduct on the part of the arbitrator were also seen as reasons that could offend public policy.[164]

The jurisprudence from Pakistan courts offers a robust explanation of the content of public policy, as per Pakistan—another example of a localized content infused into the law premised upon terms that are laced with localized understanding. Note that while doing so, the courts were cautious of not reading an expansive content into public policy, realizing the paramountcy of the principle of freedom of contract. In *The Official Assignee of the High Court of West Pakistan v The Lloyds Bank Ltd., Karachi & Others*,[165] the court was of the opinion that claims on subject-matters that allude to public policy shall hold high consideration in favour of avoidance of harm

---

160 No. F.9(3)/2011-Legis. Dated 19.7.2011 [Gazette of Pakistan, Extraordinary, Part-I, 19th July, 2011]. https://www.wipo.int/edocs/lexdocs/laws/en/pk/pk069en.pdf, accessed 10/01/2021.

161 See, generally, Ghouri [31].

162 Arbitration and Conciliation Act, 2015, introduced on 18-01-2016. https://www.pakarbitrationlaw.com/laws-rules/arbitration-and-conciliation-act-2015-draft/, accessed 30/01/2011.

163 **Section 7. Conditions for enforcement of foreign awards**—(1) In order that a foreign award may be enforceable under this Act it must have—(a) been made in pursuance of an agreement for arbitration which was valid under the law by which it was governed, (b) been made by the tribunal provided for in the agreement or constituted in manner agreed upon by the parties, (c) been made in conformity with the law governing the arbitration procedure, (d) become final in the country in which it was made, (e) been in respect of a matter which may lawfully be referred to arbitration under the law of [Pakistan], and the enforcement thereof must not be contrary to the public policy or the law, of [Pakistan]. (2) A foreign award shall not be enforceable under this Act if the Court dealing with the case is satisfied that—(a) the award has been annulled in the country in which it was made, or (b) the party against whom it is sought to enforce the award was not given notice of the arbitration proceedings in sufficient time to enable him to present his case, or was under some legal incapacity and was not properly represented, or (c) the award does not deal with all the questions referred or contains decisions on matter beyond the scope of the agreement for arbitration; Provided that if the award does not deal with all questions referred the Court may, if it thinks fit, either postpone the enforcement of the award or order its enforcement subject to the giving of such security by the person seeking to enforce it as the Court may think fit.

164 AFM Maniruzzaman & Ijaz Ali Chisti, *supra* 32, 201.

165 *The Official Assignee of the High Court of West Pakistan v The Lloyds Bank Ltd., Karachi & Others*, PLD 1969 SC 301.

to general public. However, courts shall only expound and not expand the content of public policy, and the doctrine shall therefore be invoked in cases where the harm to the public is substantial and beyond doubt. The decision in *Sultan Textile Mills v Mohd. Yusuf Shamsi*[166] restated the same with lucidity.

> a. judges shall desist from inventing content into public policy, and rather stay by the precedent, by moulding to fit the new conditions.
> b. the law shall hold the contract not void, despite it impinging upon one of the recognised heads of public policy unless it is likely to result in an indisputable harm to the community.[167]

Noting the impreciseness of the concept, the courts have interpreted notions of public good and possible injury thereto as the situations that would necessitate invalidation of a contract for being contrary to public policy.

In *WAPDA v Kot Addu Power Co. Ltd*,[168] public policy was explained in the context of public welfare. The court held that the freedom of contract could be restricted by law for the societal welfare.

In *Sardar Muhammad Yasin Khan v Raja Feroz Khan*,[169] the court addressed the validity of an arbitration compromis wherein parties specifically contracted out of criminal prosecution. While holding that such agreements, generally, are contrary to the sovereign functions of administration of justice, and therefore contrary to public policy and void, the court nevertheless found, in the instant case, that the parties were not bereft of a legal remedy. However, the court restricted such agreements to be prevalent insofar as the conduct could amount to compoundable offences. Acts that fall against the general interests of the community or impede the development of a harmonious society impinge upon the standards of morality that have been accepted by the community—all these contribute to the content of public policy.[170]

The decision in *Nan Fung Textiles Ltd. v Sadiq Traders Ltd.*,[171] finding inspiration in the definition of public policy in Chitty on Contracts (24th edition), identified a set of criteria to analyse the public policy challenges presented against the foreign award.

- commercial engagements with the enemy in times of hostilities;
- acts that are otherwise illegal, as per common law or statute;
- acts injurious to governance—domestic and foreign affairs;
- acts or purposes that interfere with the administration of justice—interfering with prosecution, champerty and maintenance;
- acts or purposes that are likely to harm family life;

---

[166] *Sultan Textile Mills v Mohd. Yusuf Shamsi*, PLD 1972 Karachi 226.

[167] Quoted from AFM Maniruzzaman & Ijaz Ali Chisti, *supra* 32, 202.

[168] *WAPDA v Kot Addu Power Co. Ltd*, PLD 2000 Lahore 461.

[169] *Sardar Muhammad Yasin Khan v Raja Feroz Khan*, PLD 1972 AJ&K 46.

[170] Ibid.

[171] *Nan Fung Textiles Ltd. v Sadiq Traders Ltd*, PLD 1982 Karachi 619.

- could be contrary to the economic public interest.[172]

Since the Arbitration Act, 1940, is applied only to domestic arbitrations, the content of section 26-A—the statutory provision related to reasoned awards—did not form the content of public policy that would apply to the challenges against enforcement of a foreign award.

In *Grosvenor Casino Ltd v Abdul Malik Badruddin,*[173] the dispute related to the execution of a foreign decree, as per section 44-A of the Code of Civil Procedure (CPC) 1908. The dispute concerned the enforcement for recovery of gambling debt. The resistance was founded upon an averment that such recovery is non-enforceable as per section 13(f), CPC, wherein foreign decrees that sustain a claim that is otherwise a breach of a law of Pakistan, need not be enforced. The judgement found the acts related to gambling and gaming in violation of the Gambling Ordinance 1961 were in violation of the tenets of the Qur'an and the Sunnah (enforced as statutory provisions), any laws/policies/acts opposed to such tenets would be void. The Constitution of Pakistan, Article 227[174] mandates upon the nullity of laws, and the same has been extensively articulated by the Federal Shariat Court (of binding hierarchy) in *Raja Khushbakht ur Rehman v The Province of Punjab,*[175] wherein betting was classified as gambling and hence prohibited by the injunction, and, in *Mushtaq Ali v Government of Pakistan,*[176] wherein a lottery scheme was held to contravene the ordainments of Islam. Therefore, in the instant case, the execution was denied for being contrary to the public policy as per section 30 of the Contract Act, section 13 (f) of the CPC and in consonance with the ordainments of the Qur'an and the Sunnah.[177]

In *Hub Power Company v WAPDA,*[178] the court held that a contract obtained by fraud and corruption is void and public policy does not permit the reference of disputes arising from such contracts to arbitration. Public policy requires that courts enter judicial findings about the alleged criminality. Criminality-related allegations remove the contract from the private space. The dispute is characterized as one relating to the validity of the contract, and not essentially a contractual dispute, therefore the injunctory relief could be provided by the courts.

Following the declaration of repugnancy towards "interest" as against Islam's fundamental tenets, the Interest Act, 1839, was declared *non est*, and the same was

---

[172] Mansoor Hassan Khan, 'Report on the Public Policy Exception to the New York Convention' (2015–16) https://www.ibanet.org/Article/NewDetail.aspx?ArticleUid=8EAAD89D-867F-4078-93DE-D30DC6465333, accessed 21/07/2020.

[173] *Grosvenor Casino Ltd. v Abdul Malik Badruddin*, PLD 1998 Karachi 104.

[174] Islamic Republic of Pakistan's Constitution, 1973, Article 227 of the Constitution—"all existing laws shall be brought in conformity with the Injunctions of Islam as laid down in the Holy Qur'an and Sunnah … and no law shall be enacted which is repugnant to such Injunctions."

[175] *Raja Khushbakht ur Rehman v The Province of Punjab*, PLD 1986 FSC 49.

[176] *Mushtaq Ali v Government of Pakistan*, PLD 1989 FSC 60. The Shariat Appellate Bench of the Supreme Court in the matter of *Federation of Pakistan v Mushtaq Ali*, PLD 1992 SC 153 reiterated the same legal position.

[177] *Grosvenor Casino Ltd.*, *supra* 173.

[178] *Hub Power Company v WAPDA*, PLD 2000 SC 841.

affirmed by Supreme Court in *Dr. M. Aslam Khaki v Syed M. Hashim.*[179] However, in 2002, the Supreme Court in *United Bank Ltd. v M/s Farooq Brothers*[180] reviewed its own affirming judgement and set it aside; the Federal Shariat Court has been asked to revisit this decision.

However, the law related to "interest on award-related payments" in the context of enforcement of award seems to be mired in indeterminacy, because of the court not taking notice of the development of the law. In *Messrs Flame Maritime Limited v Messrs Hassan Ali Rice Export,*[181] the court refused to take note of the above-mentioned review judgement of the Supreme Court and proceeded to hold that enforcement of the award, that included interest on the award, was unIslamic and against the law prevalent in Pakistan. The Supreme Court, it is expected, should clarify the law with more rigour. Interestingly, the ordering of interest is not unlawful as per section 29 of the Arbitration Act, 1940, wherein the enforcement court may order the same in addition to the award.[182]

Recently, the Lahore High Court in *Orient Power Company (Private) Limited v Sui Northern Gas Pipelines Limited,*[183] dealt with the recognition and enforcement of foreign awards in Pakistan. The judgement is pertinent for the present discussion because it clarifies and establishes the true contours of the public policy exception's meaning and scope in Pakistan. In the instant case, Orient Power Company ("Orient") and Sui Northern Gas Pipelines ("Sui Northern") entered into a Gas Supply Agreement ("GSA") for the supply of gas to the Appellant for its power generational plant. Pursuant to the same, certain disputes arose between the parties concerning pending payments under the GSA. In accordance with the terms of the GSA, the dispute was referred to the London Court of International Arbitration ("LCIA"), which passed two awards dated 27.02.2017 and 13.06.2017, respectively. Thereafter, the Appellant challenged the award before the Civil Court under the 1940 Act, and the Respondent approached the High Court under the 2011 Act for the recognition and enforcement of the Awards. Notably, the High Court observed that it was the exclusive authority for enforcing foreign arbitral awards and any challenge to a foreign award must be brought before it and the civil courts do not have jurisdiction over foreign arbitral awards. On the same note, the High Court enforced the award. Thereafter, aggrieved by the decision of the single judge of the Lahore High Court, the Appellant filed an intra court appeal to the division bench of the High Court.

In the appeal, the Appellant argued that the High Court is not the exclusive repository of the jurisdiction in relation to foreign arbitral awards and that the civil court also possesses parallel jurisdiction to recognize and enforce foreign arbitral awards.

---

[179] *Dr. M. Aslam Khaki v Syed M. Hashim*, PLD 2000 SC 225.

[180] *United Bank Ltd. v M/s Farooq Brothers*, PLD 2002 Supreme Court 801.

[181] *Messrs Flame Maritime Limited v Messrs Hassan Ali Rice Export*, 2006 CLD 697.

[182] **Section 29**—Interest on award—Where and insofar as an award is for the payment of money the Court may in the decree order interest, from the date of the decree at such rate as the Court deems reasonable, to be paid on the principal sum as adjudged by the award and confirmed by the decree.

[183] *Orient Power Company (Private) Limited v Sui Northern Gas Pipelines Limited*, PLD 2019 Lahore 607.

Further, in the context of public policy, the Appellant had averred that the second claim of Respondent under the GSA was against the provisions of the Contract Act and if the arbitral award directing payment of the amounts under the second claim were enforced, then it would lead to violation of the public policy of Pakistan. According to Appellant, the Respondent should not be awarded damages more than above of the actual loss suffered as the same would amount to unjust enrichment and would be contrary to the constitutional principles of reasonable compensation as envisaged in the Contract Act.

The division bench of the High Court in relation to the issue of the exclusive jurisdiction observed that it is impracticable to vest both High Court and Civil Courts with parallel jurisdiction for enforcing foreign arbitral awards as the same would not only be contrary to the pro-enforcement policy enshrined under the 2011 Act but also might lead to conflicting judgements regarding the same award. With regard to the public policy argument of Appellant, the High Court, pursuant to a detailed examination of the New York Convention and several decisions of the New York Convention, concluded that the applicability of the public policy exception is solely restricted to exceptional circumstance and particularly in a case which has a direct impact on the most fundamental values of a state. The High Court also stated that the public policy exemption should not be used as a back door to review the merits of the foreign arbitral award and create imaginary grounds for challenging the foreign award's sanctity. Hence, in the above backdrop, the High Court ultimately held that no case for public policy was made by the Appellant and accordingly dismissed the appeal and the decision of the single judge of the High Court was reinstated.

The foregoing narrative shows that while Pakistan's courts have found favour with the concept of freedom of contract, and a limited content to public policy, there is still an attempt to ground the content in the local laws, including the religious law, via the provisions of the Constitution.

5.3.4 Nepal—The Arbitration Act, 1999—The Curious Case of Public Interest, and of Public Policy

Nepal's tryst with arbitration is anecdotal—traditionally the dispute resolution was handled by *panchayat* (an informal tribunal of five men chosen from amongst the villagers).[184] In modern times though, documented history of arbitration law dates to 1981 when Nepal enacted its first arbitration-related legislation. Arbitration as a method of dispute resolution was known in Nepal and existed in a diffused manner for resolving various kinds of disputes, including commercial and contractual. An example of such diffused existence is section 9 of the Development Board Act 1957 that provided for the resolution of a dispute under a contract to which the board is a party. The presence of arbitration in these legislations could be attributed to the developmental needs of the country, and a realization that addressing dispute

[184] Karki [32].

resolution provisions in the law could be the path to reinforce investor interest in the economy.[185] Other such examples include the provisions related to arbitration within the Royal Nepal Airlines Corporation Act, 1962, and The Petroleum Act, 1983, wherein arbitration existed as a layer in a tiered dispute resolution process.[186]

Nepalese businesses adapted to the presence of arbitration clauses/procedures in their contracts, a fact recognized by the judiciary as well[187] despite the fact that Nepalese legal system did not have law relating to arbitration and enforcement mechanisms for arbitral awards, and the awards had to be enforced through the procedure of filing for decree before District Courts.[188] In 1981, there were two important legislations in Nepal related to Arbitration—the Arbitration Act, 2038 (1981), and the Foreign Investment and Technology Transfer Act, 2038 (1981) that included a dispute resolution provision, specifying arbitration of disputes between the foreign and domestic investors (Section 17).[189] Disputes, between the foreign investor, concerned industry and the Department of Industry[190] failing mutual settlement, will be arbitrated under the prevailing UNCITRAL rules.[191] The tribunal shall be seated in Kathmandu, Nepal and the governing law, and the lex arbitri had to be the Nepalese Law.[192] The FITTA was amended to lend more clarity to the arbitration-related provisions therein.[193] As per the law, party autonomy extends to the choice of arbitral rules, not contrary to the law.[194]

The 1981 Act was repealed in 1999 through the promulgation of the Arbitration Act, 2055 (1999)[195] because it was found to non-efficacious and was critiqued as promoting excessive judicial interference in the arbitral process.[196] This legislation was inspired by the UNCITRAL Model Law and the New York Convention; however,

---

[185] Uprety [33].

[186] Ibid., 211; Also, see generally, Pandit and Pant [34].

[187] *Anang Man Sherchan v Chief Engineer of RTO*, Ne.Ka.Pa. 2020, issue 1, part 6, decision no. 220, 13/03/2064.

[188] The General Code (Muluki Ain), 1920 (1963) governs the mechanism for enforcement of court judgments in Nepal. However, till date, the provision of the General Code, 1963 has not been updated in line with availability of different modes of dispute resolution.

[189] Foreign Investment and Technology Transfer Act, 2038 (1981), section 17(1).

[190] The foreign investment is approved under the authority of the Department of Industry (Section 17, FITTA, 2019 (2075), similar to the earlier version of the law). Investment less than six billion rupees could be approved by the Department of Industry, and investments exceeding that amount are approved by The Investment Board under the Investment Board Act, 2011 (2068). Section 40, FITTA, specified that the Department is responsible for facilitating dispute resolution, including a tiered dispute resolution procedure, involving mandatory arbitration of unsettled disputes, as per clause (5) of Section 40, according to UNCITRAL Rules, unless otherwise agreed by the parties. http://www.lawcommission.gov.np/en/wp-content/uploads/2019/09/The-Foreign-Investment-and-Technology-Transfer-Act-2019-2075.pdf.

[191] FITTA, s 17(2).

[192] Ibid., s17 (3).

[193] Foreign Investment and Technology Transfer Act, 2047 (1992), section 17(2).

[194] Arbitration Act, 1981, s 5(2); Also, Yadav [35].

[195] Arbitration Act, 2055 (1999), s 10(1).

[196] Karki, *supra* 184, 09.

there remain substantial differences with regard to law on enforcement of arbitral awards.

Recognition and Enforcement of Foreign Arbitral Awards

When acceding to the New York Convention in 1998, Nepal made the following declaration:

> [Nepal] will apply the Convention, on the basis of reciprocity, to the recognition and enforcement of awards made only in the territory of another contracting state. [The Government of Nepal] further declares that the Kingdom of Nepal will apply the Convention only to the differences arising out of legal relationship, whether contractual or not, which are considered as commercial under the law of the Kingdom of Nepal.[197]

The declaration impacts the enforcement of foreign awards, as it allows reasons beyond those mentioned in Article V, New York Convention to influence a decision related to the awards recognition and enforcement. It is not in sync with the recommendations of the Model Law, the inspiration for Nepal's arbitration law, as the Model law called for recognition of arbitral awards irrespective of their country of origin.[198] Note that the Model Law did not include reciprocity within the Model Law, since it was recognized that the place of arbitration has "limited importance … in international cases"[199] and the UNCITRAL had "the desire to overcome territorial restrictions."[200]

A foreign award is defined as a "decision taken by arbitrators in foreign countries."[201] Enforcement applications shall be heard by the Appellate court,[202] and they shall be submitted along with an official Nepalese translation of the award.[203]

The Appellate court, upon satisfaction that the foreign award fulfilled the criteria set forth in section 34(2),[204] would direct the District Court for enforcement. The Appellate Court would also ensure that the award fulfils the twin requirements of section 34(4)[205]—the arbitrability of the dispute under the laws of Nepal[206] and the

---

[197] http://www.newyorkconvention.org/list+of+contracting+states, accessed 15th September 2021.

[198] Explanatory note by the UNCITRAL Secretariat on the Model law on international commercial arbitration, January 2008, United Nations Publication, 36 http://www.uncitral.org/pdf/english/texts/arbitration/ml-arb/07-86998_Ebook.pdf, accessed 31/10/2020.

[199] Ibid.

[200] Ibid.

[201] Arbitration Act, 1999, s 34(2). https://arbitrationlaw.com/sites/default/files/free_pdfs/Nepal%20Arbitration%20Act%201999.pdf.

[202] Ibid., s 34(1).

[203] Ibid., s 34(1)(c)—[…] (c) In case the arbitrators award is not in the Nepali Language, an official translation thereof in Nepali language.

[204] Ibid., s 34(3).

[205] Ibid., s 34(4).

[206] Ibid., s 34(4)(a).

foreign award not being "detrimental to the public policy."[207] Unlike the UNCITRAL Model Law, the 1999 Act specified a timeline for presenting an enforcement application—"within 90 days from the date of the award."[208]

While these criteria, as stated above, are similar to the UNCITRAL ML's provisions on enforcement of arbitral awards,[209] there is a substantial difference in the manner in which these criteria have been provided in the 1999 Act. Unlike the Model Law Nepal's arbitration law specifies that the Appellate Court must be "satisfied that the conditions … have been fulfilled in the application"[210] thus placing the onus of proof for the same on the Appellant.

There has been a couple of interesting judicial dicta from Nepal on the issues of challenges to an arbitral award's enforcement. In *Krishna Chandra Jha v Dinesh Bhakta Shrestha*,[211] it was specified that the Appellate Court's authority is limited to correctional jurisdiction when an arbitral award is challenged. In *Anil Kumar Pokhrel v District Court Kathmandu*,[212] the Supreme Court of Nepal held that the time limitation provided in the 1999 Act with regard to implementation of arbitral awards is calculated from the date the award is final, which technically, is after the Appellate court has adjudicated and disposed the matter. The District Court would then proceed with the enforcement processes.

In *Hanil Engineering & Construction Co., Ltd. v KONECO Pvt. Ltd. et. al.*,[213] the Supreme Court of Nepal, for the first time, heard an appeal on an issue pertaining to the enforcement of a foreign arbitral award under the 1999 Act. The brief factual background of the case was that Hanil Engineering & Construction Co. Ltd ("Hanil") entered into a contract with Melamchi Water Supply Department Board ("Melamchi") to construct roads for the Melamchi Water Supply Project. Thereafter, Hanil subcontracted the work to KONECO Pvt. Ltd ("Koneco") and pursuant to the same, on account of delays in completing the work by Koneco, Melamchi forfeited the Bank Guarantee submitted by Hamil. Accordingly, Hanil suffered a financial loss totalling USD 1,758,578 with interest. Notably, the agreement entered into between Hanil and Koneco also included an arbitration clause that provided that the arbitration would be according to Korean Law. The above agreement also stipulated a pre-arbitration procedure by way of amicable settlement of disputes. Be that as it may, Hamil, *ex-parte*, applied to the Korean Commercial Arbitration Board to adjudicate the dispute with Koneco and was awarded damages amounting to USD 17,58,578 plus interest.

Consequently, Hamil applied to the Appellate Court, Patan for enforcing the award granted by the Korean Commercial Arbitration Board, which the court declined. In response, Hamil filed a Writ Petition before the Supreme Court of Nepal

[207]Ibid., s 34(4)(b).

[208]Ibid., s 34(2)(f).

[209]Model Law, *supra* 6 Article 36(1)(a).

[210]Arbitration Act, s 34(3).

[211]Ne.Ka.Pa.2059, Decision no. 7089, 285.

[212]*Anil Kumar Pokharel v District Court Kathmandu and others*, Ne.Ka.Pa, Decision no. 7836 (2064/460).

[213]Case No. 067-WO-0419, Supreme Court decision dated 2075/9/11 (December 26, 2017).

requesting the quashing of the Appellate Court's decision and enforcing the award passed by the Korean Commercial Arbitration Board under the NYC. The Supreme Court, after hearing the arguments advanced by both parties, in addition to discussing the fundamental tenets of international arbitration, opined that the foreign arbitral award in the present case was unenforceable in Nepal because: (i) the pre-arbitration amicable settlement procedure was not adhered to thereby depriving Koneco of its right to settle its dispute with Hamil amicably; (ii) the appointment of arbitrators in the present case was not made in accordance with the will of both the parties as Koneco had not consented for the Korean Commercial Arbitration Board to adjudicate the dispute, and (iii) Koenco was deprived of a fair opportunity to be heard as the notice could not be served on Koneco's office in Nepal.

A unique feature of Nepal's arbitration law is the ground of public interest specified within section 30(3)(b) to set aside an arbitral award. There has been no judicial delineation of the same as yet, and the absence of legislative clarity could unwittingly contribute to the circumvention of the arbitral process. Law reform should consider rewording and explaining the contours of such terminology. It could also consider aligning Nepal's arbitration law with common international practice as suggested in scholarship on the subject.[214] The only known example of the usage of the term public interest along with the term public policy was in the English Arbitration Act, 1996. In the English law, both terms were adopted in section 1(b) and 33 of Arbitration Act, 1996, but the law acknowledged there could be a possible overlap.[215]

5.3.5 *Sri Lanka—Public Policy—A Pro-enforcement Stance*

Sri Lanka, a unitary republic, is an island nation located near the Indian peninsula. It has a thriving alternative dispute resolution tradition at the most basic community level through the "gam sabhava."[216] Judge Saleem Marsoof explained that this institution had a rich history of more than two millenia.[217] An Arbitration Ordinance of 1866, and the provisions in Civil Procedure Code, 1889,[218] related to reference of disputes to arbitration and an exclusive procedure for enforcing arbitral awards form the foundation for the modern arbitration architecture in Sri Lanka.

In 1995, the Parliament of Sri Lanka enacted the Sri Lanka Arbitration Act[219] ("SL Arbitration Act") to regulate arbitrations conducted in Sri Lanka, other than

[214]See, generally, Anil Kumar Sinha, Chapter on Nepal, Global Arbitration Review, http://globalarbitrationreview.com/chapter/1036913/nepal, accessed 01/09/2020.

[215]See, John Sutton et al. [36].

[216]Amarasinghe [37]; cf. Saleem Marsoof [38].

[217]Saleem Marsoof, *supra* 216, 392.

[218]Civil Procedure Code, Ordinance No. 2 of 1889, s 676–698.

[219]No. 11 of 1995, (Certified on 30th June-1995) http://www.commonlii.org/lk/legis/num_act/aa11o1995183/, accessed 21/03/2021.

industrial,[220] co-operative[221] and investment[222]-related arbitration. The legislation, inspired by the New York Convention and the UNCITRAL Model Law, repealed and replaced the pre-existing law on arbitration. Its content reflects a commitment to party autonomy and a recognition of the fact that arbitration is a party-driven and consensual dispute resolution procedure[223] and requires minimal judicial intervention in arbitration proceedings.[224] The legislation is aimed at achieving efficiency in the recognition and enforcement of arbitral awards.[225]

Before the enactment of the SL Arbitration Act, the regulatory regime on enforcement of foreign awards was the Reciprocal Enforcement of Judgments Ordinance.[226] It defined the term "judgement" to include an arbitral award if such award has, "in pursuance of the law in force in the place where it was made, become enforceable in the same manner as a judgement given by a court in that place."[227] Apart from the fact that the provisions of the ordinance applied only to an award "whereby any sum of money is made payable,"[228] the need to prove that the debtor was resident or carried on of business in the place of arbitration or voluntarily submitted to the jurisdiction of the tribunal[229] and the requirement of reciprocity[230] were major constraints on enforceability.

Sri Lanka, unlike other South Asian nations, did not make any declarations related to reciprocity and commercial reservations while acceding to the New York Convention.[231] The legislation mandated

> A foreign arbitral award *irrespective of the country to which it was made*, shall subject to the provisions of section 34 be recognized as binding and, upon application by a party under section 31 to the High Court, be enforced by filing the award in accordance with the provisions of that section.[232] (Emphasis added by Judge Saleem Marsoof)

---

220 As per Industrial Disputes Act No. 43 of 1950.

221 As per Co-operative Societies Act No. 5 of 1972.

222 As per Board of Investment of Sri Lanka Law No. 4 of 1978.

223 Saleem Marsoof, *supra* 216, 393; also see, Marsoof [39].

224 Arbitration Act, *supra* 219, sections 4–5.

225 Arbitration Act, *supra* 219, The legislation's preamble, also, states—WHEREAS it is necessary to make comprehensive legal provision for the conduct of arbitration proceedings and the enforcement of awards made thereunder:.

226 Reciprocal Enforcement of Judgments Ordinance No. 41 of 1921.

227 Ibid., s 2(1).

228 Ibid.

229 Ibid., s 3(2)(b). See also, *Prins Goonesekere v Associated Newspapers of Ceylon Ltd.,* [2000] 3 SLR 122.

230 Ibid., s 6.

231 Sri Lanka acceded to the New York Convention on 30 December 1958, and the ratification of the same was achieved on 9 April 1962. https://www.newyorkconvention.org/countries, accessed 21/07/2020.

232 Arbitration Act, *supra* 219, s 33; cf. Saleem Marsoof, *supra* 216, 403; See, S. Marsoof, Recognition and Enforcement of Foreign Arbitral Awards: Some Salient Points (2005) *LCLR* 27.

Section 50 defined a foreign arbitral award as one made in an arbitration proceeding that were held outside Sri Lanka, thus marking the seat of arbitration as the deciding factors in characterization of a foreign award.

Section 34 enumerated the grounds for refusing recognition and enforcement of foreign arbitral awards, on lines similar to Article V of the New York Convention. The High Court shall hear all such applications and could be pending a set aside proceedings adjourn the hearing related to recognition and enforcement of the foreign award. While doing so it may also consider an application from the award-holder for ordering appropriate security from the award-debtor.[233] The decisions of the Supreme Court in *Light Weight Body Armour Ltd. v Sri Lanka Army*[234] *Kristley (Pvt) Ltd v State Timber Corporation,*[235] and *Kiran Atapattu v Janashakthi General Insurance Co. Ltd.*,[236] evidence a pro-arbitration attitude amongst the Sri Lankan judicial system. Further, as Judge Marsoof explained, "Sri Lankan courts, therefore, would not "second guess" the arbitral tribunal, particularly on questions of facts.'[237]

5.3.5.1 Public Policy—The Law and Praxis

An arbitral award could be denied execution for being repugnant to the public policy of Sri Lanka.[238] The delineation of the exception of public policy has been attempted by almost all jurisdictions faced with the enforcement of foreign arbitral awards. However, it may be noted that amongst the diversity of parameters related to public policy, a common feature has been the utilization of this principle to appeal to local content. The Sri Lankan Arbitration Act specifies the following as the law on public policy.

Grounds for refusing recognition or enforcement

> 34.
>
> (1) Recognition or enforcement of a foreign arbitral award, irrespective of the country in which it was made, may be refused only
>
> [.....]
>
> (b) if the Court finds that
>
> (i) the subject matter of the dispute is not capable of settlement by arbitration under the law of Sri Lanka; or
>
> (ii) the recognition or enforcement of the award would be contrary to the public policy of Sri Lanka. (emphasis supplied)
>
> [....]

---

[233] Arbitration Act, *supra* 219, s 34(2).

[234] *Light Weight Body Armour Ltd. v Sri Lanka Army*, [2007] Sri L.R. 411.

[235] *Kristley (Pvt) Ltd v State Timber Corporation*, [2002] 1 Sri L.R. 225.

[236] *Kiran Atapattu v Janashakthi General Insurance Co. Ltd.*, SC Appeal 30–31/2005, 22.2.2013.

[237] Saleem Marsoof, *supra* 216, 404.

[238] Arbitration Act, *supra* 219, s 34(1)(b)(ii).

Mr Tilakawardane J in *Light Weight Body Armour Ltd. v Sri Lanka Army*[239] observed that the grounds under subsection (b) of 34 permit the High Court to arrive at a finding, on its own accord, for want of subject-matter arbitrability or if the award was repugnant to the public policy of Sri Lanka. Finding no conflict with the public policy of Sri Lanka, the court made noteworthy observations about the content of public policy in/of Sri Lanka. It may be noted that while the legislation specified "public policy of Sri Lanka," the court attempted to read the general understanding of this term within the New York Convention, leading to a derivation that the understanding given by the Convention has been appropriated into the Sri Lankan law.

> The concept of public policy is not immutable. Rules which rest on the foundation of public policy, not being rules of fixed customary law, are capable on proper occasion of expansion or modification depending on the circumstances. Public policy is generally those moral, social or economic considerations which are applied by Courts as grounds for refusing enforcement of an arbitral Award.
>
> [...]
>
> It is generally understood that the term public policy which was used in 1958 New York Convention and many other treaties covered fundamental principles of law and justice in substantive as well as procedural aspects. Thus instances such as corruption, bribery and fraud and similar serious cases would constitute a ground for setting aside. However, the facts of this case do not bear out any such incident of illegality, fraud or corruption in order to validate a challenge on the ground of public policy.[240]

In *Kristley (Pvt) Ltd v State Timber Corporation,*[241] the court, hearing an appeal against a set aside order of the High Court, held that the High Court was wrong in setting aside the award on ground of public policy because it had erred in framing an issue related to forgery. The Supreme Court held that the High Court was wrong in reviewing the merits of the award and directed it to file the award and order accordingly. It went on order costs in favour of the claimant. The court observed

> It would be an oversimplification to describe the question for determination as being "Is it contrary to public policy to enforce the majority award on the ground that it was based on a forged 450 document?"
>
> [...]
>
> I hold that, in the circumstances, the majority was justified in refusing to consider the question of forgery without a specific issue, and the High Court was not entitled to review that decision on the ground of public policy or otherwise, under section 32 (1) of the Act.[242]

In *Lanka Orix Leasing Company Limited v Weeratunge Arachchige Piyadasa (Ellegoda Gamage Lamala Rani Weeratunge),*[243] the Supreme Court heard an appeal against an High Court order that invoked public policy provisions to set aside an arbitral award. The reason for invoking the grounds of public policy was that the award contained an amount as interest that was awarded to the Appellant which

[239] *Light Weight Body Armour Ltd., supra* 236, 416.

[240] Ibid., 419.

[241] *Kristley (Pvt) Ltd, supra* 237.

[242] Ibid., 243–44.

[243] SC Appeal No. 113/2014 /SC Appeal No: SC (HC) LA 67/2013 (05th April 2019).

exceeded the principal amount due and therefore was in violation of the section 5 of the Civil Law Ordinance. The High Court found fault with the award for reasons of public policy, as being against the law of the land, the award impinged upon public policy, hence the application for enforcement of the award was dismissed. The Supreme Court faulted the High Court for an erroneous exercise of jurisdiction with regard to the application of the public policy exception when there was no application for the set aside of the award by the Respondent, as per section 32(1) of the SL Arbitration Act. The court observed

> In the present case, the respondent has not made an application under section 32 (1) of the Act to set aside the arbitral award at any stage - not prior to the appellant's application to enforce the arbitral award nor after notice of that application [together with a copy of the arbitral award] was served on the respondent. The fact that notice of the application under section 31 (1) to enforce the arbitral award [together with a copy of the arbitral award] was served on the respondent, is not in dispute.
>
> In these circumstances, the learned High Court Judge was not empowered to set aside the arbitral award on the ground that the arbitral award was in conflict with the public policy of Sri Lanka, which is a ground set out in section 32 (1) (b) (ii) of the Act.[244]

5.4 Few Pointers for Improving the Regime on Recognition and Enforcement of Foreign Arbitral Awards in South Asia

While the enforcement of the New York Convention through national laws and localized interpretations has significantly helped in acclimatizing to the harmonized legal regimes, there is an immense need to upgrade the arbitration law and streamline it as per best international practices, especially in the context of articulating the content of public policy exception.

The upgradation effort could address these few aspects, where South Asian jurisdictions have encountered pertinent concerns.

- characterization of a foreign award;
- judicial intervention—the role of the courts in foreign-seated arbitrations;
- clarity on the gateway/threshold questions of jurisdiction of the arbitral tribunal—the principle of competence–competence;
- enforcement of provisional measures/conservatory orders from foreign-seated tribunals;
- clarity with regard to the "concurrent jurisdiction" of the local courts;
- the characterization of foreign awards;
- powers to arbitrators to decide a case *ex aequo et bono* or as *amiable compositeur* if authorized by the parties; and to apply the substantive law of any country chosen by the parties and

[244] Ibid., 09.

- the classification of international commercial arbitration to include the nationals choosing a foreign seat.

References

1. Greenberg, S., Kee, C., & Weeramantry, J. R. (2011). In *International Commercial Arbitration—An Asia-Pacific Perspective*. CUP.
2. Mattli, W. (2003). Private justice in a global economy: From litigation to arbitration. *International Organization, 55*(4), 919.
3. Hanotiau, B., & Caprasse, O. (2008). Public policy in international commercial arbitration. In E. Gaillard, & D. Di Pietro (Eds.), *Enforcement of arbitration agreements and international arbitral awards* (Vol. 1, p. 787). Cameron May.
4. Gaillard, E., & Savage, J. (Eds.) (1999). *Fouchard, Gaillard, Goldman on international commercial arbitration* (Vol. 1, pp. 996–997). Kluwer.
5. Van den Berg, A. J. (Ed.) (1997). *Yearbook commercial arbitration 1997—Volume XXII, yearbook commercial arbitration* (pp. 725–726). ICCA & Kluwer Law International.
6. Moses, M. (2019). Public policy under the New York convention: National, international and the transnational. In K. F. Gómez, & A. M. L. Rodriguez (Eds.), *60 years of the New York convention: Key issues and future challenges*. Wolters Kluwer.
7. Ghodoosi, F. (2016). Arbitrating public policy: Why the buck should not stop at National Courts. *Lewis & Clark Law Review, 20*, 237.
8. Maniruzzaman, A. F. M., & Chisti, I. A. (2019). International arbitration and public policy in the Indian subcontinent: A look through the English common law and international lenses. *Manchester Journal of International Economic Law* 16(2), 183–193.
9. Kumar, A., Upadhyay, R., Jegadeesh, A., & Chheda, Y. (2017). Interpretation and application of the New York convention in India. In G. A. Bermann (Ed.), *Recognition and enforcement of foreign arbitral awards, the interpretation and application of the New York convention by national courts* (pp. 445–467). Springer.
10. Sattar, S. (2011). Enforcement of arbitral awards and public policy: Same concept, different approach? https://www.employmentlawalliance.com/Templates/media/files/Misc%20Documents/Enforcement-of-Arbitral-Awards-Public-Policy.pdf. Accessed 21/01/2021.
11. Aragaki, H. N. (2018). Arbitration reform in India: Challenges and opportunities. In A. Reyes, & W. Gu (Eds.), *The developing world of arbitration* (pp. 3.1.1–3.1.2). Hart Bloomsbury.
12. Steinbruck, B. (2015). India. In S. Balthasar (Ed.), *International commercial arbitration—A handbook* (Vol. 1, p. 448). Beck, Hart, Nomos.
13. Rankin, G. C. (1946). *Background to Indian law* (Vol. 1, p. 30). Cambridge University Press.
14. Rao, R. (1958). Conflict of laws in India. *Rabels Zeitschrift Für Ausländisches und Internationales Privatrecht, 23*, 259, 260–62.
15. Garimella, S. R. (2019). India. In A. Reyes (Ed.), *Recognition and enforcement of judgments in civil and commercial matters* (Vol. 1, pp. 291, 293), Hart-Bloomsbury.
16. Khambata, D. J. (2021). Chapter 10: Challenge and enforcement of awards: The brooding omnipresence of public policy. In D. Dave, M. Hunter, et al. (Eds.), *Arbitration in India* (pp. 195–234). Kluwer Law International; Kluwer Law International.
17. Rab, A. (2019). Defining the contours of the public policy exception—A new test for arbitrability in India. *Indian Journal of Arbitration Law,* 7, 161.
18. Arfazadeh, H. (2001). Arbitrability under the New York convention: The lex fori revisited. *Arbitration International,* 17(1), 73.
19. Born, G. (2015). *International arbitration: Law and practice* (Vol. 1, 2nd ed., p. 82). Kluwer.
20. Mustil, & Boyd. (1989). *Law and practice of commercial arbitration in England* (2nd ed., Vol 73).

21. Hariani, A. (2020). Indian arbitration and the shifting sands of public policy. *Asian International Arbitration Journal, 16*(2), 159.
22. Khambata, D. J. (2021). Challenge and enforcement of awards: The brooding omnipresence of public policy. In D. Dave, et al. (Eds.), *Arbitration in India* (Vol. 1, p. 195). Kluwer Law International.
23. Nariman, F. (2011). Ten steps to salvage arbitration in India: The first LGIA-India arbitration lecture. *Arbitration International, 27*(2), 115.
24. Mathew, D. (2016). Situating public policy in the Indian arbitration paradigm: Pursuing the elusive balance. *Journal of National Law University, Delhi, 3*(1), 105.
25. Garimella, S. R. (2017). Issues of jurisdiction, choice of law and enforcement of foreign arbitral awards: An Indian perspective. In S. R. Garimella, & S. Jolly (Eds.) *Private international law: South Asian state practice* (Vol. 1, p. 344). Springer.
26. Sattar, S. (2017). Enforcement of foreign arbitral awards in Bangladesh: The Law, its implementation and challenges. In S. R. Garimella, & S. Jolly (Eds.) *Private international law: South Asian state practice* (Vol. 1, p. 303). Springer.
27. Maniruzzaman, A. F. M. (2003). The new law on international commercial arbitration in Bangladesh: A comparative perspective. *American Review of International Arbitration, 14*, 139.
28. Khan, M. A. (2017). Issues of jurisdiction, choice of law and enforcement of foreign arbitral awards: A Bangladesh perspective. In S. R. Garimella, & S. Jolly (Eds.), *Private international law: South Asian state practice* (Vol. 1, p. 285). Springer.
29. Maniruzzaman, A. F. M. (2004). Bangladesh embraces the UNCITRAL model law on international commercial arbitration—But not quite! *Mealey's International Arbitration Report, 19*(3), 1–3.
30. Van den Berg, A. J. (Ed.), *Yearbook commercial arbitration 1998—Volume XXIII* (p. 624). ICCA & Kluwer Law International.
31. Ghouri, A. A. (2013). Law and practice of foreign arbitration and the enforcement of foreign arbitral awards in Pakistan. Springer.
32. Karki, B. B. (2005). UNCITRAL model law on international commercial arbitration (1985) and Nepalese arbitration law. *NEPCA Half Yearly Bulletin, 15*, 8.
33. Uprety, B. P. (2008). Evolution of commercial arbitration in Nepal. *Nepal Judicial Academy Law Journal, 2*(1), 205, 208.
34. Pandit, G., & Pant, A. (2017). Issues of jurisdiction, choice of law and enforcement of foreign arbitral awards: A Nepal perspective. In Garimella, S. R., & Jolly, S. (Eds.), *Private international law: South Asian state practice* (Vol. 1, p. 347). Springer.
35. Yadav, B. (2004). Problems faced in Nepal in the settlement of disputes through arbitration. *NEPCA Half-yearly Bulletin, 11*(2059), 8.
36. Sutton, D. St. J., et al. (1997). *Russell on arbitration* (Vol. 3, p. 17). Sweet & Maxwell.
37. Amarasinghe, A. R. B. (2007). Sri Lanka arbitration act. In K. Kanag-Isvaran, & S. S. Wijeratne (Eds.), *Arbitration law in Sri Lanka* (3rd ed., p. 9–13). ICLP.
38. Marsoof, S. (2017). Issues of jurisdiction, choice of law and enforcement of foreign arbitral awards: A Sri Lankan perspective. In S. R. Garimella, & S. Jolly (Eds.), *Private international law: South Asian state practice* (Vol. 1, p. 391). Springer.
39. Marsoof, S. (2008). Judiciary and the arbitral process. In S.Marsoof, & N. Wigneswaran (Eds.), *In pursuit of justice* (p. 33, 35). Kamalasabayson Foundation.

Chapter 6
Conclusion and Observations

Overview
The concluding chapter draws attention to the primordial issues addressed in the book in relation to the enforcement and recognition of foreign arbitral awards. In particular, it explains the following:

- The dispute mechanism devised by the New York Convention and the Model Law is an essential part in the successful application of arbitration in South Asia.
- It maps the changing geopolitical landscape in Asia, namely the Belt and Road project and its legal challenges.
- It takes particular care to note the difference between the application of the Model Law and the New York Convention and the importance of the seat.

The exceptions to the enforcement of foreign arbitral awards are explained by taking note of the jurisprudence from State practices.

6.1 Introduction

This book has discussed the significance and contribution of the New York Convention on the Recognition and Enforcement of Foreign Arbitral Awards, 1958, and the UNITRAL Model Law on commercial arbitration. Of special importance is that the book highlights the importance of understanding the effects of the recognition and enforcement of foreign awards in a changing landscape. One of its focal points has been an attempt at mapping the enforcement regime in the context of the grounds for refusal of the same, within the otherwise lesser known jurisdictions of South Asia. Towards this, the book also presents interesting insights into how courts in the South Asia Region have enforced and set aside arbitration awards where the seat was not in the enforcing country. This book sets out the current State of the influence exerted on each other by the NYC and the UNCITAL Model Law, as nations grapple with operationalizing their commitments towards these instruments. It further examines the

B. Zeller et al., *Enforcement of Foreign Arbitral Awards and the Public Policy Exception*,
https://doi.org/10.1007/978-981-16-2634-0_6

effect of this impact on domestic courts and will be of importance to practitioners as well as academics in understanding the geopolitical change in the region. This book is especially important as it also notes that despite adhering to these two instruments, courts in South Asia have not demonstrated enough consistency in their approach and hence the jurisprudence from this region is an important source of analysis and suggest remedying the inconsistencies in an area where changes and clarifications are still forthcoming. In addition, the fact that once the setting aside or enforcement process is enlivened, privacy and confidentiality are lost as the process moves from the arbitral tribunal to the court system.

6.2 Chapter 1

The background to the increased importance in arbitration in the Asian region due to the effects of the Belt and Road Initiative (BRI) is explained. The Hong Kong Trade and Development Council noted that more than sixty countries could be impacted by this omnibus trade and economic partnership, covering the land and sea routes, and therefore included them in their project on country profiles in the context of the BRI. These countries span across Southeast Asia, South Asia, Central Asia, Northeast Asia, Central and Eastern Europe, Africa, Australasia, and the Middle East.[1] The project that has had a collateral change impact on the geopolitical climate, nevertheless, highlights the importance of a neutral dispute settlement mechanism. Simply put, goods travelling along the nations[2] signed up to the BRI[3] move across many jurisdictions and legal systems, and hence the seat of a dispute in most cases is not the same as where an award needs to be enforced. It is not disputed that London, Singapore and Hong Kong are and will continue to be the most influential seats/place of arbitration dealing with conflicts but enforcement in legally high-risk countries is always an issue. This chapter also highlights the importance of trade connections which has drawn Australia into the economic sphere of South Asia. The important impetus was the Free Trade Agreement such as the AANZFTA, 2010, ASEAN, Australia and New Zealand Free Trade Agreement[4] and the Indonesia-Australia Comprehensive Economic Partnership Agreement (IA-CEPA) which entered into force on 5 July 2020.[5] Increasingly, important will be the settlement of infrastructure and investment matters which will be directly linked to BRI and the emergence of new economies in the Asian region.

[1]See, The Hong Kong Trade and Development Council, 'Belt and Road: Country Profile'. http://beltandroad.hktdc.com/en/country-profiles, accessed 27/08/2020.

[2]Lim Tai Wei [1].

[3]See, Sooksripaisarnkit and Garimella [2].

[4]ASEAN-Australia-New Zealand Free Trade Area (AANZFTA), 2010, https://aanzfta.asean.org/general-review, accessed 17/11/2020.

[5]Indonesia-Australia Comprehensive Economic Partnership Agreement, 2020, https://www.dfat.gov.au/trade/agreements/in-force/iacepa/Pages/indonesia-australia-comprehensive-economic-partnership-agreement, accessed 17/11/2020.

The importance of arbitration as a flexible tool is highlighted due to being "neutral" that is not bound to a singly legal system of law but still enjoys the enforceability in any system where the parties have an inherent interest. Foremost the principle of confidentiality which is important in many business disputes is highlighted.

This chapter also draws out the importance of the word "may" which is contained in Article V(1)(e) as well as in Articles 34 and 36 of the Model Law. The chapter further argued that these articles allow local courts to apply a more favourable provision in a local law than is found in the New York Convention or in the Model Law. Such judicial practice, foremost, strengthens the binding nature of arbitral awards without losing sight of the transnational effect of the Convention. However, on the flip side, the courts might also adopt a domestic law interpretation to the binding nature of arbitral awards, thus testing the awards on reasons and interpretations that are necessarily not part of the international Conventions and international legal regimes. Importantly, this chapter also explains the distinction between court assistance and court intervention especially in light of the interrelationship of setting aside and enforcing an award.

6.3 Chapter 2

The chapter maps the work of the Working Group of the UNCITRAL in order to understand the underlying philosophical mandate as it revolutionized the arbitral landscape. The Model Law was drafted in 1985, and it is is a sign of its success that there has been no revision until very recently. It is also of value to note that the UNCITRAL Arbitration Rules, 1976—as the forerunner—provided for a rule structure to manage arbitration of a broad range of disputes.[6]

The success of the Model Law can be measured by the fact that it has been included into domestic legislation by 76 countries comprising 107 jurisdictions.[7] The relevant articles for the setting aside of the awards and the enforcement process are Articles 34 and 36. The two articles can be usefully be divided into two main groups: the first group lists grounds that have to be proven by the party invoking them, whereas the second group names grounds which the court can take into consideration itself.[8] Also the wording appears to be the same as in the New York Convention, but care must be taken as some variations are included. The importance of this chapter lies in the explanation of the distinction and hence interplay between the seat and the place of enforcement exists. As Lord Mance explained:

[6]UNCITRAL, UNCITRAL Arbitration Rules, 1976, https://uncitral.un.org/en/texts/arbitration/contractualtexts/arbitration, accessed 01/02/2021.

[7]UNCITAL, Model Law on International Commercial Arbitration, 1985, http://www.uncitral.org/uncitral/en/uncitral_texts/arbitration/1985Model_arbitration_status.html, accessed 01/02/2021.

[8]F. Liebelt, 'The Courts' Discretion under UNCITRAL Articles 34 and 36/, LLM Research Paper, Victoria University of Wellington, 2. http://researcharchive.vuw.ac.nz/xmlui/bitstream/handle/10063/3248/thesis.pdf?sequence=2.

> a deep distinction should be drawn between cases where the intrusion comes from the court at the place of the arbitration and cases where a "foreign" or "third" court interferes with an arbitration that is seated in a different country.[9]

The Working Group II found that the issue of setting side an award was "amongst the most difficult ones to be settled in the Model Law."[10] As highlighted in the chapter the *travaux préparatories* of Article 34 are longer than any other provision of the Model Law, except for Article 1.[11]

In relation to Article 36, and in general as well, the argument was that the Model Law was "not a simple repetition of the 1958 New York Convention but an innovation in that it established a unified common regime for international commercial arbitration."[12] The chapter attempted to map the discussions at the Working Group meetings in the context of the language of Articles 34 and 36, especially the usage of the words "may" and "only" within these specific provisions. The chapter, albeit briefly, discusses the issue of public policy exception to enforcement of arbitral awards, highlighting the discussion at the above-said meetings.

Pertinently, this chapter discussed the importance of the word "exclusive" in Article 34. Simply put the exemptions listed in Article 34 are exhaustive and are the sole recourse against an arbitral award; however, it is also recognized that this Article creates more problems than it solves but is still of significance.

6.4 Chapter 3

The New York Convention, the subject of this chapter, recognized that enforcement of the award, apart from the setting aside of an award, can be sought also at the seat of arbitration (courtesy, the second sentence of Article I). Hence, care needs to be taken to understand that as an example, the procedural reasons contained in Article V (1) is only valid at the seat where Article V(2) lists the grounds such as public policy where a court, wherever it is situated, might refuse enforcement. The *travaux preparatoires* are clear on the aspect that the basic legal rights of a party must be safeguarded without rehearing the case which would defeat the purpose of arbitration.

---

[9] Carbone [3].

[10] Yearbook of the United Nations Commission on International Trade Law, 1981, Volume XII, 'Report of the Secretary-General: possible features of a model law on international commercial arbitration, A/CN.9/207', [107] https://undocs.org/pdf?symbol=en/A/CN.9/207, accessed 20/10/2020. ("Yearbook of the UNCITRAL"), 924.

[11] 'UNCITRAL Model Law, Chapter VII, Article 34 [Application for setting aside as exclusive recourse against arbitral award]', in Holtzmann and Neuhaus [4].

[12] See, generally, United Nations Commission on International Trade Law (UNCITRAL), 'Summary records for meetings on the UNCITRAL Model Law on International Commercial Arbitration, 329th Meeting'. ("Summary Records-329th Meeting") https://uncitral.un.org/sites/uncitral.un.org/files/media-documents/uncitral/en/329meeting-e.pdf, accessed 08/08/2020, [69].

As the enforcement and setting aside procedures have moved the dispute from the arbitral tribunal to the courts, this chapter explained the interplay between granting basic legal rights that is due process to a losing party without allowing the losing party to frustrate the legal process and importantly courts have also understood not to engage in an appeal process. Article V(1)(a), namely the issue of incapacity has—despite lacking a clear definition—has been rarely used as seen in the jurisprudence offered in this chapter which also indicted that in doubt courts would use the conflict of laws rules to ascertain the issue of incapacity. In relation to proper notice, the important aspect is that the duty rests on the Respondent himself because "placing the burden of proving the grounds for refusal under the Convention on the applicant seeking enforcement of the award is not in accord with international treaty or procedural law."[13]

The chapter identified the import of the provisions like Article V(1)(c), per which an arbitration cannot proceed "beyond the scope of the submission to arbitration" otherwise enforcement could be denied; Article V(1)(d) gives the court power to refuse enforcement if the arbitral tribunal was not constituted according to the agreement to arbitrate; and, that an award cannot be contested if the award has not yet become binding on the parties as such a request would constitute a legal nullity acceding to Article V(1)(e).

The chapter also discussed the important issue of the interplay between Articles V and VII. The problem is that an award is enforceable under the laws where enforcement is sought. The issue is that the award might have been set side at the seat hence a "renvoi" issue arises. The solution accepted by courts appears that comity will prevail except if there existed a concern related to the public policy is at issue. The issue as discussed in this chapter brings forth the conflict between a traditional or territorial view and a denationalized view. This is best described by Jacobs CJ in *Corporación Mexicana De Mantenimiento Integral, S. De R.L. De C.V., v. PEP–Exploración Y Producción*[14] where he stated:

> this case requires us to reconcile two settled principles that militate in favour of opposite results: a district court's discretion to confirm an arbitral award, and the comity owed to a foreign court's ruling on the validity of an arbitral award rendered in that country, here, Mexico.[15]

This issue is not settled yet as seen in vastly different approaches by courts in the USA, France and Holland as seen in the *Yukos* dispute.[16]

---

[13] *Codest Engineering v OOO Grupa Most* (Presidium of the Supreme Arbitrazh Court of the Russian Federation 2005), in Yearbook Commercial Arbitration XXXIII (2008) (Russia no. 17), 666–672.

[14] *Corporación Mexicana De Mantenimiento Integral, S. De R.L. De C.V., v. PEP–Exploración Y Producción,* 823 F 3d 92 (2nd Cir, 2016).

[15] *Ibid.*, [1].

[16] See, *Yukos Capital s.a.r.l. (Luxembourg) v. OAO Rosneft* (Russian Federation) (Court of Appeal 2009), in Yearbook Commercial Arbitration XXXIV (Netherlands no. 31), 703–714. See also Northern River Shipping Lines v. Kompas Overseas Inc. (District Court 2010), in Yearbook Commercial Arbitration XXXVI (Netherlands no. 36) and *Nikolai Viktorovich Maximov v*

This chapter concludes by examining the effects of Article V(2)(a), namely the words of "that country." In effect, the right of enforcement ads shifted from the seat to the country where enforcement is being sought specifically in light of the public exclusion in subsection (b). The US circuit court in *Corporación Mexicana De Mantenimiento Integral, S. De R.L. De C.V.*[17] noted succinctly:

> The public policy exception does not swallow the rule: "[t]he standard is high, and infrequently met"; "a judgment that 'tends clearly' to undermine the public interest, the public confidence in the administration of the law, or security for individual rights of personal liberty or of private property is against public policy." The exception accommodates uneasily two competing (and equally important) principles: [i] "the goals of comity and res judicata that underlie the doctrine of recognition and enforcement of foreign judgments" and [ii] "fairness to litigants." [18]

In effect, public policy as explained by the Swiss and Spanish judgements is only a tool of last resort.

6.5 Chapter 4

The public policy exception is the subject of this chapter. The issues and problems with public policy have been observed for a long time. In 1824, the court in *Richardson V Mellish* noted that "I, for one, protest … against arguing too strongly upon public policy; it is a very unruly horse, and when once you get astride it you never know where it will carry."[19] Nevertheless, the opinion of Burrow J is not correct insofar as public policy does play an important role as the interest of the public has always been safeguarded.

The only issue is how is public policy defined and when is the public interest overriding the private interest of litigating parties where a foreign law is applied. Lauterpacht concisely explained the legitimacy of the public policy by stating that 'public policy is the part and parcel of the entire doctrine of and practise of Private International Law almost from its very inception … the State needs a "safety valve" so that its courts might, if thought necessary, decline to apply a particular foreign law.'[20] As public policy is a State's safety valve, it will by definition be impossible to define in an international sense. This so as each State has different "sacred cows" it wants to protect, hence this book argues it is impossible to accurately define public policy. Public policy like good faith is recognized as principles which are applied but the best definition which can be offered is that courts recognize it when it is absent like the absence of good faith when we find bad faith conduct.

OJSC Novolopetsky Metallurgickesky Kombinat (District Court 2011), in Yearbook Commercial Arbitration XXXVII (Netherlands no. 41), 274–276.

[17] *Corporación Mexicana De Mantenimiento Integral, supra* 14.

[18] *Ibid.*, 107.

[19] *Richardson v Mellish* (1824) 130 E.R. 294.

[20] *Netherland v Sweden*. http://www.icj-cij.org/docket/index.php?sum=145&code=nls&p1=3&p2=3&case=33&k=37&p3=5.

As this book explained, courts have a limited ability to interfere in the process which has also been recognized by the New York Convention and the Model Law. Courts have always understood the limited involvement only in areas where judicial powers are needed. In essence, the courts recognized the distinction between an appeal and an enforcement or setting aside:

> We do not owe deference to the district court's legal conclusions, but we afford "maximum deference" to the arbitrators' decisions."[21] It follows that "[a]n arbitrator's erroneous interpretations or applications of law are not reversible.[22]

Article III of the New York Convention was drafted with the intention to discourage courts to apply standards of extreme difficulties. However as this chapter explained, the standards of public policy should be contoured on international standards, rather than extrapolating its meaning in domestic circumstances to international arbitration.[23] It discussed the scholarly approach to determining the boundaries of public policy by either following the maximalist or the minimalist approach. Simply put the maximalist approach tends towards but does not extend to a review of the point so law is applicable to the arbitration. The minimalist approach conscious of the purpose of arbitration in not rehearing the dispute only overturns the award if there is a fundamental breach of public policy in line with OECD recommendations.[24] The problematic issue which is recognized is the fact that public policy devised to be a "safety valve" has in some instances become a "gateway for undesirable obstructions." Contracting States have refused recognition and enforcement of foreign arbitral awards on a "back door approach" denying enforcement or setting aside, hence impeding the pro-enforcement policy of the New York Convention.[25]

Public policy is also an exception in the Model Law, hence it affects the internal effect of arbitration, whereas as noted above the New York Convention reflects the transnational approach. However, the issue of a lack of definition of public policy has not been diminished by the Model Law. In relation to a lack of definition in domestic little alone international documents, the conclusion drawn by the IBA is instructive:

> In the vast majority of jurisdictions covered by this report, a violation of public policy implies a violation of fundamental or basic principles. These principles seem, however, to be differently expressed by courts (and scholars) depending on whether they are in civil law or common law jurisdictions. In the first group, the definitions of public policy generally refer to the basic principles or values upon which the foundation of society rests, without precisely naming them. In the second group, on the other hand, the definition often refers to more precisely identified, yet very broad, values, such as justice, fairness or morality.[26]

---

[21] *EEG (Shanghai) Solar Science & Technology Co., Ltd. v LUMOS LLC n/k/a/ LUMOS Solar LLC*, the US Court of Appeals for the Tenth Circuit. Only the Westlaw citation is currently available. United States Court of Appeals, Tenth Circuit. 2016 WL 3909579. [3]–[5].

[22] *Ibid.*

[23] Hanotiau and Caprasse [5].

[24] OECD Hearings—Arbitration and Competition 2010 http://www.oecd.org/competition/abuse/49294392.pdf.

[25] Wolff [6].

[26] Mayer and Sheppard [7].

(a) Public Policy as envisaged in New York Convention and UNCITRAL Model Law

As the limitation articles are similar in both instruments, this chapter sets out the only important difference between the two instruments. The NYC uses the words "*that country*" and the Model Law public policy of "*this State*". This distinction allows each Contracting State to interpret the public policy independently whether the enforcement or setting aside as the case might be is sought at the seat via the Model Law or in another country relying on the New York Convention. It is also argued—relying on section 19 of the Australian Arbitration Act—that if a *breach of natural justice* is proven, it automatically equates to a breach of public policy. However, a breach of natural justice is not to be confused with revisiting the facts it is strictly only to applied to the "public policy" issue as noted by Lord Mustil in *Pupuke Service Stations Ltd v Caltex Oil (NZ Ltd.*[27] He stated:

> Having agreed at the outset to take his dispute away from the Court the losing party may afterwards be tempted to think better of it, and ask the Court to interfere because the arbitrator has misunderstood the issues, believing an unconvincing witness, decided against the weight of evidence or otherwise arrived at the wrong conclusion. All developed systems of arbitration have in principle set their face against accommodation such a change of mind. … the findings of the arbitrator are impregnable.[28]

Additionally as the New York Convention is drafted in English, the question of different language and their translation of the English version has been averted by noting that the French *"ordre public"* is to be understood to mean the same.[29] However, this book also explains clearly that not all national arbitration legislations distinguish between "*this State*" or "*that State*" relying on several legislative examples. However, the arguments put forward in this book follow the observations of the court in *Hebei Import and Export Corp v Polytec Engeneering Co Ltd.*:[30]

> … there must be compelling reasons before enforcement of a Convention award can be refused on public policy grounds…[the reasons do not need to be extreme] … But the reasons must go beyond the minimum which would justify setting aside a domestic judgment or award. [31]

The facts which emerge in jurisprudence is that natural justice or public policy is not a precise science but rather a determination of instances which arguably are "feeling not right" or offend fundamental notions of justice and fairness as noted in *Emerald Grain Australia Pty Ltd v. Agrocorp International Pte Ltd (Emerald Grain).*[32]

[27] *Pupuke Service Stations Ltd v Caltex Oil (NZ Ltd.* [2003] 3 NZLR 338 (PC).
[28] *Ibid.*, 338–339.
[29] Chen [8].
[30] *Hebei Import and Export Corp v Polytec Engeneering Co Ltd.* [1999] 2 HKC 205.
[31] *Ibid.*, 215.
[32] *Emerald Grain Australia Pty Ltd v. Agrocorp International Pte Ltd* [2014] FCA 414.

This chapter is concluded by examining the major decision in the South East Region of Asia. The overall impression which can be gained is that courts in applying the New York Convention and the Model Law have adopted a narrow view of public policy, hence courts do not have much room to initiate a review of the award which is in line with the underpinning philosophy of both arbitral instruments.

6.6 Chapter 5

This chapter explained in particular the "State of play" in India and selected emerging South Asian economies such as Bangladesh, Pakistan, Nepal and Sri Lanka in relation to the public policy exception.

This chapter in particular examines whether the diversity with the conceptual understanding of the public policy exception is discernible in the treatment of the policy by the selected South Asian countries. The starting point is the notion expressed in *Parsons and Whitemore Overseas Co. v Societe Generale de L'Industrie du Papier*,[33] where the court held that the public policy exception is enlivened if the enforcement of the award would violate the State's most basic notions of morality and justice. However, the prevalence of constructing an understanding of public policy using a dual vision like in France, namely *ordre public interne* and *ordre public international* appears to be observable in South Asia. One example, namely India, is instructive where in the past courts have judged awards which in the view of the Indian courts seemed to be inconsistent with an understanding of the Indian law as being illegal, hence falling under the public policy exemption. In effect, these decisions on merit are merely disguised as violation of public policy and hence not correct. This has now been corrected.

(a) **India**

India having been a colony inherited the regulatory regime on arbitration from England. The Indian Arbitration Act was enacted in 1940, and the New York Convention entered into force in 1960. A new legislation, guided by the Model Law, the Arbitration and Conciliation Act, entered into force in 1996. An important change was that an arbitration award is now treated as a decree and enforced as such and in addition Part I of the Act deals with domestic arbitral awards, whereas Part II is reserved for the recognition and enforcement of foreign awards. In addition, the new act does not define "public policy." The chapter traces the development and application of public policy. Earlier decisions were based on a restrictive interpretation. Hence, words "opposed to public policy" have always been construed in a local context. The struggle of Indian Courts is well highlighted in a catena of decisions, wherein the courts have assumed that public policy is a concept that they control

[33] *Parsons and Whitemore Overseas Co. v. Societe Generale de L'Industrie du Papier* 508 F. 2d 969 (2nd Cir. 1974). See, generally, Greenberg et al. [9]; see, generally, Mattli [10].

albeit acknowledging the inherent dangers of paying heed to the concept of public policy for nullifying commercial transactions.[34]

A paradigm shift towards expanding the scope of public policy was expounded in *Central Inland Water Transport Corporation & another v Brojo Nath Ganguly and another*[35]. In essence, the court noted:

> Practices which were considered perfectly normal at one time have today become obnoxious and oppressive to public conscience. If there is no head of public policy which covers a case, then the court must in consonance with public conscience and in keeping with public good and public interest declares such practice to be opposed to public policy.[36]

In 1996, another change took place in *Renusagar*[37] wherein the Supreme court, as a matter of first impression, concretized the judicial views on enforcement of international awards in India. According to the Court the term public policy under the Foreign Awards (Recognition and Enforcement) Act, 1961 denotes:

(i) fundamental policy of Indian law;
(ii) the interests of India; or
(iii) justice or morality.

Pertinently, the Court was also of the opinion that contravention of law in itself is not a sufficient ground to attract the defence of public policy and 'something' more is required to set aside an arbitral award.

In 2012, another change took place in *Bharat Aluminium Company v Kaiser Aluminium Technical Services, Inc.*[38] where the court ruled that foreign judgements do not need to conform anymore to the provisions and standards specified in Part I. This brought the Indian jurisprudence in conformity with international norms.

A further development in 2013 in *Shri Lal Mahal v Progetto Grano Spa*[39] where the court declined to rule on the merits of a foreign award as stated in *Renusagar.* It in effect significantly reduced the ability of Indian courts to interfere in foreign awards by reason of a public policy consideration. However, it appears that recent decisions such as in *National Agricultural Co-operative Marketing Federation of India v Alimenta SA*[40] are not a step forward but are viewed to be retuning to a notion

---

[34] See, generally, Khambata [11].

[35] *Central Inland Water Transport Corporation & another v Brojo Nath Ganguly & another* (1986) 3 SCC 156.

[36] *Ibid.*, 213.

[37] *Renusagar Power Plant Co. v General Electric Corporation* (1994) Supp (1) SCC 644.

[38] *Bharat Aluminium Company v Kaiser Aluminium Technical Services, Inc.* Civil Appeal No. 7019 of 2005. Decision of the Indian Supreme Court dated 06/09/2012.

[39] *Shri Lal Mahal v Progetto Grano Spa* Civil Appeal No. 5085 of 2013.

[40] *National Agricultural Co-operative Marketing Federation of India v Alimenta SA* 2020 SCC Online SC 381. The award related to a contract for shipment of certain commodities in which there was a partial performance by the Appellant. Upon denial of the permission by the Government of India for carrying forward the supply to the following year, the Appellant failed to supply the goods. Consequently, the Respondent initiated arbitration at the FOFSA, London, in 1981. The 1989 award in favour of the Respondent granted damages to them, and the same was applied for enforcement

of localization of the content of public policy exception, often coming into conflict with the stated vision of the national law and international law as well.

(b) Bangladesh

When Bangladesh gained independence form Pakistan in 1971, it also inherited the then governing laws on arbitration which in effect gave the courts scope to interfere in awards. The New York Convention was only adopted in 1992, and the Model Law was the base to enact the domestic Arbitration Act 2001. Only though the Arbitration Act was the New York Convention given legal force. It makes it obligatory for the national courts of Bangladesh to enforce foreign arbitral awards, as if they were a decree of the court,[41] subject to the exceptions provided in Section 46. Recently, several decisions in Bangladesh indicate a positive approach to the enforcement of foreign reign arbitral awards.

In *Uzbekistan Airways and another v Air Spain Ltd*,[42] the High Court Division of the Bangladesh Supreme Court reiterated the general rule that a foreign arbitral award can be enforced in Bangladesh. The pro-arbitration approach was again demonstrated in 2013 in *Goenka Impex S.A. v Tallu Spinning Mills Ltd*,[43]

(c) Pakistan

Pakistan has not made much progress in the field of arbitration. It is still relying on legislation based as an example on the Indian Contract Law (1872) and Arbitration Acts form the 1940s. The New York Convention has only been adopted into Pakistani law in 2005. It did shift the perception on issues of of jurisdiction, choice of law and enforcement of foreign arbitral awards. However, the Model Law has not yet been adopted in Pakistan, and jurisprudence is example of a localized content infused into the law premised upon terms that are laced with localized understanding. It needs to be understood that public policy in Pakistan is also shaped by Islamic laws. However, freedom of contract has found favour and reasons to refuse enforcement on public policy grounds have been narrowed.

(d) Nepal

Nepal promulgated its first statute specifically dealing with arbitration, i.e. the Arbitration Act, 2038 (1981), which was repealed in 1999 due to inefficiencies, interference of courts and delays in dealing specifically with foreign firms. The 1999 Act is based on the Model Law as well as the New York Convention, however substantial differences exist. Only awards which are made in a New York Convention country are given reciprocity which is contrary to the mandate in the Model Law. Enforcement

---

in India under the Foreign Awards Act, 1993. The Delhi High Court heard the Appellant twice but turned down their appeal, hence the appeal before the Supreme Court.

[41] AA 2001, Section 45.

[42] *Uzbekistan Airways and another v Air Spain Ltd* [2005] 10 BLC 614, [5].

[43] *Goenka Impex S.A. v Tallu Spinning Mills Ltd.* [2013] 33 BLD 340.

is only granted if all requirements in section 34(2) of the 1999 Act are fulfilled such as that the award must be translated into Nepali language.

(e) **Sri Lanka**

Sri Lanka is a unitary Republic and has a robust tradition of alternative dispute resolution. The 1995 Arbitration Act was inspired by the Model Law as well as the New York Convention. Each act is very much aligned with international practices such as it does not allow an appeal against the merits of the award as the award is declared to be final and binding. Decisions such as *Light Weight Body Armour Ltd. v Sri Lanka Army*[44] reflect a strong pro-arbitration stance. In relation to the issue of public policy, the Sri Lankan Arbitration Act are materially the same as in the New York Convention.

6.7 Concluding Remarks

This book has demonstrated that the New York Convention and the Model Law in relation to enforcement or setting aside an award have been differently applied in various jurisdictions. Specifically, the issue of public policy has played an unsettling effect in the enforcement process of foreign awards. However, it is becoming more obvious that many countries are applying foreign judgements and comity of courts in this respect is becoming a feature. South Asia also has more and more aligned itself with the global pro-arbitration stance by courts, and it is rare to see a "patently" wrong decisions in relation to the enforcement or setting aside of awards despite the fact that the "field" is not settled.

However, it needs to be noted that the reputation of a jurisdiction in the context of enforceability of awards could be adversely impacted by a constant and deliberately inconsistent positions on matters like public policy. It also needs to be noted that while the doctrine's presence and utility are not a matter of question, it also needs to self-regulate in the context of enforceability and thereby upholding contractual freedom, which happens to be the foundational element of all international economic interaction. States need to legislate upon the content of public policy exception to ensure that reasons that are not primal to international commerce and dispute resolution shall not impact the binding nature of an arbitral award. Such endeavours produce two results that effectively rein in the unruly horse that public policy was characterized as.

(a) It would ensure that the public policy exception is grounded within the national firmament, but is in effect denuded of the localized content.
(b) It would also prevent the extraversions that occur in the dispute resolution processes before the courts, as the law would provide signposts to guide decisions of courts in engaging with the public policy exception. Courts would

[44] *Light Weight Body Armour Ltd. v Sri Lanka Army* [2007] Sri Lanka Law Reports 411.

therefore be prevented from (over)indulgence with the enforceability and public policy based upon localized content.

References

1. Wei, L. T. (2016). Introduction. In Wei, L. T., et al. (Eds.). *China's one belt one road initiative* (p. 3). Imperial College Press.
2. Sooksripaisarnkit, P., & Garimella, S. R. (2018). 'Introduction'. In Sooksripaisarnkit, P., & Garimella, S. R. (Eds.). *China's one belt one road initiative and private international law* (Vol. 1, pp. 2–5). Routledge.
3. Carbone, G. (2012). The interference of the court of the seat with international arbitration. *Journal of Dispute Resolution.* 217, 219. https://scholarship.law.missouri.edu/cgi/viewcontent.cgi?article=1128&context=jdr.
4. Holtzmann, H. M., & Neuhaus, J. (1989) *A guide to the UNCITRAL model law on international commercial arbitration: Legislative history and commentary* (Vol. 1, pp. 910–1003). Kluwer Law International.
5. Hanotiau, B., Caprasse, O. (2008). Public policy in international commercial arbitration. In E. Gaillard, & D. Di Pietro (Eds.). *Enforcement of arbitration agreements and international arbitral awards* (Vol. 1, p. 787). Cameron.
6. Wolff, R. (Ed.) (2012). *The New York convention: Convention on the recognition and enforcement of foreign arbitral awards of 10 June 1958—Commentary* (Vol. 1, p. 406). Hart Publishing.
7. Mayer, P., Sheppard, A. (2003). Final ILA report on public policy as a bar to enforcement of international arbitral awards. *Arbitration International, 19*(2), 249. ("ILA's Final Report"), 6.
8. Chen, H. H. -C. (2017). *Predictability of 'Public Policy' in Article V of the New York convention under Mainland China's judicial practice* (pp. 11–26). Kluwer Law International.
9. Greenberg, S., Kee, C., & Weeramantry, J. R. (2011). *International commercial arbitration—An Asia-Pacific perspective.* CUP.
10. Mattli, W. (2001). Private justice in a global economy: From litigation to arbitration. *International Organization, 55*(4), 919.
11. Khambata, D. J. (2021). Chapter 10: Challenge and enforcement of awards: The brooding omnipresence of public policy. In Dave, D., et al. (Eds.). *Arbitration in India* (p. 195). Kluwer Law International.